WORSHIP IN THE BEST OF BOTH WORLDS

'In this hugely important book, Philip Greenslade challenges the either/or of contemporary worship and offers us instead a paradoxical vision of worship that is both/and: both liturgical and spontaneous; tearful and festive; reverent and intimate. It is a great riposte to so much "middle-of-the-road" Christianity.'
Ian Stackhouse, Senior Pastor, Guildford Baptist Church, UK

'Greenslade issues a call for integrating the structure of the liturgical approach with the freedom of the charismatic approach to corporate worship, as the best way to reflect and celebrate the "polarities" which characterize our perspective of God, our view of reality, and our way of gathering together. This is an erudite guide to a new (and yet perhaps old) way of thinking about how we do church.'
Ron Man, Worship Resources International

'Here is a biblical vision of worship at the extremes that is ancient yet ever new. Worship as God-centered, passionate, intimate, world-shaping, explosive, politically subversive, brutally honest, prophetic, Spirit-led and yet rooted in tradition. If this does not inspire you to worship then you may be dead!'
Robin Parry, author of *Worshipping Trinity*

'A timely and important challenge to the contemporary church to recognise the limitations of polarised, one-dimensional worship.'
David Peacock, Head of Music and Worship Department, London School of Theology

'In this highly readable book Philip Greenslade has made a strong case for worship that integrates both liturgical order and charismatic freedom. Drawing on a wide range of resources from Scripture, theology and ritual studies, he has convincingly demonstrated that integrated worship is not an option but a necessity because it is true to everything that God reveals about himself. I highly recommend it to pastors and church leaders who are concerned about the question of truth in worship.'
Simon Chan, Earnest Lau Professor of Systematic Theology, Trinity Theological College, Singapore

WORSHIP IN THE BEST OF BOTH WORLDS

An Exploration of the Polarities of
Truthful Worship

Philip Greenslade

Paternoster:
thinking faith

MILTON KEYNES ● COLORADO SPRINGS ● HYDERABAD

First published 2009 by Paternoster
Paternoster is an imprint of Authentic Media
9 Holdom Avenue, Bletchley, Milton Keynes, Bucks, MK1 1QR, UK
1820 Jet Stream Drive, Colorado Springs, CO 80921, USA
Medchal Road, Jeedimetla Village, Secunderabad 500 055, A.P., India
www.authenticmedia.co.uk

Authentic Media is a division of IBS-STL U.K., limited by guarantee, with its
Registered Office at Kingstown Broadway, Carlisle, Cumbria CA3 0HA.
Registered in England & Wales No. 1216232. Registered charity 270162

British Library Cataloguing in Publication Data

A catalogue record for this book is available from the
British Library

ISBN: 978-1-84227-614-3

Cover design by James Kessell for Scratch the Sky Ltd
(www.scratchthesky.com)
Print Management by Adare
Printed and bound in Great Britain by J F Print Ltd., Sparkford, Somerset

Contents

Series Preface

Many are exasperated with what they perceive as the fad-driven, one-dimensional spirituality of modern evangelicalism and desire to reconnect with, and be deeply rooted in, the common historical Christian tradition as well as their evangelical heritage – welcome to what C.S. Lewis called 'Deep Church'.

Deep Church is far more than an ecumenical dream of coming together across the barriers of ignorance and prejudice: it is predicated upon the central tenets of the gospel held in common by those who have the temerity to be 'Mere Christians'. This commonality in the light of post-Enlightenment modernism is greater and more fundamental than the divisions and schisms of church history . . . Deep Church, as its name implies, is spiritual reality down in the depths – the foundations and deep structures of the Faith – which feed, sustain, and equip us to be disciples of Christ.

Andrew Walker, Series Editor

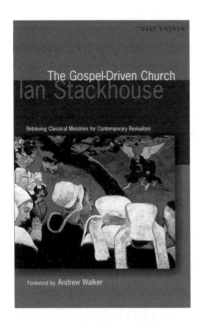

The Gospel-Driven Church

Ian Stackhouse

Retrieving Classical Ministries for Contemporary Revivalism

Foreword by Andrew Walker

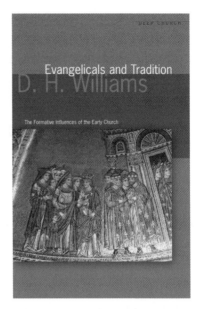

Evangelicals and Tradition

D. H. Williams

The Formative Influences of the Early Church

Edited by Andrew Walker
and Luke Bretherton

Remembering
Our Future

Explorations in Deep Church

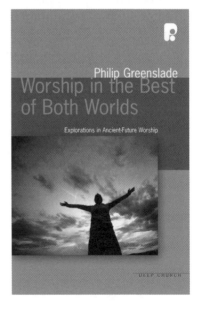

Philip Greenslade

Worship in the Best
of Both Worlds

Explorations in Ancient-Future Worship

Foreword

Worship that is characteristically open to the surprising moves of the Spirit while being, at the same time, ordered and shaped liturgically by the outline of the redemptive narrative – this, idealistic as it may seem, is still my dream and the driving force behind this study. Though rooted in earlier years of teaching seminars on the subject, it is an expanded version of a Master's thesis undertaken through the London School of Theology and accepted by Brunel University in which the Old Testament theologian, Walter Brueggemann was the chief conversation partner. Not surprisingly, Brueggemann's insights still feature prominently in the ensuing discussion.

I am grateful to Derek Tidball, then Principal of the London School of Theology, for so shrewdly and sympathetically supervising my thesis; to Robin Parry for commissioning and encouraging its emergence in book form; to Andrew Walker for so generously commending it for inclusion in the Deep Church series; and to Mick Brooks, CEO of CWR for supporting its publication. None of them, of course, are in any way responsible for my mistakes, or my views, and certainly not for any polemical opinions I have let show!

What I offer is a mere contribution to the debate, and there is comfort in knowing that. But I think I can safely say that I make up in experience what I lack in expertise. Nurtured on the classical hymnody of revivalism (Wesley, Watts, et al.), I came early to relish the freedom and playfulness in God's presence of charismatic praise. Of late, I have come to appreciate the serious joy of cathedral choral worship. I have truly 'smelt the roses' in many places.

I am mindful, also, of New Testament scholar Mark Allan Powell's riposte to a Christian rock fan from their old 'Jesus Freak' days who told Powell that he loved Jesus so much he would do anything, even die, for him, but that the church and its worship was like an old black-and-white TV show and was irredeemably boring. So said Powell: 'You would die for him, but you won't be bored for him?'

My good friends, Trevor Martin, Stuart Reid and Ian Stackhouse continue to console, correct and cheer me along the way, and Kathy Overton goes the extra mile in smoothing that path for my work at Waverley Abbey House.

My wife, Mary, is the worshipper in the family and should take most credit for encouraging me in the theory and practice of loving God both charismatically and liturgically. I am forever thankful to God for her.

Recently, we have mourned the death of two dear friends: after lingering Alzheimer's, Dacre Wicks, the most exuberant celebrator I knew, and, prematurely, Alex Sutherland, the most sensitive worship leader I knew. The year 2007 also marked the fortieth anniversary of the graduation of the 'Applegate Batch' from Spurgeon's College: Keith Applegate, David Coffey, John Hayes, Peter Hicks, Peter Judd, Gustav Kon, Rob Riden, Bob Scott, Boyd Williams – and *in memoriam*, Trevor Martin, Athol Gill, John Murray and most recently, my first room-mate, Peter Edwards.

I dedicate this book to them all. I dare to believe that, having already passed from death to life in baptism, the 'Band of Brothers' is not diminishing, merely relocating . . . in 'the sure and certain hope of the resurrection of the dead'. *Sursum Corda*.

Now in my sixth decade, and having 'come back from the dead' (metaphorically speaking) more than once, I am glad to be able to testify with Tolkein's Aragorn that 'deep roots are not touched by the frost'.

Philip Greenslade
Waverley Abbey House
January 2008

Introduction

Why the Best of Both Worlds?

Worship wars are nothing new. They have been with us since the Garden of Eden and the Judean Wilderness. And if John's witness in Revelation is anything to go on, the battle with imperial idolatries continues until the consummation. The crisis of contemporary evangelical/charismatic worship purports to be of a lesser order: a conflict over *styles* rather than substance. But I wonder. Is this all such conflict reveals? A preference based on musical taste or personality type? A cross-generational disagreement over sound volumes?

Maybe in some cases it is. In which case the matter can be solved by turning down the amplification, boxing the drummer in a see-through plastic cage, letting the sedate and grey-haired have their own 'alternative' service, or – and this is least likely – by a greater show of Christian charity all round.

But, based on my own history, I suspect that something more is going on than meets the critical eye. I suspect that in such conflicts deep misconceptions are surfacing about the nature of worship. I would suggest that deeper issues are involved – issues of ecclesiology and biblical theology.

My positive proposal is to suggest that a greater grasp of the *necessary polarities inherent in worship* might serve us better than surface antagonisms. I use the word 'polarities' – though perhaps 'paradoxes' or 'dialectic' or 'bipolar' might serve equally well – in ways which I hope become clearer as we go on.

My interest in the polarities of worship has been roused by a number of concerns. Firstly, personal experience of different types of worship has left me satisfied with none but fascinated by all – and has whet my appetite for a new synthesis. Two contrasting memories of 'sung Eucharist' spring to mind: one on Easter Day in Ely Cathedral, the other in a Pentecostal church in Scotland. In one, the mixed-voice choir led us through Haydn's *Nelson Mass* accompanied by orchestra, soprano soloist, trumpeters, incense, and sunlight streaming through the great lantern for which Ely is noted. In the other, the local assembly, bread was broken, wine was shared, songs of praise were sung to guitar, keyboard, flute and drums. In both, I felt, genuine worship was offered.

The basic reflection is just this: since at their best, both cathedral and 'charismatic' worship are God-centred, why is it not possible to embrace both classic and contemporary worship in what some commentators style 'blended worship'? As a fully consenting adult worshipper, I want something of the best of both worlds. But is this possible?

Voices have recently been raised that give cause for hope. These voices are not only those of mainstream liturgical theologians but also from within the evangelical tradition. The late Robert Webber, of Wheaton College, who for a long time taught and researched the theology of worship, approvingly reports a new phenomenon in North America in which he sees 'a convergence of worship traditions taking place'.[1] Webber finds a reason for this in a post-Enlightenment freedom from what is merely cerebral, and the emergence of what is a more holistic – and to him, more biblical – approach to worship.[2] He sees traditionally liturgical churches becoming increasingly more open to 'the active presence of the supernatural'[3] including the charismata. A number of such churches, Webber observes, are discovering that 'liturgy was never meant to be a closed order with no room for spontaneity . . . but a guide'.[4] By the same token he now finds charismatic pastors, weary of 'performance-driven ministry', who are looking 'for more structure, more content, and more connection with the past'.[5] For them the rhythm of the Christian Year and the recognition of creation inherent in sacramental practice have fresh appeal. Webber applauds this development as spiritually enriching.

Another significant thinker within Evangelicalism moving in this direction is Marva Dawn, now adjunct professor at Regent College, Vancouver. She has argued that to develop worship which genuinely adores God and forms faithful people is not to narrow but to expand our repertoire. 'That is why worship must be filled with all kinds of sounds, new music and old, faithful fountains of praise, powerful retellings of the biblical narrative, an ever-widening river to convey the grandeur of God.'[6] British worship consultant Andrew Maries agrees, if in somewhat more measured tones: 'It could be exciting to think of rediscovering some of the ancient Christian heritage while integrating the freshness and vibrancy of the new.'[7]

All this would be mere grist for the polemical mill were the issue not deeply serious. The insights of sociology suggest that worship is a powerful agent of human change. If so, then how we worship matters profoundly. Will not worship which is merely formal, emotionless and lacking in human dynamics tend to reproduce people as formal and self-inhibited as itself? Equally where worship stays one-dimensional, affecting only at a visceral level by its mantra-like repetitions and rhythms, there is a lack of soul, creating passing moods rather than lasting emotions. Will not such theologically shapeless worship tend only to confirm people in an already thoughtless, impressionistic lifestyle? Even the word 'alternative', as applied to so-called 'alternative services', may prove a misnomer. Does such 'worship' really offer any genuine alternative to the techno-music culture that is already shrinking the imagination of the young?[8] It is questions like these that this book seeks to probe.

In biblical terms, blandness is a sin against the rich texture of God. To be neither hot nor cold, neither one thing nor the other is possible for idolatry but is not an option for worshipful response to the Living God. The Golden Calf was Israel's tragic 'fall' from grace. But what Moses said to Joshua as they came down the mountain together to confront the ugly idolatrous scene makes for disturbing reading. Joshua tries to make sense of the turmoil beneath him. In John Durham's translation,

> Joshua heard the racket of the people celebrating and he said to Moses: 'a noise of battle in the camp!' But Moses answered:
> 'not the sound of heroes exalting,
> not the sound of losers lamenting,
> but the sound of random singing is what I hear.'[9]

This is truly blowing neither hot nor cold. This is, in Durham's words, 'the disorganized, conflicting, answering of random singing'. In this loss of vital connection with the Living God in all his toughness and tenderness lies the seed of worship that is a mere singing of songs, a worship with no thought-out sequence, that has lost touch with its vivid reasons for praise or lament. This is a worship with no theological rationale, worship which tends to being jarring and meaningless. This is celebration without victory, rejoicing without reality – the offering of worshippers who are merely having a good time.

Ongoing theological consideration about the kind of God it is we worship is crucial to the health of worship. Otherwise worship – like middle-of-the-road music – becomes bland and middlebrow, both intellectually and emotionally. Worship is, as it were, reduced to 'easy listening'. Embracing the extremes in God will keep worship alive and well. Marva Dawn raises important issues when she asks: 'Does our worship focus one-sidedly on comfortable aspects of God's character, such as his mercy and love without the dialectical balancing of his holiness and wrath? Is Jesus reduced to an immanent "buddy" or "brother" without the accompanying transcendence of God's infinite majesty?'[10] These are issues which will be considered later. For the moment it is enough to say that worship needs to reflect not only the richness and scope of God's character but the range and scale of human experience, too.

Israel's worship tradition seems to suggest that the lesson of the Golden Calf was a bracing challenge to subsequent generations of prophetic singers. Walter Brueggemann has characterised Israel's praise as 'going to the extremes'.[11] In the Psalms – the songbook of Israel's Temple worship – are found songs for all seasons, praise and prayer that cover the whole emotional spectrum, celebration and lament that embrace the polarities in human experience.

Worship is the place where the polarities of our human experience are drawn redemptively into the polarities of all God is. This can and needs to be reflected in the way worship is structured. In the words of liturgical theologian Gordon Lathrop:

> The various paradoxical pairs that have been so necessary to Christians to speak faithfully of God – human and divine, letter

and spirit, now and not yet, immanent and transcendent – correspond, in conceptual language, to the ways the liturgy presents the
faith.[12]

Exploring this proposition is just what this book seeks to do.
Though Brueggemann's overall approach to biblical interpretation is open to substantial criticism – of which my thesis took note
– his stimulating body of work has undeniably inspired a whole
generation of students to hear with greater acuteness the sharp
testimony of the Old Testament. Drawing on his work has proved
useful in rooting my case in specific biblical texts, in linking it to
larger biblical theology themes, and in relating it to wider cultural and social issues. Brueggemann's angle of view draws our
attention to three aspects of biblical interpretation which are
relevant to my case: the *rhetorical* dynamics, even, tensions in
scriptural text, the *sociological* context, even conflict, reflected in
the text, and the inescapable *dialectical* dimensions of biblical
theology.[13]

Testimony and Counter-testimony

Rhetorical criticism is a method of approach to the text that goes
beyond form-critical analysis of sources into a study of language
itself, discerning how the genre, style and assembly of a text com-
municate its message. This method examines those speech-
patterns crafted into the text which explain its persuasive and
transforming impact upon the reader or hearer.[14] Exposing
rhetorical tensions in the text will enable us to hear the angular
and odd witnesses in Scripture and prevent us from a premature
flattening out of its varied contours.

We are alerted to listen to the dissonant voices, to the counter-
order prophetic speech. Renewed recognition of the reality-mak-
ing power of speech will inform our understanding of the
prophetic nature of Israel's praise and of her counter-cultural
liturgical witness to the reality of Yahweh's rule. Brueggemann's
interest in the literary function of Scripture bears affinities with
George Lindbeck and the so-called 'Yale' school of post-liberal-
ism.[15] In Lindbeck's words, it is not that 'believers find their

stories in the Bible, but rather that they make the story of the Bible their story'. What Lindbeck calls 'intertextual theology' works by redescribing 'reality within the scriptural framework rather than translating Scripture into extrascriptural categories. It is the text, so to speak, which absorbs the world, rather than the world the text'.[16]

Preaching and liturgy, I shall argue, are primary means of grace precisely because they provide access to that biblical world: through them we enter to 'indwell' the story of God and reidentify ourselves as the people of God. To take Israel's worship life seriously is to recognise that 'it is in worship, and not in context-less, cerebral activity, that Israel worked out its peculiar identity and sustained its odd life in the world'.[17]

Narrative, too – it goes without saying – is fundamental to our experience of life. This was true for Israel, except that in Israel's case, the narrative was a redemptive one in which Yahweh was the chief actor in the drama. In keeping with post-modern fashion, which remains incredulous towards all metanarratives, Brueggemann claims that the narrative world of the Bible has no special privileged position but must compete with other accounts. Somewhat tentatively, Brueggemann concedes that the Old Testament offers the materials for constructing a metanarrative with certain qualifications.[18]

One qualifier is to insist – as Brueggemann does repeatedly – on taking the story of Israel as 'history' told from the underside in contrast to the way in which history is usually presented as a tale told by the winners! This has important ramifications for worship: it implies there is no celebration without victory but at the same time that such celebration be without complacent triumphalism. Israel, the nation of former slaves, thereafter sang the song of freedom and perpetuated the Passover Lamb in the ongoing sacrificial worship associated with both Tabernacle and Temple. Christian worship, likewise, can only reflect the cross-and-resurrection-shaped narrative that saves us.

Brueggemann draws on the work of Amos Wilder in contending that 'stories generate story-worlds' which govern the development of the characters in it. 'Derivatively,' he argues, 'those who hear and trust these narratives are invited to live as well in a world where the same sort of characters are available and the same sort of transactions are possible'.[19] This is a large claim – one which will reappear shortly when we consider the sociological underpinnings of Brueggemann's insights. But it is a claim – as I hope to show – that offers one way of understanding the impact of worship as the magnetic field which draws worshippers into the alternative world of reality which is God's kingdom.

Transformed Imagination

Accessing this 'alternative world of reality' requires a revitalised and re-educated imagination. It is, argues Brueggeman, 'the vocation of the prophet to keep alive the ministry of imagination' so as to evoke an alternative scenario of reality – one that critiques the prevailing culture and empowers people to think the unthinkable and opt for change.[20]

Brueggemann applies this insight brilliantly to the exilic prophets Jeremiah, Ezekiel and Second Isaiah as they seek by dazzling flights of rhetoric and imagination to lift the sights of the downcast exiles, closed in to the dominant Babylonian definitions of reality. 'These poets', he writes, 'not only discerned the new actions of God that others did not discern, but they wrought the new actions of God by the power of their imagination, their tongues, their words. New poetic imagination evoked new realities in the community.'[21] Or again, 'Poets have no advice to give people. They only want people to see differently, to re-vision life.'[22]

In this regard Brueggemann acknowledges a debt to the philosopher Paul Ricoeur, who taught that people are changed not by ethical urging but by transformed imagination,[23] and to Craig Dykstra for whom it was the 'function of revelation to provide us with images by which to see truthfully and realistically'.[24]

Of course, as Trevor Hart reminds us, imagination is also 'the source of fantasy and untruth'.[25] Some versions of seeing 'as' will be found in practice to be in competition with others and we need some means of making imagination accountable.

Hart repudiates as inadequate the minimalist view that Christian imagination is stocked with bits and pieces of particular biblical text. Seeking a larger and surer basis, Hart points to paradigm theory which suggests, Hart argues, that new wholes, new overall patterns, are 'not built up from a gradual accumulation of fragments. Rather the shift to a new construal, a new way of seeing "as", happens all at once as our imagination lays hold of a pattern in its entirety and is consequently able to make sense of the fragments as belonging to this pattern precisely by locating them in it.'

Isaiah's life-changing experience in Temple worship springs to mind in this connection – an experience in which a sudden realisation of an open heaven puts Uzziah's death into perspective and launches a new era of God's activity. Rescripting the liturgy then becomes a key prophetic task. To evoke the deep memories of a redeemed people and to envisage a greater exodus for an exiled nation is to give them a new song to sing.

Socially Constructed Reality

As well as paying attention to the rhetorical features of the text, a consideration of its *sociological context* proves useful, too. The *sociological* implications for worship are significant in rooting Israel's cultic life in actual reality, something that prophets like Amos had cause to remind the nation and which it is no embarrassment to an incarnational faith to acknowledge either. Social tensions are reflected as affirmations of divine stability and order and are matched by the counter-melody of subversive praise and prayerful dissent. Liturgy cannot be detached from the realities of power and the struggle for justice. Worship in the Old and New Testaments is a political act.

Also relevant to the project in hand is the theory of knowledge expounded by Peter Berger and Thomas Luckmann in *The Social Construction of Reality* (1966) and in Berger's *The Sacred Canopy* (1967).[26] Here 'Reality' stands for that framework of organised social life that is accepted and relied upon. 'Construction' implies that this does not drop from the sky but is humanly produced, is often jealously guarded but can be altered, albeit through struggle. 'Social' recognises the communal effort needed to grasp and maintain this construct.[27] Berger himself recognised the crucial role played by religion and in particular by religious ritual in sustaining this constructed world. Through 'theology embedded in worship', the vital societal tradition is remembered.[28]

But if liturgy can act to reinforce the status quo, it can also serve prophetically to declare the imaginative construction of an alternative world. Such a defiant world-remaking function of worship proves especially crucial to the survival of exiled and beleaguered believers.[29] In Brueggemann's words, 'Praise is not a response to a world already fixed and settled, but it is a responsive and obedient participation in a world yet to be decreed and in process of being decreed through this liturgical act.'[30] It scarcely needs emphasising that this is no mere wishful thinking but the creative response of a faithful and worshipping community to an authoritative and given story which names Yahweh as the chief actor and speaker.

The theme of 'Exile' functions at a number of levels: as a real and traumatic historical experience, as a governing paradigm for subsequent Jewish faith, and as a metaphor applicable to the post-Constantinian situation of the post-modern Western church and – by further extension – to the alienation and needed homecoming of those as yet outside of faith.[31]

Walter Brueggemann, for one, explores these levels to great effect. He points out what is becoming a scholarly consensus that 'the exile became the matrix in which the canonical shape of the Old Testament faith is formed and evoked'. Its shadow looms over the whole corpus of Scripture. The trauma of exile inspired in Israel 'a surge of theological reflection and a remarkable production of fresh literature' – including, we might add, fresh praise and new songs.[32] We may feel too the metaphorical power of the exile as a 'dramatic, liturgical event of marginality, alienation and displacement'.[33] The 'new' psalms it evokes – says Brueggemann, commenting on Psalm 117 – challenge even the Babylonians to join in Yahweh's praise. As he says, 'exiles take music seriously and they sing dangerously'.[34] Even more intriguingly, Brueggemann draws an analogy between Exile and the events of Easter by suggesting that 'the Jewish model of exile and homecoming received a Christological equivalence in terms of crucifixion and resurrection'.[35] All these are significant clues to that richer biblical understanding of worship this project seeks to unfold.

Making Both Ends Meet

Lastly, we note the dialectical dynamics of biblical theology. This may be acknowledged without necessarily entering into a debate about a contentious theological tradition that flows through Barth to Kierkegaard and back to Hegel. Modern dialectical theology – that of Barth and Brunner in particular – viewed our inability to know ultimate reality as a result of sin. Be that as it may, at a popular level, the term dialectic may serve as a way of acknowledging the paradoxical nature of truth. In what Donald Bloesch styles the *'via dialectica'*, polar pairs are held together in the tension of faith. Savingly, all contradictions in the human condition are absorbed into the supreme paradox of eternity entering into time in the incarnation of God in Jesus Christ. 'Unlike philosophical thinking,' Bloesch adds, 'theological dialectic refuses to resolve contradiction; instead, it strives to keep them in creative tension with each other'.[36]

It is evident from the language he uses that Brueggemann follows the broad thrust of the dialectical method: 'hurt and hope', 'accessibility and freedom', 'assurance and precariousness'. These are characteristic of what Brueggemann terms his 'bipolar' approach.[37] The paradoxes of faith are precisely the junction points of God's self-revelation. God is known only in the crisis of faith created by the convergence of opposites. This bipolar scheme, Brueggemann claims, provides a true shape for Old Testament theology; it is the tension between 'structure legitimation' and 'the embrace of pain'.[38] In so far as the Old Testament shares in the common theology of the Ancient Near-Eastern world, it is 'structure legitimating' and presents a God who is 'above the fray'. This 'common' theology – which appears later to be identified with 'creation theology' – posits a lofty God of justice and mercy whose will imposes a strict deed-consequence system of morality on humans.

At the same time – and in tension with it – from within the Old Testament, this common theology is resisted and an openness to pain occurs in which God is disclosed as a God who is 'in the fray'. Here the Old Testament reflects experience from the 'underside', especially as felt in social conflict. To be true to the canonical witness of Scripture, we must not dissolve this tension.

The dominant thread portrays a world in which Yahweh rules supreme. As spelt out by the Mosaic Covenant, Deuteronomy and the Deuteronomic history, as well as the classical prophets of Israel, it establishes a non-negotiable link between commandment and curse. In this order of things, obedience is submission to the 'maker's instructions' so that morality is based on creation theology and encoded in Torah.

In Brueggemann's view, the stance of the exilic prophets to the effect that Exile is the judgement of God on the people's covenant unfaithfulness, serves only to undergird the moral structure. This is reflected in the Proverbial wisdom in a practical way, and in an overly dogmatic and overstated way by Job's friends. The act-consequence view of ethics suggests a morally coherent world and represents the contractual side of covenant theology. Contractual theology is an aspect of creation theology and 'creation theology readily becomes imperial propaganda and ideology'.[39]

Brueggemann then links creation theology directly to royal theology, suggesting that creation theology is exploited to maintain the status quo. The building of the Temple to celebrate Yahweh's rule, for example, can be construed as a legitimising of the current king's regime by the endorsement of divine presence. Again it needs to be noted that worship is inextricably bound up with political realities.

This legitimising tendency, Brueggemann argues, needs strong critique. 'The main dynamic of the Old Testament is the tension between the celebration of that legitimation and a sustained critique of it. The reason the contractual theology must be sharply criticised is that it lacks a human face when it is articulated consistently. It is a system of theology that allows no slippage, no graciousness, no room for failure.'[40] But the system is not foolproof nor the theology leakproof. What is to be done with those aspects of reality which do not readily submit to the legitimised regime and the ideology that supports it? Is there room for dissent from 'beneath', from the disadvantaged and the disenfranchised? Is there room for lament and complaint within the worship of a sovereign, just and merciful God?

Contractual theology – a distortion of creation theology – did not die with Job's friends. It is alive in many modern guises: for example, in contemporary forms of prosperity teaching, which guarantee to faith certain results and blessings, and even treats worship in a pragmatic way as a weapon of warfare. It is reflected in the exchange mechanism of modern consumerism, an attitude which lies behind much of the so-called 'worship wars' where pressure is experienced to shape worship to the felt needs of the guests. It is reflected in our confidence in technological control and the application of this cause-and-effect mentality to the arena of worship in what Eugene Peterson calls the 'technology of the supernatural' where by ritual activity we seek to harness spiritual power for our own ends.

The dialectical tension inherent in biblical faith not only effects worship; it ultimately concerns the character of the God who is worshipped. How worship handles pain, protest and perplexity is crucial for its authenticity. 'The presence of pain-bearers is a silent refutation of the legitimated structures.' Worship that is overly triumphalist or socially indifferent dissolves the tension short of resolution and ultimately balks at the cross. 'The liturgy in Israel subverts imperial ideas of a god who neither hears nor obeys pain.' By doing so worship makes possible true resolution by opening up God's alternative future where grace reigns and a vision beckons of a saving reality beyond present demands and failures.[41] As Gordon Lathrop argues, since worship utilises the dialectic that is so central to the communication of meaning, the 'paradoxical appositions of liturgy . . . ought to be the preferred medium'.[42]

Contemporary cultural developments contribute to making this an appropriate time to consider the potential of 'blended worship'. Definitions of post-modernity are as difficult to grasp as wet soap. But, as Leonard Sweet has recently urged, one significant feature of the post-modern condition is its oxymoronic character – its relish for the and/also rather than the either/or or even the both/and. He cites the conjunction of the liturgical and the Pentecostal as an example of how the post-modern church works. 'What if the church,' he asks, 'were to embrace extreme worship (the freedom and the liturgical)? . . . Any community without the tang of "realness" is too insipid for post-modern tastes – not to speak of Jesus himself.'[43]

Yet to seek 'blended worship' is to seek more than a patchwork quilt of traditional rubrics skilfully – or otherwise – interwoven with contemporary ingredients. It is to seek for worship which recognises both the heights and depths in God and in human experience; worship which attempts both to embody the long historic narrative and the broad creational scope of God's covenant love. Here liberated shouting and love-saturated silence live together. The wild exuberance of joy, song, laughter and music goes hand in hand with the deep anguish of repentance, tears, groaning and hope-filled prayer. Robert Webber appreciates 'a growing consensus that, in the future, Christian worship will be characterised by the blending of the traditional and the contemporary into a vital experience of worship and praise'.[44]

1

God-sponsored Hedonism: Self-fulfilling *and* God-glorifying

Is worship for God? Or is worship, in some way, for us? Of course, these two questions are not strictly a matching pair. No one would seriously argue that blessing God adds to his stock or enriches him in any way. After all, 'who has ever given to God that God should repay him?' (Rom. 11:35). In this sense God is never put in our debt by the praise we offer him, however lavish; nor is he deprived or impoverished by the lack of it.

On the other hand, it is undeniable that worship impacts the worshippers and may be beneficial to them. Archbishop William Temple famously described worship in terms of its effects on the worshipper: 'To worship is to quicken the conscience by the holiness of God, to feed the mind with the truth of God, to purge the imagination by the beauty of God, to devote the will to the purpose of God.'[1]

Yet the questions we have raised are worth asking if only to expose a tension at the heart of worship which is worth preserving, and a confusion which is worth avoiding. The issue concerns the *ultimate direction* of worship. Ephesians 1:1–14 is one long eulogy in which Paul celebrates the fact that what originates in blessing returns in blessing (1:3). The long outworking of salvation all tends in one direction: 'to the praise of his glorious grace . . . for the praise of his glory . . . to the praise of his glory' (1:6, 12, 14). Liturgy, by definition, is 'service to God' – the people's work of offering to God grateful appreciation for his gifts of grace and awed acknowledgement of God's august majesty and glory which is worthy to be praised.

Yet edification cannot easily be discounted. After all, it is precisely in Ephesians with its strongly God-directed doxological thrust that our attention is drawn to the edifying effects of corporate worship. By singing speech and making music, worshippers speak *'to one another* with psalms, hymns and spiritual songs' which, according to Colossians, is an extension of the teaching and admonition of the Body of Christ (Eph. 5:18; Col. 3:16).

This reaffirms a point made elsewhere in this book about the instructional power of worship in shaping our understanding of the faith. Think of the hymns which teach *bad* theology![2] Think, too, of the potential of a faithful credal hymnody that transmits the faith – as in the so-called 'hymns to Christ' (for example Col. 1:15–20). So praise can never be reduced to private self-expression; it is shared experience with mutual effects. Worship in this practical sense is not uni-directional. And yet, the mutual edification of believers that occurs in worship is nevertheless still drawn into the stream that flows 'to the Lord' and gives thanks to God the Father (Eph. 5:19–20; Col. 3:16c).

One way of embracing the creative tension that lies at the heart of worship is offered by the recent work of John Piper.[3] Piper's take on the Westminster Confession, which echoes that of Jonathan Edwards, is that we are most blessed when God is most glorified. God is the only being who has a rightful duty – so to speak – to seek his own glory, and God would not be God without doing so. Paradoxically, we human creatures are most fully ourselves when we seek to live to the praise of that same glory, and without doing so we would not become fully human and fully ourselves.

If 'the chief end of man is to glorify God and to enjoy him for ever', Piper argues, God's glory and my gladness are not antithetical. The human heart's passion for pleasure and God's passion for praise converge in a way that makes sense of human existence and brings Godly self-fulfilment. Piper has termed this 'Christian hedonism'. To pursue God's holiness is to pursue our highest good and happiness. The chief end of man is to worship God by enjoying him forever. This, says Sam Storms, following Piper, answers to our God-given 'inescapable hunger for joy and satisfaction and delight'.[4]

There is, in this view, a relentless God-centredness which often cuts across our modern or post-modern cultural predispositions. Donald Bloesch – while generally appreciative of Piper's aims – questions whether even 'Christian hedonism' sufficiently challenges the 'motifs of self-aggrandisement that are so ubiquitous in our culture'.[5] From a mainstream church standpoint, Lutheran liturgical theologian Frank Senn has argued that the Enlightenment's turn towards 'the human' is reflected liturgically in a definite turn away from adoration to edification. Such a move has accelerated within Evangelicalism especially with its populist bent to reach out to unbelievers. In the process, edification has itself been superseded by evangelistic and seeker-friendly services in which inherited language and iconic props are pared down to the minimum or dispensed with altogether in an attempt to engage the interest of the unchurched.

Much is said to be gained by this move in bridging the secular gap – and mega-churches can do the number-crunching to prove it. But frenetic attempts to make worship 'relevant' invariably run the risk of compromising the God-directedness of worship. The outcome is a dilution of worship which tends to soften the encounter with God so that God no longer looms over us in majestic grace or stands over against us in confrontational challenge or judgement. And the loss is ours: we lose the *real* God. But the key here is to make the pursuit of God in worship the priority direction in which worship flows. Then we see the benefits that accrue to us worshippers as 'spin-offs' of the focus on God.

Simon Chan makes just such a point in criticising worship that is driven by pragmatism into being 'useful' to serve some other end than God's glory. 'Worship itself,' Chan writes, 'has become the means by which one hopes to induce God to act on our behalf. It is not uncommon hear "worship leaders" telling the congregation that praise will bring down the glory of God, or, that if we wait on the Lord long enough we will receive healing.'[6]

It is only when we accept that worship is of no earthly use at all that we get its point. Only when we 'actualise the "aimlessness" of worship that we know what it means for the church to exist "to the praise of God's glory"'.[7] Only when we prioritise worship in this way do we benefit.

When we forego the idea that we worship God in order to be better people, we begin to appreciate that 'certain good things do happen to people when they worship God in spirit and truth'. But such 'good things' are 'byproducts' of worship, 'intrinsic goods', the added value accrued by seeking first God's kingdom.[8] In worship which is self-consciously designed to appeal to us, what could conceivably prevent worship from lapsing into entertainment? Frank Senn warns that to turn worship into entertainment leaves the audience satisfied and confirmed in what they already feel and know. In place of entertainment, he presses for worship as *enchantment*.[9]

The utilitarian demands that drive so much contemporary worship tend to jettison all beautiful artefacts as a frivolous irrelevance. What – in our multi-purpose, functional worship centres and pragmatic worship – speaks of the *beauty* of God?

Worship surely includes inquiring in God's sanctuary long enough and lovingly enough to begin to behold the beauty of the Lord (see Ps. 27:4). This necessitates being given time and space to gaze and contemplate, to savour and relish – as well as being swept up in the crowd as it gatecrashes the festive party! Such a stance in worship should not be regarded as static and demotivating: quite the reverse.

It is entertainment that induces passivity. Enchantment captivates and entices us beyond ourselves; it opens our eyes wide with wonder and stirs the imagination of the heart. Senn suggests that, whatever its deficiencies, even the medieval mass at least 'gave worshippers a glimpse of another, brighter, heavenly world that lifted their spirits, at least momentarily, out of the drab and brutal world in which they eked out their daily existence'.

Worship then is multi-directional because this is how things are in relation to God. Everything flows *to* God; everything does so *through* God, through God's Spirit *to* and *through* one another; and all this only because everything flows *from* God.

Every worshipful move we make is a response: we love because we are first loved; we sing and pray because we are first addressed and even 'sung over' (cf. Zeph. 3:17).

We worship, in the end, because we are taken up – and into – the loving life-force and fellowship of the Blessed Trinity – even as this God is 'with us'. 'I think we delight to praise what we enjoy because the praise not merely expresses but completes the enjoyment; it is its appointed consummation.'[10]

2

Worship as Politics: Attending Heaven's Throne *and* Confounding Earthly Powers

The second of the polarities of worship I want to consider is the way in which worship reflects the tension inherent in the life of faith of being either *world-denying* or *world-reflecting*. Failure here is readily apparent in worship that sticks at either of the two poles. On the one hand is worship which is almost world-denying in its provision of escapism. It offers worshippers a liturgical cocoon, insulating them from reality so that one is often exhorted at the Benediction: 'Now go out and face the real world'! William Willimon tells of a child psychologist in his congregation who complained that children's addresses never deal with children's real concerns such as death, abandonment, fear of adults, adult injustice and violence.[1]

At the opposite extreme is liturgy which is self-consciously designed to be relevant. What springs to mind is that 'God-of-concrete-God-of-steel' type of worship so obviously 'designed by a committee' that was in vogue in the 1960s and 70s. The great liturgical scholar, Alexander Schmemann, was unimpressed. As an Orthodox theologian for whom worship is the earthly interaction with the Divine Liturgy, Schmemann deplored this trend, which he saw as the secularisation of the sacred. Experimental liturgies obsessed with current issues or crises – environmental pollution or the latest earthquake – fail, he argued, in presupposing that 'traditional worship can have no "relevance" to these themes and has nothing to reveal about them and that unless a "theme" is somehow clearly spelled out in the liturgy or made into its "focus", it is obviously outside the spiritual reach of liturgical experience'.[2] Contemporary 'alternative' services might well face the same stricture: strobe lights and the banging of dustbin lids are no less kitsch. As Schmemann urges, 'to anyone who has had, be it only once, the true experience of worship, all this is revealed immediately as the ersatz it is. He knows that the secularist's worship of relevance is simply incompatible with the true relevance of worship'.[3]

Kathleen Norris records her distaste for this overly self-conscious and pretentious approach to worship, which she experienced at a conference on the subject. 'We knew that the worship had begun,' she recalls, 'when our "Worship Facilitators", so designated in our conference programs, marched up to the lectern, briefcases in hand.' Norris goes on to describe words that 'were pure abstractions and all but unsayable', and hymns that 'veered off into psychobabble', which were 'sodden with good intentions . . .' She describes her survival technique: 'I satisfied myself by mentally devising a Modest Proposal for a remedial course on the difference between a workshop and worship.'[4]

Worship as World-making

One way to hold this creative tension in worship is to see worship as a *world-shaping* activity. Walter Brueggemann, in a key discussion of the point, speaks of 'praise as a constitutive act' and of the 'social reality of praise' which 'effects the shape and character of human life and community'.[5] He follows the Old Testament scholar of a previous generation, Sigmund Mowinckel, in speaking of worship as 'world-making'. Brueggemann himself debates the use of quotation marks in 'world-making', wanting to resist the notion that worship merely alters our perception of things rather than impinging directly on reality to affect a transformation of the way things are.

Brueggemann appears to merge the two as his use of world-making without citation marks indicates. Liturgy is, in itself, sacramental in being the channel through which God does world-making work.[6] In developing this theme Brueggemann

relies on insights drawn from several disciplines: literary theory
– which posits that 'speech leads reality' to create alternative sce-
narios for the imagination to indwell; personality theory – in
which the infant learns to project another reality or where therapy creates a new 'world' of hope and meaning for the client; and
theology – which, while not determining the ontology of God,
does to a large degree 'shape the life-world in which we
encounter God'. But it is sociology which provides Brueggemann
with his strongest root and, once again, the work of Berger and
Luckmann to which he draws our attention.[7] In Peter Berger's
words, 'Every human society is an enterprise in world-making.
Religion occupies a distinctive place in this enterprise . . . by
which a sacred cosmos is established.'[8]

Of course, merely to stay at the sociological level is to shut ourselves into anthropology. If society is a human product that con-
tinuously acts back upon its producer then dialectic offers us only
a hermetically sealed system in which 'I am' and 'I am acted upon'
reinforce each other. How can we break out of our own 'socially
constructed reality'? How can we break through our own self-
described 'plausibility structures'? These are the questions David
Burrell has raised in his critique of Berger and Luckmann as he
seeks to press beyond the limitations which he perceives their
analysis sets on creative intrusion. Where does change intrude?
How does transformation take place? 'Nothing short of a conversion is required; an expansion of the parameters of one's experience so that it cries for a new language to articulate it.'[9]

Whether or not Burrell's criticism of Berger and Luckmann is
fair is open to question. They, undoubtedly, make room for some
form of transcendence in their emphases on objectification and
externalisation. They would surely agree with Burrell that it is
precisely here that worship plays its key role. Worship is not
merely a human product but the dynamic interaction of the
human with the divine. Worship is the matrix for major paradigm shifts. Liturgy is that new language Burrell suggests is
needed. Liturgy is, in Brueggemann's defining words, 'the intentional public nurture and practice of communal images and
metaphors'.[10]

Hence worship provides the context for a reconnection with
heavenly and ultimate realities as Isaiah discovered. Isaiah's

world, destabilised by the death of Uzziah, is restabilised on the throne of a sovereign God. As John was to find on Patmos, Isaiah in the Temple rejoins a worship that is already going on, encountering in the process the intense and focused holiness of God that transforms, cleanses and recommissions, transfiguring the prophet's world and connecting the prophet to the passionate heartfelt concerns of God. Worship makes a 'hole in the fabric of things',[11] through which pours ultimate reality reordering the dysfunctional world we ordinarily inhabit and reassigning our place in it. Brueggemann concludes somewhat effusively: 'It is the act of praise, the corporate, regularised, intentional, verbalised, and enacted act of praise, through which the community of faith creates, shapes, imagines, and patterns the world of God, the world of faith, the world of life, in which we are to act in joy and obedience.'[12]

Worship and the Reordering of Creation

Turning to biblical reflection, my first case in point is Genesis 1:1–2:4 – the so-called Priestly account of creation. In general terms creation narratives – both in ancient religions and in the Bible – stem from concerns about the stability of life as experienced by those recalling such accounts. Their setting in life is likely to be 'those occasions when such narratives served to assure and stabilize the state of the world, of life, of human existence'.[13] One such key setting in life was the cult, where the Babylonian Enuma Elish myth, for example, was recited as part of a New Year Festival. Speculation about the existence of a similar festival in Israel was for a long time the object of much scholarly energy. What is clearer is the consensus about the generally liturgical nature of Genesis 1:1–2:4. Although the passage lacks the linguistic features characteristic of poetry, its overall structure does give it an almost hymnic quality.[14] It is a stylised text with repeated 'sevens' whose rhythms and repetitions give it the feel of a litany or 'festive overture' in which can be detected 'an undercurrent of praise'.[15] Bernhard Anderson remarks that the 'atmosphere pervading the first chapter of Genesis is that of the community of worship'.[16] In his view 'the priestly account of creation, like the creation psalms of the Psalter, is a sublime expression of Israel's praise. The creation story is most at home in a setting of worship' and the form of the narrative 'suggests it was shaped by liturgical usage over a period of many generations'.[17]

Brueggemann concurs by stating that Genesis 1:1–2:4 is a 'liturgical text in which the community "remembers" God's creating event, but also re-enacts and participates in it in order to give pattern to present experience, presumably in the exile'.[18] The point about exile will be taken up later. Here we note only how well Genesis 1:1–2:4 as a liturgical texts fits the consistent emphasis in Israel's worship experience on praise for all God's created works. This stream of praise for the goodness of creation flows most fully in the Psalms, notably in psalms such as Psalm 104. This appears to place worship clearly on the world-affirming side of our equation.

Dangers of Creation Praise

But there is danger here and Walter Brueggemann has been vocal in pointing it out. He alerts us to how readily creation praise can degenerate into passive acceptance of the status quo. Brueggemann has long argued that creation praise was susceptible to exploitation by Israel's kings as a means of buttressing their own position. This forms the heart of his protest in *Israel's Praise*,[19] that creation theology when placed at the centre of the cult was turned into ideology. When the reasons for praise are lost and the root of Israel's praise in liberation is obscured, then the way is open for praise – even of God's goodness in creation – to be an uncritical affirmation of the way things are. When 'unanswered disorder and unconsoled suffering' are screened out of the liturgy then a false peace and a phoney world have been made.[20]

Brueggemann recognises and approves of the recent rehabilitation of creation theology. In a useful summary he traces the unease with it back to Barth's rejection of natural theology. This was re-enforced in the 1930s by von Rad who, writing against the backdrop of Nazi ideology of 'blood and soil', made the redemptive credo the firm centre of Israel's faith and confession. The Biblical Theology movement subsequently made an anti-Canaanite, anti-fertility stance central to their view of the prophetic protest in Israel. In the light of the increasing mystery of the cosmos, the debate between science and religion, and growing environmental concerns, creation theology has undergone a necessary renaissance in recent decades. All this Brueggemann readily acknowledges but while he may have softened his tone he remains wary. He still insists that Israel's praise of creation was subverted by royal propaganda, and that it remains vulnerable to political, ideological or technological misuse.[21]

But this need not be. Various considerations suggest themselves as safeguards. Firstly, it is worth recalling that, at least, two of Israel's key feasts – Pentecost and Tabernacles – were once harvest festivals which were adapted for commemorating redemptive events. The conjoining of praise for creation and redemption was precisely what enabled prophets like Deutero-Isaiah to invoke the Creator God as the Redeeming God and to envisage salvation as an act of *New* Creation.

Secondly, prophetic protest is always needed to inveigh against worship that gives thanks for the gifts and forgets the Giver. Nor is it acceptable, as Hosea protested, to honour Baal alongside Yahweh, the Creator, as a way of covering all your options! Yet, at the same time, Hosea did not eschew the bold, and erotic imagery used by the Baalites and never wavered in his portrayal in word and deed of Yahweh as Lover and Husband of his people. Yahweh was not to be confused with any fertility god but he was not for that reason any less fertile! True worship in responding to holiness rules out both cynical detachment from the social world and autonomy and self-sufficiency within it.

Thirdly, worship must never be detached from ethics. This was the famous critique of Amos (see chapter 8). When 'all is patently not right with the world' – especially from the viewpoint of the victims of social injustice – then some decidedly prophetic 'unmaking' and imaginative 'remaking' of that world become necessary. To that end, and quite deliberately, there is in Amos no rejection of creation praise. Quite the reverse: praise of Yahweh as Creator is reaffirmed as central to the prophet's protest by the insertion of passionate creation hymns into the sequence of prophetic oracles (Amos 4:13; 5:8–9; 9:5–6).

A prophetic re-envisioning of the liturgy, it seems, is crucial to a prophetic reordering of the social world.

'A world of justice, mercy, peace, and compassion is created in the imaginative act of liturgy.'[22] This is the real world, such worship declares. And it is precisely those who would evade the claims of justice by escaping into religion who need reminding of the Creator's concern for the wider world and his refusal to condone 'business as usual' when social righteousness is being betrayed in it.

Fourthly, the 'setting in life' of Israel's creation praise must be noted. It is not hard to see how Genesis 1:1–2:4 might function in the Babylonian Exile when construed as a liturgical polemic against the gods, offering an alternative world-view to that held in the Ancient Near East. Particularly where life is experienced as disordered, unfruitful and not good, the 'contrast-world' of creation most needs to be expressed in worship. In Brueggemann's words, 'The liturgy cuts underneath the Babylonian experience and grounds the rule of the God of Israel in a more fundamental claim, that of creation.'[23] This counter-experience of worship, he argues, permitted the exiles 'who gave themselves fully over to the drama and claims of the creation liturgy to live responsible, caring, secure, generative, and (above all) sane lives, in circumstances that severely discouraged such resolved living'.[24] Creational monotheism is reborn in song. The world is refigured, the astral deities are put firmly in their place, the gods are deposed, their stewardship over earthly affairs entrusted to God's human creatures who become the 'secretaries of nature's praise'.[25]

Fifthly, creation beckons beyond itself. The current creation, though good, is flawed and provisional not yet having reached its perfected potential. Significantly, the creation narrative of Genesis 1:1–2:4 reaches its crescendo in the rest of God. If human ones are the crown of creation then Sabbath is its climax. On the one hand work is dignified and our working-week with it; on the other, we are reminded that we are not to be workaholics but worshippers who continually reach out for the final 'rest' of God. This is the eschatological energy within creation praise, which saves it from ritualised complacency. The Sabbath, which harks back to creation, also points the people of the covenant – of which it is the sign – towards the future grace of rest in the land and ultimately in the consummated kingdom.

The feast that marks times past also makes time for a new world coming. In Brueggemann's words 'Praise is not a response to a world already fixed and settled, but it is a responsive and obedient participation in a world, yet to be decreed and in process of being decreed through this liturgical act.'[26] Paradoxically, as Gordon Lathrop has reminded us, it was when Sunday was just another working day, that it more powerfully pointed beyond itself, beyond the working week itself, to something that will not be achieved simply by a mere succession of seven days. 'Sunday is not the same thing as the week; Easter is not the same thing as springtime.'[27] Sunday is the 'eighth day', the eschatological day of resurrection, the first day of a new creation. By transcending time, Sunday – like Sabbath before it – sanctifies time, affirming the goodness of the old creation while heralding the new. In these ways worship which includes praise for creation's gifts and goodness need not succumb to the temptation to be indulgently affirmative of the world as it is but can contribute to the remaking or reshaping of the world as it shall become.

Worship and the Reordering of the World in the Tabernacle

Further confirmation of the world-making possibilities in worship can be gained from considering the narrative which outlines the planning and building of the Tabernacle in Exodus 25–31 and 35–40. Several scholars have helpfully shown that this Tabernacle narrative is a counterpart to the Genesis creation account we have just been considering, bringing to a climax the Priestly account to which both belong.[28] Jewish scholar John D. Levenson has focused a good deal of this reflection. For him the Tabernacle represents a 'microcosm or miniature world'.[29] In Terence Fretheim's view, Exodus 35–40 'invites us to see the building of the tabernacle . . . in terms of re-creation'.[30]

The points of correspondence between the two accounts are, indeed, striking and fascinating.

(i) The dedication of the Tabernacle on the first day of a New Year (Ex. 40:2, 17) corresponds in liturgical celebration to the first day of creation.

(ii) Repeated emphasis on the direction given by God's word – 'as the Lord commanded Moses' (e.g. Ex. 40:16–32).

(iii) A seven-fold pattern of speeches made by Yahweh matching the seven days of creation (Ex. 25:1–30:10; 30:11–16; 30:17–21; 30:22–33; 30:34–38; 31:1–11; 31:12–17).

(iv) The empowerment by the Spirit of God of Bezalel and other craftsmen reflects the creative role of God in creation's beauty and order (Ex. 31:1–2; 35:31–36:2; Gen. 1:2).

Levenson profitably compares textual details.[31] 'Moses saw . . . and blessed . . .' (Ex. 39:43) corresponds to 'The Lord blessed . . . and saw that it was good' (Gen. 1:22, 28, 31). 'And Moses did everything as the Lord had commanded him' (Ex. 40:16, 19, 21, 23, 25, 29, 32) connects directly with 'And God said . . . and it was so' (Gen. 1:3, 9, etc.). 'And so Moses finished the work' is reminiscent of 'when God had finished the work he had been doing' (Ex. 40:33; Gen. 2:2). The sanctifying of both sanctuary and priests echoes the setting apart as 'holy' of the seventh day (Ex. 40:9–16; Gen. 2:3).

Two further points particularly stand out:

(i) Sabbath climaxes both accounts (Ex. 31:12–17; Gen. 2:2–3). As a covenant sign, Sabbath (Ex. 31:16) asserts that in the worship of Yahweh by a people he has made holy, the Creator's original intentions for his creation are being reinstated and furthered. On this point it is worth noting that Nahum Sarna, in typical Jewish fashion, strongly asserts the priority of the Sabbath over the Tabernacle since the latter was only a mobile and temporary structure.[32]

(ii) The glory which marks the dwelling of God in the Tabernacle matches the 'rest' of his completed creation work (Ex. 40:34–35; Gen. 2:2–3). 'This is one spot in the midst of a world of disorder where God's creative, ordering work is completed according to the divine intention just as it was in the beginning.'[33] 'The pattern shown on the mount', when implemented, enables worship to act as a

kind of cosmic gyroscope, realigning and restabilising the
turbulent and off-centred world around it. 'Collectively,
the function of these correspondences is to underscore the
depiction of the sanctuary as a world, that is, an ordered,
supportive, and obedient environment, and the depiction of
the world as a sanctuary, that is a place in which the reign
of God is visible and unchallenged, and his holiness is pal-
pable, unthreatening and pervasive'.[34] William Brown sums
up the significance of this literary pattern: 'In addition to
informing each other, creation and tabernacle form perhaps
the bookends of an original Priestly layer of Israel's formation or, at least, a magisterial *inclusio* that imbues everything within its narrative bounds with cosmic and cultic
significance.'[35]

Even the immediate context sets up a contrast between the
Tabernacle and the idolatrous worship of the Golden Calf.
Fretheim lists the human initiative, commanded offerings,
unplanned and hasty activity, user-friendly accessibility, and the
impersonal, if visible, object of worship, as characteristics of the
worship of the Calf. In contrast, the Tabernacle, born of God's initiative, is built with willing offerings, after careful planning, over
a long period, and safeguards the divine holiness, presenting an
invisible yet personal God.[36]

Furthermore, the slave-driven Egyptian imperial oppression
which at the beginning of the book of Exodus made brick-mak-
ing and construction an enforced and severe activity is, by the
close, eclipsed by the Spirit-inspired energies of a redeemed and
free people voluntarily contributing to and engaging in the work
of sanctuary construction under the benign rule of Yahweh. The
God-defying chaos into which the world has fallen is reordered
by liturgical space and ritual into a God-glorifying cosmos once
more. To take this one stage further, as William Brown does, is to
see Israel's ultimate occupation and division of the Land of
Canaan as creation's mirror image: 'Yahweh's holy dwelling
established in the sanctuary leads to the establishment of Israel's
land, divided and filled.'[37]

Symbolic, liturgical world-shaping, then, can be construed as
re-enacting original creative world-making. This is in line with

Berger's sociological assessment that through liturgy 'the sacred cosmos emerges out of chaos and continues to confront the latter as its terrible contrary'.[38] Worship is the key to the reordering of creation. Brown cites a Rabbinic source as declaring: 'Before the sanctuary was erected, the world shook, but from the moment the sanctuary was erected the world was firmly established'; thus, Brown concludes, 'The establishment of Yahweh's dwelling-place finalises creation, and a Sabbath stasis is reached.'[39]

Original sin is to refuse to sing the original song – and the social consequences are dire. As Romans 1:19–32 makes clear, the God-constructed social fabric disintegrates when the creation order is, as it were, put into reverse by human rebellion and refusal to praise. What emerge are the hyphenated sins of the human heart: self-love and self-idolatry which corrupt social relationships, obliterate the 'other' and render narcissism the order of the day, finally descending to the ultimate narcissism of same-sex acts. 'The world,' as Berger argues, 'begins to shake in the very instant its sustaining conversations begins to falter . . . Religion' – especially, we might add, 'worship' – 'is the audacious attempt to conceive of the entire universe as being humanly significant'.[40]

The Christological hymn of Colossians 1:15–20 celebrates the recovery of that human significance by putting a human face on the wisdom of the creation-order – Jesus the image of the invisible God. The hymn acclaims the reunification of what sin has torn asunder. The rebellious powers are pacified to the divine will and the alienated are reconciled to God through the blood of the cross. The cosmos is straightened out in Christ, realigned with its origins ('by him') and destiny ('for him'). To sing of this is to celebrate the world's renewed coherence and to hymn its restored harmony and wholeness.[41]

Worship and 'Empire-building'

By continuing in the New Testament it is possible to take further the concept of worship as world-making. Central to the credal confession and liturgical expression of the early church was the acclamation of Jesus as 'Lord'. Nowhere more than in Philippi would such a claim have been made with awareness of its political overtones.[42] Philippi was a 'colony of Rome', predominantly settled by veterans from the army, and granted the high honour of the *'ius Italicum'*, that is, of being governed by Roman law. Ironically, as it turns out, it was in Philippi that Paul exploited his Roman citizenship to avert unjust punishment, leaving behind the tiny first church in what we would now call Europe.[43] Richard Horsley has urged that we take more seriously the heavily political nuance to the Pauline notion of church as 'assembly'. The roots are indeed in the Old Testament Septuagintal description of Israel as the 'assembly of the Lord'. But this, in Horsley's view, is conjoined with what was its normal connotation in the Greek-speaking Eastern Roman Empire – the 'citizen' assembly which formed the key element in the local government of the Greek 'polis'. Christian *ekklēsiai*, then, must be viewed as the counterpart to these local political assemblies, the gathering by contrast of those whose 'citizenship' (*politeuma*) was in heaven (Phil. 1:27; 3:20), who worship together as alternative communities, who owe a higher allegiance than to the Emperor, who constitute the sign, foretaste and agent of a superior kingdom.[44]

For the early church in first-century Philippi, therefore, to confess Jesus as 'Lord' (Phil. 2:5–11) and to await him as 'Saviour' (Phil. 3:20–21) was to commit a political and counter-cultural act. It meant – and means – to 'cultivate explicitly an alternative consciousness, to maintain a sense of reality running against the stream of the unquestioningly accepted commonplaces of the age'.[45] It is still a matter of much debate whether Philippians 2:5–11 is a pre-Pauline hymn or indeed, whether it is hymnic at all. But there is no doubt that Paul, with the early church, celebrated that Jesus, the Jewish Messiah (as was his destiny according to Psalm 2), had been installed as Ruler of the World. 'Rejoice the King is Lord' represents an outrageous realignment of political realities: Jesus, not Caesar is Lord. To hymn the praise of Jesus as Lord (*kurios*) and Saviour (*sōtēr*) – both terms familiarly applied to the Caesars – was to relativise the Emperor and the Empire that went with him.[46]

The same dynamic can be detected in Paul's daring revision of the Shema in 1 Corinthians 8:6. He is arguing for the 'oneness' of God in typical Jewish fashion – not so much, that is, to assert a

mathematical unity in God as to reaffirm his unrivalled suprem-
acy with 'no other gods beside me'. But this newly confessed oneness in God includes 'one Lord, Jesus Christ' but excludes all
other 'so-called gods, in heaven or on earth', not least the deified
Emperor on earth.[47]

To await this one Lord's 'presence' or 'arrival', his *parousia* – a
word regularly used for an imperial visit[48] – was to look beyond
what Rome offered for ultimate hope. As it was similarly to be in
eager anticipation of going out and meeting him (1 Thes. 4:17) –
apantēsis being the technical word for the welcoming committee
of leading citizens going out to meet a visiting dignitary in order
to escort him back into their city.[49] The 'parousia' would explode
the myth of Roman propaganda that all was 'peace and security'
(1 Thes. 5:3) and bring everything – presumably including the
Roman Empire – under his control (Phil. 3:21). To evoke and
incite this 'royal visit' at the Eucharistic feast with its eschatological shout of 'maranatha' (1 Cor. 16:22) was to rob Rome of its ulti-
macy and transcendence and to re-centre the world around the
Lordship of Jesus.

Such a potent mix of confessional praise and liturgical
expectancy contradicted the prevailing view of how the world
was framed. Diplomacy and conquest partly account for how the
Caesars refigured the world in their favour and made their
names. As S.R.F. Price has shown, 'The Imperial cult was another
way by which the Emperor was constructed.'[50] 'The Imperial
cult,' Price goes on, 'stabilised the religious order of the world.
The system of ritual was carefully constructed; the symbolism
evoked a picture of the relationship between the emperor and the
gods. The imperial cult, along with politics and diplomacy, constructed the reality of the Roman Empire.'[51]

The Roman 'social construction of reality' was an efficient and,
to many, an attractive package of order, prosperity, protection
and patronage, gift-wrapped in religion. 'Political power rests
not only in armies, taxes, and administrative apparatus. Power
can be constructed or constituted in religious forms, of temples,
shrines, images, sacrifices, and festivals. Not only does power
order, sustain, threaten, and dominate, but people also desire
order, sustenance, direction, and protection.'[52] To this end Rome
practiced a controlled economy, fixing prices and guaranteeing

trade. The Emperors even subsidised grain shipments and gave insurance cover to shipping importers in order to maintain the flow of goods to Rome.[53] All this was undergirded and shot through with the Imperial cult. 'It simply was good business to show loyalty to the Emperor who made maritime trade possible.'[54] Adopting Peter Berger's language, Wes Howard-Brook and Anthony Gwyther describe the 'sacred canopy' of the Imperial cult as characterised by the prevailing 'myths' of empire, peace, victory, faith and eternity.[55] The association of *'pax'* with *'Romana'* for instance was no mere feat of arms but a triumph of 'marketing', the hijacking of language so as to subsume whole areas of human activity under the Empire's logo, sustained by incessant 'advertising' of the Emperor's fame. The Empire was a well-spun web in more senses than one.

And central to it was the all-pervasive Imperial cult. Christian worship could only stand as opposed to the lie and the liturgy which perpetuated this mythology. 'If then, we can see the theatre of Christian beginnings in terms of a "war of myths", one can identify it even better as one of liturgy against liturgy or liturgies, with an understanding that liturgy involves a whole life-style, acts and ethic, as well as recital.'[56] The Imperial cult was the glue that held together the intricate network of social, economic, political and cultural activities. Sport, games, festivals, markets, concerts – all were marked with the seal of the Emperor. His image was everywhere and stamped on everything, not least the coinage. In this way the Imperial cult, while not always directly idolatrous, became pervasively idolatrous in demanding absorption in a 'domination system'.[57]

Worship as Politics

Worship, then, is an indisputably political act. Nowhere can this be seen more clearly than in John's Revelation and in the vision of liturgy and worship shown us there. Praise calls the bluff of the idolatrous powers-that-be. It declares the Emperor has no cosmic clothes on! But to see this calls for the development of 'apocalyptic eyes', eyes which, like John's, have 'grown young with eternity'.[58] Apocalyptic unveils the eschatological and transcendent truth behind the scenes of earthly and historical realities. In doing so it invests those historical eventualities with ultimate significance as magnets of either judgement or grace.

As we worship, the ultimate 'there and then' of God's rule impinges on the immediate 'here and now' in our world. Worship purifies our imagination and keeps the heart's eyes and ears open to these apocalyptic sights and sounds. Susan White urges that 'part of the liturgy's work is to invite people to envision the world in a different way, to imagine it as God intended it to be; indeed, to imagine the world "as if" the reign of God had already been fully realised'.[59]

In this way we are enabled to transcend the cultural closed systems, the current 'plausibility structures' of society that seek to contain and control what we can or cannot perceive. 'To see history doxologically', as John Yoder characteristically put it, 'demands and enables that we appropriate especially, specifically, those modes of witness which explode the limits that our own systems impose on our capacity to be illuminated and led'.[60] Doxology, again in Yoder's words, 'is more than liturgy. It is a way of seeing; a grasp of which end is up, which way is forward'.[61] Worship offers us access to the 'real' world. As Richard Bauckham says, 'The most elemental forms of perception of God not only require expression in worship; they cannot be truly experienced except as worship.'[62] To adapt John's own language – and indeed Aldous Huxley's – worship, not drugs, opens the true 'doors of perception'.

To be 'in the Spirit on the Lord's day', then, is the language of both prophecy and worship. It implies the invitation and privilege of the church to ascend in worship into the heavenly liturgy, to join a worship that is already and always going on. To sing

> Wherefore with angels and archangels,
> and the whole company of heaven,
> We laud and magnify your glorious name

is to give voice to the conviction that 'Christian collective worship participates in the heavenly cultus . . .'.[63] This kind of Ascension language as applied to liturgy is typically part of the Orthodox testimony. 'When the witness of the revelation writes:

"I, John, was in the Spirit on the Lord's day . . . then I saw a new heaven and new earth . . ." it is as if he were saying to us: I, John, your brother took part in Divine Liturgy. The Liturgy brings us to an open window of revelation, of incorruption.'[64] 'The early Christians,' declared Schmemann,

> realised that in order to become the temple of the Holy Spirit they must first ascend to heaven where Christ has ascended . . . For there in heaven they were immersed in the new life of the king-dom; and when, after this 'liturgy of ascension', they returned into the world, their faces reflected the light, the 'joy and peace' of that kingdom and they were truly its witnesses.[65]

John's communities are encouraged by John's prophetic insight into the 'Divine Liturgy' to 'set their worship head-to-head with the worship of the mighty Roman Empire'.[66] This worship is not so much world-denying as world-deconstructing. Rome's wor-ship is a parody of heaven's praise, its pomp is a sham, its peace an enforced placebo, its vaunted permanence a front.[67] True wor-ship destroys this illusion and remakes the world in God's image.

We now know that the initiative for the Imperial cult did not lie with the Emperor but was, in effect, a form of religious flattery devised by the 'worshippers'. It is significant in grasping the impact of John's vision – particularly of the centrality of worship – to realise that Asia Minor was in the front-line of this response. Smyrna and Pergamum were among the first cities eager show their gratitude for the Emperor's patronage by erecting temples in his honour. Yet the danger facing Christians in John's world was not the temptation to convert, even under duress, to a differ-ent religion, bowing down at a pagan shrine to a false god. We now know that there was little outward pressure to do this, and indeed, no evidence of widespread persecution of Christians under Domitian. The test was how to be 'in' this Imperial world and not 'of' it. The challenge faced by John's readers was how to carry on normal life, including conventional commercial transac-tions, within the system while not buying into its idolatrous values and mores. What was at stake was assimilation, spiritual 'fornication', and succumbing to the seductive charms of a sys-tem which John viewed as the 'Great Whore' (Rev. 17–18).[68]

Faithfulness in worship framed the church's parameters and measured its resistance. 'To see history doxologically meant for John's addressees that their primordial role within the geopolitics of the Pax Romana was neither to usurp the throne of . . . Domitian . . . nor to pastor Caesar prophetically, but to persevere in celebrating the Lamb's Lordship and in building that community shaped by that celebration.'[69] John's pastoral vision sought to alert his readers to the fact that 'as kings and priests' they already shared through worship in ruling the world. This is to fly in the face of the facts as the Empire broadcasts them. 'Worship wars' are not a twentieth-century Western phenomenon but a perennial conflict of sovereignties – whether in Eden, Canaan, crucially in the Judean wilderness and at Calvary, or, as here, in Asia Minor.

There are, not surprisingly, seven scenes of worship in Revelation all located in 'heaven' (4:2–11; 5:8–14; 7:9–17; 11:15–18; 14:1–5; 15:2–4; 19:1–8). These scenes act like the chorus in a Greek drama or Broadway musical. They have a strategic place in the literary structure of the book, often explaining the preceding vision. They can be said to constitute the overall theme of John's vision and message: by exposure to the worship of heaven, his readers can be assured of the ultimate sovereignty of God and Christ in redeeming and judging the world, and so be motivated to enter into worship with greater passion and purpose and to live out that worship in patient obedience and suffering love.

Worship which connects with ultimate sovereignty and holiness teaches us the script of heaven and superimposes the map of the new world on the old one. And at every point these hymns subvert the cult of Empire. As David Aune points out, the similarity between them and the Imperial hymns is reflected in the terminology employed: 'the holy one', glory', salvation', 'authority', 'worthy to receive power', 'righteous are your judgements', 'our God the Almighty' and so on.[70] In every case, the language is recycled, redeemed and put to its true use.

Of the seven liturgical segments, those in chapters 4 and 5 are the most significant, summarising what John has seen and setting the scene for what follows. First the Creator is praised in the trisagion, then the Lamb as alone worthy to open the scroll of God's redemptive plan for history, then both the enthroned Creator and the Lamb together are honoured and adored. Revelation 4:2–11 records a 'liturgical ascension' which gives John his first glimpse of heaven's worship. The vision, set in the Temple, is of the heavenly, prophetic council of God gathered around the throne. This, too, reflects an imperial court scene with the king's advisors grouped around him. 'Just as the Roman Emperor surrounded by the court was depicted as holding a *libellus*, a petition or letter in the form of an open scroll, so God is seen as holding a *biblion*, a scroll with seven seals.'[71] In John's vision, the concentric circles of praise around God's throne only serve to emphasise its centrality in the scheme of things. It is this throne-centred worship to which the church on earth has access and on which its own liturgy is intended to be modelled. By worship, our world – which has spun off its axis – is symbolically realigned with the will and purpose of its Creator. Worship re-centres our lives – indeed all of life – around the throne of the One Creator God.

The elders who possibly represent the twelve tribes and twelve apostles – in fact the whole people of God – prostrate themselves at this throne. The historian Tacitus tells us the Parthian King, Tiridates did likewise when he placed his royal diadem before the image of Nero.[72] The sea of glass symbolises the truth that all chaotic forces of evil are subjugated to God's sovereignty. The adoration of the cherubim echoes the praise of all animate life, and the four living creatures offer praise as forerunners of what all creation is meant to fulfil. The God who is worshipped is the one 'who was, who is and who is to come' – the Lord of history and the future. His ascription as the 'one who lives forever and ever' (4:9c) is almost certainly polemical, relativising the 'eternal' empire of Rome. The title 'Lord and God' (4:11c), *'dominus et deus'*, currently being applied to Domitian, is reclaimed for its rightful Owner.[73]

Revelation 5:8–14 is a description of worship which illuminates the worthiness of the one who, uniquely, qualifies to open the scroll of God's redemptive purposes for history. Here the singing is in praise of a slain lamb. And which Empire has ever had this emblem on its coat of arms! Yet it was by crucifixion that the Roman Empire disposed of its most socially dangerous 'loose cannons' – runaway slaves and political rebels. The *Pax Romana* was ultimately founded on the crosses Rome erected. So is the

Empire of God. But in this version of the story, our Emperor conquers by dying on the cross in place of all victims and rebels. In doing so he subverts the domination system, expunging the myth of sacred violence with the reality of redemptive love. At the crucifixion the powers that be played their ace card – sacred violence – and were trumped by suffering love. One Empire exalts the love of power; the other the power of love. Needless to say, if I have all the right ideas, the superior myths, the truly sacred canopy, but have not love, all I have is a clash of symbols! Worship centred on the Lamb reorientates the worshippers and recentres the world around this paradoxical *pantokrater*.

The seeming uselessness – even passivity – of such 'acts of worship' when compared to the all too active power of the Empire, is precisely the point. As Eugene Peterson has pointed out, 'When we worship, it doesn't look like we are doing much – and we aren't. We are looking at what God is doing and orienting our action to the compass point of creation and covenant, judgement and salvation.'[74] By its very nature, worship of God and the Lamb on the throne is the still point of the world, a holding of the breath, to acknowledge that, despite all continuing suffering and injustice, the casting vote is already in, the ultimate issues already settled.

The further hymnic sections serve the symbolic rearrangement of the world as we look into the world as God sees it. Revelation 7:1-9 portrays the one eschatological people of God from two aspects: as a completed, perfected company ('144,000') and, in fulfilment of the Abrahamic promise, as an international multitude ('whom no one can count') gathered for an eschatological feast of Tabernacles. Verses 7:9–12 voice the praise of this completed but innumerable crowd as celebrating that true *sōtēria* – parodied by the Empire's totalitarian benefaction – which belongs to the enthroned God and the Lamb and those daring enough to forsake Rome's 'protection racket' for the lasting shelter they provide (v. 15). 'Participants in the imperial cult organised regional choral societies and sang praises to the Emperor. John now sees a vast choral society of people who worship God and the Lamb for their generosity, power and love.'[75] The strange 'silence in heaven' (8:1) only highlights the paradox of the non-pragmatic offering of prayers, which turn out to be instrumental in the unleashing of God's judgements on earth. In this way the powerful correspondence between heavenly worship and its earthly counterpart is confirmed. Prayers really do 'get through' and contribute to the 'answer' given. The traffic really does flow in both directions.

The next three songs form a chiasm – with 11:15–19 and 15:2–8 – where the heavenly sanctuary is opened, bracketing 14:1–5. In 11:15–18 the announcement of the subjugation of world empires to the transcendent sovereignty of God is greeted by another surge of worship. No longer is God the 'coming one' for he has taken his great power. The time has come for judgement and for reward. From one angle, this is the terminus of history as Revelation sees it, acclaimed in a victory chant and a subsequent prayer of thanksgiving, headed by the only certain liturgical formula (*eucharistoumen soi*) used in Revelation.[76] Verses 14:1–5 witness to the overwhelming music which accompanies the followers of the Lamb as they sing the new song, born of their own unique experience of redemption, their virginity a metaphor for lives uncorrupted by the domination system. The worship here in song and self-sacrifice constitutes a total lifestyle offered up as the first fruits of a renewed humanity.

In 15:2–8 the song of Moses and the Lamb are creatively combined, both to affirm the oneness of God's true covenant people across the dispensations, and to celebrate the new and greater exodus. John's readers can be heartened and challenged by the praise of the same Lord as Lord over Caesar and Rome as he was over Pharaoh and Egypt. When John hears the heavenly worshippers acclaiming the downfall of 'Babylon' (19:1–7), he touches the ultimate in worship where God's people, without glee or gloating, can celebrate, in humble maturity, the will of God being done on earth, in judgement as well as grace. Worship truly has the capacity to reshape the spiritual and political landscape.

In the words of Christian activist, Bill Wylie Kellerman, 'praise is no Sunday School pastime. It rises on the raw edge of common history, acknowledging and even affecting it'. Commenting on the astonishing 'Hallelujahs' uttered over the demise of Babylon (Rev. 19:3, 6), Kellerman notes that the 'liturgy signifies and celebrates the end of one world and the beginning of another. In that sense, faithful worship is inherently subversive'.[77]

Again and again throughout Revelation, certainly at crucial points, the liturgically structured visions re-emphasise that 'glory and power' belong to God, not the Emperor – that the Lamb, not Caesar, is Lord. And it is chapter 13 which most vividly pictures the battle for worship that is raging. The three monsters – dragon, sea beast and land beast – form an 'unholy trinity'. Usurping God's place, the beast from the land abrogates to itself the world's astonished adulation, 'who is like unto you', plagiarising the repeated Old Testament acknowledgment of God as incomparable. It masquerades as unique but has, in truth, only a borrowed authority and an imitation glory. This first beast's resilience (symbolised perhaps by the rumoured revivification of Nero) parodies the death and resurrection of Jesus; his permitted authority and well-nigh universal acclaim parodies the Lamb's investiture (chapter 5).

The second beast, perhaps in parody of the role the Holy Spirit plays in glorifying Jesus as Lord, seems to represent the provincial imperial cult, including its priesthood which acted as the local enforcement agency and propagandist for the Empire's blasphemy. The saints are challenged by this blasphemous worship to counter-cultural distinctiveness even if this means embracing exile with all that entails of confinement and suffering (13:10). It is perhaps because the increasing social isolation of John's readers echoes that of Israel in a previous 'Babylonian captivity' that John draws so heavily on the book of Daniel for his imaginative reconstruction of what he has seen and heard. The distinct echoes of the heroism of the three young Hebrews in resisting Nebuchadnezzar's idolatrous demands to bow down to his image, only served to reinforce John's call for patient endurance and counter-cultural faithfulness on the part of the saints. Focused in its worship of God and the Lamb, the church utters 'one mighty NO to imperial Caesar and all his idolatrous works and ways'.[78]

It is the Emperors who are the 'hollow men'. To worship them, even second-hand, by uncritical subservience to their system is to perpetuate a charade. The verb *proskuneō* was used of the Roman senators who were compelled to worship an empty chair representing the absent Emperor Gaius.[79] But the throne John sees is not unoccupied: on it sits the Last Emperor in 'real presence'. It was while 'in the Spirit' on this Emperor's day (*kuriakos*, 1:10)[80] that John 'ascended' to the heavenly worship of the One Creator God and the Lamb, there to encounter the ultimate reality which could refigure his world and that of his beleaguered readers. 'Think of Easter as a political rally. Think of Sunday worship, our handling of the broken body and the shed blood, as our attempt to get our politics right.'[81]

3

Crossing the Threshold: Charismatic Freedom *and* Liturgical Order

This chapter explores further the polarities inherent in worship by addressing the issue of what may broadly be called strangeness and familiarity and – more specifically – freedom and order. This will be done with the aid in particular of the sociological concept of liminality.

The Concept of Liminality

The concept of liminality was popularised in the 1960s by the social anthropologist Victor Turner as a result of detailed fieldwork with the Ndembu people of north-western Zambia. His findings have been utilised profitably by a number of liturgical theologians and have a particular bearing on this thesis. In a number of studies, notably the ground breaking book *The Ritual Process*, Turner resurrected and developed ideas first put forward by Arnold Van Gennep in his investigation into the dynamics of rites of passage. These ideas converge particularly on the term 'liminal' which derives from the Latin word *limen* meaning a 'threshold'. For individuals and societies, Gennep had observed, 'there are always new thresholds to cross: . . . thresholds of birth, adolescence, maturity, and old age, the threshold of death and that of the after life'.[1] Van Gennep likened rites of passage to a journey in which the old securities were left behind in hope of arrival at a new status, a process which involves traversing a liminal landscape. He wrote that 'a complete scheme of rites of passage theoretically includes preliminal rites (rites of separation), liminal rites (rites of transition), and postliminal rites (rites of incorporation)'.[2]

Turner took the original idea of Van Gennep and broadened it – helpfully for our interest – to apply to ritual as a whole, and even further to those who, by participating in ritual, mark themselves out as 'threshold people'. The clear implication is that each event of corporate worship can be construed as a regularised and extended rite of passage. Viewed like this, worship becomes the renewal in its vocation of a people who are constantly crossing and recrossing the boundaries of church and world. Tom Driver has summarised Turner's findings: 'when people engage in ritual activity, they separate themselves, partially, if not totally, from the roles and statuses they have in the workaday world. There is a threshold in time and space or both, and certainly a demarcation of behaviour, over which people pass when entering into ritual'.[3]

Liminal experiences have the capacity to loosen ties both of inhibition at a personal level and of social status at a communal level. For those who embark on them, liminal journeys have the potential to recreate new social forms in the experience of what Turner calls 'communitas'. By entering into ritual liminality, people experience a new bonding, an awareness of becoming 'one heart and mind', in a shared sense of common humanness. Such people and such ritual defy traditional classification. 'Liminal entities', Turner wrote, 'are neither here nor there; they are betwixt and between the positions assigned and arrayed by law, custom, convention, and ceremonial'.[4] At the personal level, such activity can be characterised by great extremes as the polarities in human existence are ritually encapsulated. So, alongside immense solemnity – as when a process of dying is being re-enacted or recalled – there is also playfulness – as newfound freedoms are explored and relished. In both cases there is something which is unsettling to rigid concepts of order, whether of liturgical correctness, rationality or civic control. Significantly for my purpose, as I hope to show, the subtitle of Turner's *The Ritual Process* is 'Structure and Anti-structure'. Driver indeed goes on to argue in ways reminiscent of our earlier argument that the very language we use to describe liminality must be paradoxical 'because of the fact that threshold phenomena have a dialectical relationship to the realities that surround them and define them; and it is this dialectic of the liminal, hinted at in Turner's term "anti-structure", that opens a way through which "communitas" and other invisible potencies may arrive upon the human scene'.[5]

Holiness and Liminality

To test the relevance of the concept of liminality it is necessary to turn first to the broad contours of the Holiness tradition in Israel. Every society has its own 'culture map' which gives it meaning and structure. This can take the form, at a minimalist level, of a consensus of relatively undeveloped dyadic statements, ranging from male and female, hot and cold, right and left, up to basic moral orders of right and wrong. Whether sophisticated or not, such 'maps' provide the means of maintaining boundaries – boundaries which are necessary for an ongoing sense of identity, security and morality. Israel's 'culture map', in broad terms, was governed by the concept of holiness as laid out in the Priestly tradition.[6] This concept was, of course, a working out in practice of the existential encounter with holiness at Sinai and radiated out from it – a regularised response to what Rudolph Otto famously termed 'the numinous'. It may indeed be true, as Philip Jenson notes, that 'the subjective and psychological aspects of holiness stressed by Otto are of secondary interest to the Priestly writers'.[7] Nonetheless, the overarching aim of holiness legislation was that Yahweh, the Holy One of Israel, might dwell in the midst of his people. It was to this end that emphasis was laid on the implementation of holiness categories as a means of bringing order to the bewildering diversity of life.

The most basic classification was the separation of the Holy and the Profane (or Common) on the one hand, and Clean and Unclean on the other. Movement was possible from one category to another under certain conditions, though this was governed by strict rules and usually entailed a 'rite of passage'. This movement may be diagrammatically represented like this:

<<<<< sanctify <<<<<

HOLY   COMMON (or PROFANE)

>>>>> profane >>>>>

<<<<< cleanse <<<<<

CLEAN   UNCLEAN

>>>>> pollute (defile) >>>>>

HOLINESS MAP

It was possible to be 'holy and clean', 'profane and clean' or even 'profane and unclean'. What was impossible was to be both 'holy and unclean'! To bring the 'holy' into contact with the 'unclean' threatened to set off the ritual equivalent of 'fusion reaction' which might incur a deadly display of Yahweh's wrath.[8] This would spark a disordering, an explosive decentring and falling apart of the normal order of things – as experienced personally by the prophet Isaiah when he felt himself dismantled by an encounter with the holiness of God. '"Woe to me" I cried, "I am ruined! For I am a man of unclean lips and I live among a people of unclean lips"' (Is. 6:5).

As has already been noted, liturgy has the effect of making and remaking the world. Much recent scholarship roots ritual in the Old Testament understanding of cosmology, in its creation theology, and therefore in the need to maintain order. Ritual enacts a particular view of the world, a context of meaning which produces and, in turn, is reflected in and re-enforced by the ritual processes. Gorman suggest that this 'symbolic world' is constructed of three elements: (i) knowledge and language which identify and evaluate the elements of the world 'out there'; (ii) the subsequent meanings and interconnections assembled to locate our human place in it; (iii) the 'system of conduct' or set of responses appropriate to our view of the world and our place in the order of things. Through this process, Gorman suggests, 'the individual and also the community in communal rituals, helps to maintain and sustain that order'.[9] Ritual is an act of social drama in which the holiness of the creation order is respected or, when breached, repaired. Ritual as dramatic action, in Gorman's view, is characteristically formal, predictable and sequenced. He adds –

giving a hint that I will pursue later – that 'the sequence of ritual often has built into its structure the possibility for free or spontaneous moments'.[10]

According to the Priestly tradition, the aura of holiness in the Old Testament cult covers four dimensions, described by Jenson as the spatial, the ritual, the temporal and the personal. Space is sanctified in holy places. Of these the Tabernacle and later the Temple were central, with zones of holiness radiating out from the Holy of Holies, through the Holy Place and Outer Court to the Holy Camp (or later Holy City) into the Holy Land. An important distinction was made in this connection between being 'inside the camp' and 'outside the camp' (Lev. 4:21; 8:17; 13:46; 14:1–8). Ritual offerings and sacrifices pay homage to transcendent holiness and restore relationship with it when it has been infringed by sin. Time is sanctified in the rhythms of weekly, monthly and annual feasts and festivals. Personnel are inducted to sanctified roles, especially, for example, in the ordination of priests to represent the priestly people of God.[11]

All such ritual actions embody the dynamics characteristic of rites of passage. They lure priests and worshippers into that ambiguous and risky 'liminal state' which exists, as Turner put it, 'betwixt and between'. Van Gennep himself had described the ritual process as a transition from Status A to Status B, which passes through this marginal state. Here, familiar order gives way to strange chaos. Here, social hierarchies melt down into status reversal. Here, social bonds are dissolved and reforged into a new 'communitas'. As an example of this, Gorman treats the ritual of the Day of Atonement ritual in Leviticus 16 as a communal rite of passage.[12] The people are called to abandon their normal working life in favour of a sabbatical rest and humility. 'On the tenth day of the seventh month you must deny yourselves and not do any work . . .' (16:29). The suspension of the daily structures of society effectively holds people in a liminal state.[13] On the Day itself, the dyadic distinctions holy/profane, clean/unclean, order/chaos – each of which has 'one element that is a dangerous, destructive, invasive power'[14] – are dismantled in a period of ritual liminality and rearranged for the blessing of cosmos, camp and cult. Crucial to the constructive outcome of this entry into the uncertain liminal condition is the priest. In Gorman's words, 'the key to this liminal confusion and the re-establishment of the categories . . . is the ritual role of the high priest who, as the representative of the people and in the context of the liminal state, sets aside the normal separations of the categories . . . and, through his ritual actions, restores the normal, ordered relations of these categories'.[15]

Priesthood and Liminality

Holiness demands the preservation of ritual demarcation. The chief means for preserving these boundaries was priesthood: 'You must distinguish between the holy and the common, between the unclean and the clean, you must teach the Israelites all the decrees the LORD has given them through Moses' (Lev. 10:10). Priests are boundary-keepers, and can be described as 'guardians of the threshold' (2 Kgs. 12:9 NASB). What makes the role of priests so pivotal and so highly charged is that priests 'live both in the profane and holy spheres, though at different times'.[16] Priests maintained the boundaries of holiness in two ways, by teaching the prescriptions of the Torah and by performing rituals. Thus the holiness tradition brought into focused connection the creational order, the social sphere of the wider tribal encampment, and the more immediate zone of holiness within the worship of the sanctuary. Thus cosmos, camp and cult are ritually joined in the vision of the Torah both through instruction in law and in worship. Ritual ceremonies re-established the creational order and thus provided a sort of 'homeostatic balance'[17] that served to preserve the wholeness and integrity of creation and society.

Priests therefore on the one hand served the 'forces of conservatism' as agents of stability. But, on the other hand, and paradoxically, 'sacrifice and ritual compelled the priest to cross these same boundaries for the welfare and safety of the people. The priest had to move back and forth between ordinary space and sacred space.'[18] The priest inhabited the volatile intersection between sanctuary and society. He grasped in each hand, as it were, the positive and negative terminals of the holiness circuit. The priests – to continue the electrical metaphor – acted as 'insulators and connectors for the rest of the community'.[19] A priest 'lived his life in the transition zone between the holy and the profane. He operated daily in the dangerous ritual areas, midway between clean and unclean, manipulating the powers released by death and blood.'[20] The priest's own lengthy ordination ceremony encapsulated the liminal condition required of the people. On the Day of Atonement, the liminality of the priest is framed by two ritual bathings (16:4, 23–24). Once having entered the liminal condition himself, the priest is armed to enter the ambiguous interstices between the holy and the profane which are perilous and powerful. His ongoing lifestyle mirrored that of a people called to live in a permanent state of liminality as those on a lifelong rite of passage.

Worship, Exile and Liminality

The concept of liminality can now be applied in two main ways to the theology of worship.

(i) Worship is a liminal activity engaged in by a liminal, priestly people in transition – whether as pilgrims in the wilderness[21] or aliens in exile – which, itself, focuses and reinvigorates their unique transcience in the world.

(ii) *Within* worship lies a dynamic experience of liminality as worship oscillates between order and freedom, structure and spontaneity. In this sense it is feasible to posit an analogous relationship – though not a strict correlation – between these two areas and Gorman's cosmos, camp and cult: cosmos (what kind of status do transients have in the order of things?), camp (what is the significance of worship to a transient people?) and cult (what goes on within worship to renew the liminality of such people?).

Worship as Liminal Event

As has been noted earlier, Brueggemann has led the way in evaluating the symbolic location of the contemporary church in the Western world as culturally in exile.[22] No longer does the church hold sway over the centres of power in politics, the media or education. Now the church is marginalised and alienated in a post-Constantinian environment. This fact is not only being recognised but heralded by an increasing number of observers as the good news of exile. Now the church is presented with a crucial opportunity to relinquish its culturally soft, accommodating mode of existence in favour of a more distinctive, sharper edged relationship to society. 'Resident Aliens'[23] strike another chord, sing and pray differently and tell a different story from permanent settlers. No one has been more influential in the emergence of this stance, than Brueggemann in his championing of the formative influence of the Babylonian Exile. Brueggemann sees Exile as having a threefold significance: as a traumatic reality, as a theological paradigm and as a cultural metaphor.

1. In his handling of the Exile, Brueggemann makes much of its canonical significance though he acknowledges the current scholarly scepticism about the extent or – in a minority of cases – the actuality of, the Babylonian Captivity.[24] He nevertheless endorses the current view that the Exilic period was the probable matrix for the canonical shaping of the Scriptures, and so sees it as definitive of Israel's faith.[25] Exile is presented to us in Scripture as a traumatic reality. The Exile was a painful, liminal experience in which Israel was suspended 'betwixt and between' two worlds. Through the Exilic prophets God called his people to a bold relinquishment and an imaginative receiving. 'Judah had two tasks in this crisis of life and faith. It had to let go of the old world of king and temple that God had now taken from it. It had to receive from God's hand a new world which it did not believe possible and which was not the one it would have preferred or chosen.'[26]

It is true that the exiles were urged by Jeremiah to make peace with Babylon, to settle down for the long haul and not to look for early release.[27] But the exile prophets also sought to rouse the exiles to imaginative construction of an alternative scenario of reality to the dominant ideology offered by Babylonian hegemony. Exiles have to live prophetically by an imaginative 'as if'. The renowned anthropologist Clifford Geertz defined religion as having the capacity to propose a 'really real world' over against, but not as escape from, the 'real world'. It is precisely in ritual activity, Geertz argues, these two worlds come together. 'In a ritual, the world as lived and the world as imagined, fused under the agency of a single set of symbolic forms, turn out to be the same world.'[28] In Israel's case the imagined world is not a construct of its own imagination but a vision drawn by the prophetic poets through whom God spoke. Samuel Balentine, in evaluating the Torah's vision of worship as forged in the aftermath of Exile in the Persian period, sums up Geertz's insights.

> By repeatedly crossing and recrossing the boundary between the world as religiously conceived and the world as politically given, one's understanding of both the sacred and secular changes, enlarges, and sharpens. Whether in ancient Yehud or at the intersection of Straight Street and Broadway in any contemporary city, the summons for the people of God is to live faithfully inside the shadow that separates the 'idea and the reality.'[29]

Here lies the essential reason why liturgy is not – or need not be – a form of fantasy or escapism. As Brueggemann observes, 'While the temptation to a dualism that divides "life" from "worship" is real, it is important to see that worship models and enacts an alternative world of sanity that prevents Israel from succumbing to the seductive insanities of a world raging against the holiness of Yahweh the Creator.'[30]

This view of liturgy as a creative point of departure from current securities and as homecoming to new realities is important because worship and praise were among the first casualties of Exile. The total disruption of normal cultic functions – not least the demise of the Temple and its sacrifices – left Israel bereft and songless: 'How shall we sing the Lord's song in a strange land?' (Ps. 137). It was eventually the trauma and reality of Exile that inspired new forms of praise, notably lamentation, of which more later. It has been pointed out also, as a further example of the impact of Exile on liturgy, how the structure of the Psalmody collection reflects a drastic re-evaluation of kingship.[31] Psalms 2–72 portray the Israelite kingship in glowing colours as God's vice-regency on earth, destined to overlordship of the whole world. These Psalms give a very positive spin to the Davidic kingship, and include the best songs attributed to him. But Psalms 73–89 reassess this in the light of the Exilic experience. Psalms 88–89 are open wounds to be grafted on only in the course of time by Easter and the Parousia. Psalm 89, in particular, faces up to the failure of human kingship in Israel and asks whether the Davidic covenant still holds. Psalm 90 appears to be a deliberate editorial answer to the questions raised by Psalm 89. It reaffirms faith in the pre-monarchical Mosaic period, which knew that Yahweh alone was King and celebrates the fact that his dominion remains undimmed and can continue to be trusted after human monarchy has been swallowed up by Babylonian imperialism. The psalms that follow, 90–100, exult in this renewed awareness of Yahweh's kingship as the hope for the future by singing of his coming to rule and judge again. Songs of aspiration then predominate as if Israel's worship is fired with fresh horizons and the feet of the worshippers set to marching once again as pilgrims on the ascent to what is to come.

In this way liturgy both reflects a changed perspective forced by Exile and serves to re-enforce it by expressing renewed confidence in God. In more general terms, the Exile, by forcing the exiles to relinquish their grasp on the previous settled order of things, paradoxically spurred them to recall the deeper, foundational, 'old, old story of Yahweh and his love' which had originally given God's people their distinctive identity. Memory gave rise to hope, prompting the singing of new songs of restored expectation. The concept of Good News – '*basar*' – which became current during this period became the token of a longing for homecoming and signalled the intrusion of fresh grace from God. So worship, which had been the first casualty of exile, becomes the spearhead of renewed vision and hope. In Brueggemann's words, 'the exile is a dramatic, liturgical event of marginality, alienation and displacement'.[32]

2. Secondly exile may be viewed as a theological paradigm for later theological literature and reflection both Jewish and Christian. At this point we can extend a quotation from Brueggemann which was earlier cited in part: 'Together with the restoration, the exile emerged as the decisive, shaping reference point for the self-understanding of Judaism. Moreover, the power of exile and restoration as an imaginative construct exercised

enormous impact on subsequent Christian understandings of faith and life as they were recast in terms of crucifixion and resurrection.'[33] Here Brueggemann indirectly anticipates the more recent and more extensive use made – notably by N.T. Wright among others – of the 'exile and restoration' motif as a key to understanding the ministry of Jesus and as the seedbed for New Testament theology.[34]

The experience and paradigmatic power of the exile evoked in Israel a surge of theological reflection and a remarkable production of fresh theological literature. Brueggemann has in mind particularly the prophetic visions of Jeremiah, Ezekiel and Second Isaiah, as well as the final shaping of the Torah and the early beginnings of canonical Scripture. But as an example of immediate post-exilic reflection on the impact of Exile in a liturgical setting, Brueggemann cites Nehemiah chapters 8–9. Everyone was at the meeting and the Torah was read and expounded. 'Ezra opened the book . . . Ezra praised the LORD, the great God; and all the people lifted their hands and responded, "Amen, Amen!" Then they bowed down and worshipped the LORD with their faces to the ground' (Neh. 8:5–6). Paradoxically, both weeping and joy break out: weeping when the Torah is read as the narrative of lost identity, joy when it is understood as a story giving fresh hope. They then celebrate the Feast of Tabernacles, the reminder of how provisional Israel's life had been in the wilderness, yet how secure in the providential presence of God.

The paradox is again acute. As Brueggemann comments,

> There is something very odd about the Feast of Booths. On the one hand it is an experience of exposed homelessness . . . of leaving our conventional securities . . . On the other hand, and at the same time, this festival is evidence of true homefulness, when Israel senses that this is the right, safe place, lived with the sojourning God who keeps God's people safe, even in dangerous exposure. Thus the festival of homelessness turns out to be true homefulness.[35]

Through fasting and penitence, the Israelites 'separated themselves from all foreigners' (9:2). This was not, Brueggemann argues, a sign of arrogant legalism but a crucial stage in the reaffirmation of their distinctive identity. 'And now,' he writes, 'in these dangerous liturgical acts, Jews are facing up to their oddity, to their strong commitment, to their distinctive obedience.'[36] The long prayer of praise, confession and recital that follows, two weeks later, climaxes paradoxically in the recognition that 'we are slaves today, in the land you gave our forefathers . . .' It is clues like this and others brought to light by recent research, that have given rise to a growing acknowledgment among biblical scholars that many Jews from the return from Babylon right up to and including the time of Jesus genuinely felt themselves to be, in a profound sense, still 'in exile' – continuing subjection to foreign domination being read as a sign of being under the ongoing judgement of God.[37] Be that as it may, Brueggemann concludes that 'Nehemiah 8 is a moment of incredible and powerful liminality for this community, when old patterns have failed, when people in their vulnerability of grief and joy could for an instant leave their conventional home and live in the booths of fragility, in the presence of many ancestors, prepared to be reconfigured and reidentified.'[38] Exile concentrates the liturgical mind wonderfully. Liturgy is recovered as a liminal event, a litmus test of one's current status, and a catalyst for change.

We might talk in a similar vein from a Christian, New Testament perspective. As followers of Christ, we have passed from death to new life in baptism. We re-enact this drastic transition in corporate worship, focused in the Eucharist, which becomes a regularised rite of passage. Passing from death to life engenders its own evidence of loving one another in a new 'communitas' of love. Singing together the alternative story binds us together in heart and voice. Symbolically we hold the old world of creation and the new creation world together. We entertain a memory of the original goodness of the created order even as we seek to heal its wounds by prayer and confession of our sinful contribution to its brokenness. At the same time we both rekindle new patience and anticipate with joy by suspending the world 'as it is' in favour of the world 'as it will be', all the while learning the skill of patient endurance to live 'in-between' the times.

3. Brueggemann, as has been said, has been at the forefront of those urging us to embrace exile as the key cultural metaphor for

understanding the church's marginalised situation in the post-modern Western world. Exiles are an interim people who must live eschatologically a life betwixt and between the present and future, the 'world as it is' and the 'world as it will become' signalled in the church. Priestly people stand at the dangerous and often ambiguous intersection of church and culture, God and world, holiness and uncleanness. This is a danger zone where 'fusion reaction' is a daily possibility. Priests live in danger from holiness on the one hand and at risk from uncleanness on the other. A priestly people is called to live in a constant state of transition, experiencing permanent liminality.

This is perhaps why the letter to the Hebrews – which, in the New Testament, most explores this dimension – prefers to describe Christians as 'pilgrims and strangers' rather than 'priests'. But pilgrim people are in priestly mode as they cross and recross boundaries all the time. They have to make fine judgements and subtle decisions along the way since the tension of living in transition cannot be avoided.

In Frank Senn's words, 'liminality celebrates transition rather than status, and therefore provides the most appropriate mode of worship for Christians who are "pilgrims and strangers" in this world, following the Christ who had "no place to lay his head"'.[39]

According to the letter to the Hebrews, having offered his own blood in a once for all sacrifice, Jesus has made the ultimate priestly journey of boundary crossing into the heavenly sanctuary and the holiest place of all, God's very presence.[40] He has transcended an earthbound ritual system and broken through temporal limitations into the eternal realm. By his sacrificial death and interceding life as High Priest over God's people, Jesus opens up a new and living way and invites believers to follow him there, enabling them to come to the throne of grace, to 'draw near to God with a sincere heart and in full assurance of faith' (Heb. 10:22). But to achieve this, as David de Silva reminds us, Jesus had first to '"go outside the camp" to a place characterised by both liminality and sacrality'.[41] This paradox is veiled except to faith. 'To the eyes of the unbeliever, Jesus dies a shameful death in a place of uncleanness, outside the lines of society; in the eyes of God, Jesus' journey outside the margins of the camp is a ritual act of sacred power'.[42] His self-offering and entrance into the holy presence of God for us consecrates believers and assures them of their status within God's house. But this is no escapist enclave for believers suffering cultural 'withdrawal symptoms'. In fact, the writer urges them to leave their own comfort zones to brave the shame and hostility of society. 'And so as Jesus suffered outside the city gate to make the people holy through his own blood. Let us, then, go to him outside the camp bearing the disgrace he bore' (13:12–13). To draw near to God, and to go where Jesus is, are mysteriously one and the same thing! Worship, in this sense, encompasses both the 'coming in' and the 'going out'. 'The addressees are called to continue in this journey and, out of gratitude to Jesus for his journey "outside the camp" on their behalf, to sacrifice the sense of at-homeness and belonging in human society and enter a place of liminality – to live in between the home they have left behind and the kingdom they are in the process of receiving.'[43] Life in the liminal state is recharged and reorientated by praise and worship. The strange interweaving of exhortations to worship with admonitions to courageous living in 12:22–13:16 show the strategic role of worship. Worship, in stretching us to God, extends us further into God's world. Liminal worship, like a coiled spring, launches worshippers into risky acts of faith: unswerving loyalty to the Christian family; unusual hospitality to strangers and visitation of prisoners; unlikely commitment to the culturally despised act of marriage and an even more surprising faithfulness to the vows taken in it; and, perhaps most distinctively, an uncommon non-acquisitiveness and contentment. All this is the extension of worship. To move outside the camp in these radical ways is to move further into the presence of the Living Lord. Confessing the name in worship means to confess the name in witness. Boldly to come together in worship to the throne of God is to 'boldly go' to the waiting world. Worship then is not an escape from the world but the entry point to a longer journey of liminality, so that we go through worship and on with Jesus out into the world.

> Not to know whether one is coming or going at this point may well be to have stumbled on the liturgical secret of liminality! The only way to hold together these 'comings' and 'goings' is to see

that all our goings to the world outside the camp are further moves in coming to God, to Jesus, to the abiding city of the New Jerusalem. In short, it is worship as ritualised liminal event that reflects, refocuses and re-energises worshippers for their liminal existence as priestly pilgrims. Exiles are sustained in their alternative passion with power and freedom by the regular practice of intentional, alternative liturgy.[44]

If worship and liturgy are so crucial a focus for the life of a liminal people, then questions are raised about importing 'Babylonian cultural values' into worship. In adapting worship too uncritically to the musical tastes and felt needs of 'outsiders' do we not sell out to the culture? Homecoming will sound a strange language and songs of homecoming strange music in the ears of those who are very far from considering themselves 'exiles' but are well settled as 'Babylonian' citizens and consumers. What is at stake in relaxing the liminal status of worship is not merely an attenuated liturgical experience but a lessened sense of God's grandeur and a loss of identity as the distinctively priestly people of God. Similarly, if we strive to make worship too ostentatiously 'relevant', we destroy its liminal capacity for regenerating our lives. As Randall Nichols reads Turner: 'the heart of worship lies in its being a communitas experience that is related dialectically and perhaps paradoxically to the world of structure but is distinctively and critically different from it'.[45] To envisage worship as sanctuary from the structure of the world is not to isolate it from reality or rob it of its effectiveness; precisely the opposite. As Nichols argues: if 'worship were the market-place instead of a sanctuary, it would lose its unique power to equip me for going back outside and grappling with the realm that is "too much with us" sometimes'. As liminal event, liturgy is a 'sanctuary' experience in service to (never as a substitute for) the exile's return to a broken Jerusalem in need of rebuilding'.[46] We carry his broken world with us into worship to be offered and sanctified but not to be endorsed as it stands. As Moltmann has it, 'The messianic feast is the Lord's song in a foreign land. Its melodies mingle thoughts of home with the sighs of exile.'[47]

Liminality within the Worship Experience

'Even within the worship experience itself it could be argued that there is an alternation between states and transitions, so that in one moment worship is more structural while later it is more liminal.'[48] The second main application of liminality theory is to the internal dynamics of worship itself, in particular, to the vexed issue of freedom and order, spontaneity and structure. Usually these polarities are played off against each other rather than held together in creative tension. It is only too obvious that rigid forms of worship can harden into mechanical ritual, which masks what is inauthentic and even hypocritical. One mainline pastor, in self-critical mood, concedes that 'too much worship in mainline churches is trivial. There is a diminished sense of God's presence, of worship as risky engagement with a peculiar God. Too often we clergy seem to construe our role as that of protecting our congregations from this God, from God's holiness and grace'.[49]

At the same time, spontaneity is certainly no guarantee of spirituality and can make worship vulnerable to the manipulative leader or worship leader, or to overly subjective worshippers. It is salutary to realise that no one escapes liturgy: it constitutes the rules of the game. But as Jean-Jacques Surmount notes, whereas established churches seem often overly conscious of these rules of the game, Charismatics and Pentecostals neglect to have any well-thought out rules. In either case, as any child knows, the game is spoiled.[50]

Although Pentecostals and Charismatics deny this, their own meetings, as Daniel Albrecht shows, tend to follow a fairly standard liturgical order inherited from Revivalism and Frontier Evangelism.[51] Albrecht's field work disclosed an underlying, though theologically uninformed, tripartite arrangement of worship, made up of preliminaries, preaching or exhortation, followed by 'ministry-time' – altar calls, laying on of hands, healing or going out in the Spirit. This latter, 'hands-on' conclusion to many contemporary charismatic worship events seems to make up for the undervalued sacrament. Evidently the need to 'touch and handle things unseen' demands satisfaction in one way or another. If Pentecostals and Charismatics were willing to acknowledge their 'liturgy' it could be examined and developed and invested with weightier theological rationale. But, in Suurmond's words, 'because they do not recognise that they are following an order in the liturgy (albeit an oral one), they cannot critically reflect upon it'.[52]

Worship in the Pauline New Testament churches – especially taking into account the correctives in the Corinthian correspondence – seems to bear this out. On the one hand there are distinct traces of 'liturgical elements', ranging from credal statements, public reading of Scripture – including reading the apostolic letters themselves – familiar prayers and ejaculations, benedictions, shared 'Amens' and the simple, inherited pattern of the Lord's Supper. At the same time Paul risks misunderstanding by going out of his way not to quench the freer elements in worship – spontaneous prayer, prophetic utterance, praise, singing, tongues and interpretation, words of instruction and revelation. Oscar Cullman's remark is apposite: 'It is precisely in the harmonious combination of freedom and restriction that there lies the greatness and uniqueness of the early Christian service of worship.'[53]

Paul's first letter to the Corinthians is a case in point. '1 Corinthians is surely a letter about achieving the right balance between Spirit and structure. Since it was structure that was lacking in Corinth, Paul tries to inject some order without quenching the Spirit.'[54] Even Paul's much maligned rubric 'Let all things be done decently and in order' (1 Cor. 14:40) – often mocked as a recipe for a graveyard – may, on closer inspection, reveal a dynamic paradox. If we take 'decently' ('*euschēmonous*') as meaning well fitted, shaped, purposeful, then a case can be made for worship which is framed by well-thought-out structure and form. As for 'in order' ('*kata taxin*'), it depends what imagery is used to exploit it. If what springs to mind is regimentation and predictability then the idea of rigidity is re-enforced. But if a water metaphor is used then 'order' becomes the sequence and fluidity of a living stream or river. 'Decently and in order' might then imply a quality of worship which gives due regard to both the fixed form of liturgy and the free flow of praise and worship within and around it. At least this would seem to be more faithful to Paul's evident attempt to hold together the pressures of freedom and the constraints of order. As Richard Hays sums it up, 'in Paul's vision for Christian worship there is neither stiff formality nor undisciplined frenzy: the community's worship is more like a complex graceful dance or a beautiful anthem sung in counterpoint'.[55] This, of course, is an example of that common paradox of human experience: discipline engenders freedom. It was characteristically expressed by Austen Farrer after watching the ballet: 'What a release and what a control and the marvel of it is that the release and the control are not two opposite factors balancing one another, they are one and the same thing.' Imagine, he suggests, a village dance, even, with pipe and drum: 'That was what releases you, something to dance to, but what is it that controls you? Why, the very same thing: you dance to the music. The control is the release, the music lets you go, the music holds you.'[56]

Carol Doran and Thomas Troeger have helpfully explored this paradox further in connection with liturgy by utilising liminality theory.[57] Their account depends on Turner indirectly through the work of Urban Holmes. Holmes himself makes use of Turner's distinction between structure and anti-structure that occurs in liminal experiences. He points out that those who put a high premium on order are uncomfortable with the anti-structure encountered in liminal experiences. But if we make idols of our structures, for fear of chaos, we lose out 'because the anti-structure is the place where the intuitive sense of God's presence and power engages us'.[58]

Doran and Troeger emphasise the twin poles which govern the dynamics of worship. One pole represents the elements which promote security: orderliness, clear definitions, predictable sequences; in short, a liturgy under human control. The other pole stands for the more uncontainable, mysterious elements, where there is a depth of feeling and intensity of meaning which goes beyond verbal description. They visualise this in a graph depicting the interchange between structure and anti-structure. Their graph (see page 46) is a modification of Holmes' adaptation of Turner's original which I have slightly altered!

'Excellent worship,' argue Doran and Troeger, 'is continually interweaving structure and anti-structure.'[59] Worshippers experience liminality by crossing and recrossing the boundary between structure and anti-structure. Worship thus involves oscillation, moving back and forth between order and freedom, criss-crossing the frontier dividing fixed forms and free space to follow the flow of the Spirit. A yachtsman plots his course with the time-honoured and well-researched maps and charts available to him but then makes room for the turn of the tide and the shifting of the winds. So blended worship is prepared to follow familiar ritual and practised routine and at the same time is ready to place itself at the mercy of the movement of the wind of God. Worship then needs to combine those regular means of grace which re-enforce our sense of security through familiar words and actions with those uncontrolled and unpredictable areas of anti-structure where we experience further mystery and grace.

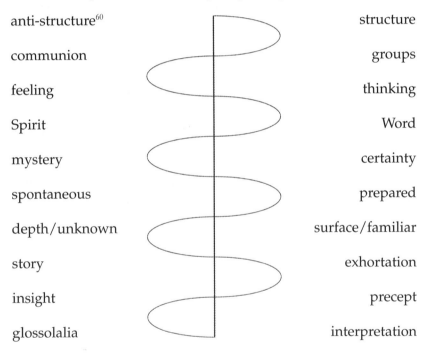

anti-structure[60]	structure
communion	groups
feeling	thinking
Spirit	Word
mystery	certainty
spontaneous	prepared
depth/unknown	surface/familiar
story	exhortation
insight	precept
glossolalia	interpretation

LIMINAL EXPERIENCE

Daniel Hardy and David Ford speak of a 'continual spiral re-enforcement' in praise, applicable in this context to the way in which freedom loops back to rest on revitalised order and order relaunches the next phase of freedom. 'Praise is always over-flowing where we have got to in thought and action, as it risks greater and greater receptivity and response, and so it becomes the catalyst of prophetic knowledge of God and his will.'[61] In worship, say Hardy and Ford, our life is always being 'thrown into the air . . . in trust that it will be caught, blessed, and returned renewed'.[62] They call this 'the jazz factor', describing activity which is neither order or disorder but non-order; yet a non-order which feeds on order by improvising on already determined themes and motifs and taking them into new realms.[63] Brueggemann picks up on this insight of Hardy and Ford, and likens Old Testament praise at its best to the making of jazz music 'that holds a story line and maintains the beat, but is endlessly inventive in what more may be said'. Israel knew, he writes, that 'the God addressed is always out front and beyond our best singing. This God is restlessly waiting for our tongue to catch up with the sovereign reality who dreams our wholeness'.[64]

Paradoxically then, 'good free worship always has a pattern and requires an immense amount of sensitivity, discipline, experience and preparation for it to ring true'. The creative interplay between form and freedom may lie behind the intriguing difference between two otherwise virtually identical passages in Paul. Colossians 3:16 reads, 'Let the word of Christ dwell in you richly as you teach and admonish one another with psalms and hymns and spiritual songs with gratitude in your hearts to God.' The parallel text in the Ephesian letter states: 'Be filled with the Spirit, speaking to one another in psalms, hymns and spiritual songs, singing and making music in your hearts to the Lord' (Eph. 5:18b–19). 'Word' and 'Spirit' seem complementary here as rich, full sources of the church's praise. The 'word of Christ' almost certainly in this context refers to the richness of the truth of the gospel which is meant to inform and shape worship. What enriches worship is not the feelings we bring to the meeting but the revelation in word and sacrament of who Christ is and what he has achieved. The deeper our experience of the word of the gospel, the better the quality of the individual's praise and indeed, the stronger the content of the songs sung. Since the Spirit acts on the word, then the richer our experience of the Word, the more the Spirit has to work on. In Suurmond's sober assessment of the playfulness of worship, 'The play of Word and Spirit seems likely to find most room in the charismatic renewal. The combination of a traditional liturgical order used critically and openness to the charismatic Spirit often inspires a creative Sabbath play which leaves few people indifferent.'[66]

The psychological effects of liminality in worship are summarised by Doran and Troeger in terms of intra-dependence and extra-dependence. Intra-dependence is that state of mind in which we are in control in a carefully managed environment – a state of mind which gets us to work every morning. Extra-dependence involves the yielding of control ultimately to God the Holy Spirit. Here worshippers explore the 'might be' in what Driver calls 'a subjunctive mode of play' and experience something of what he terms 'sacramental effervescence'.[67] Again both factors are needed. If charismatic worship seeks to abolish intra-dependence in favour of randomness, then chaos and disorder ensue so that either praise drifts or dribbles on without meaningful direction, or worshippers indulge in blatant attention-seeking or self-indulgence with no thought to the building up of the Body of Christ and corporate nature of its worship. Lacking the extra-dependence dimension, so failing to expose people to liminality, traditional worship is likely to insulate worshippers from lively encounter with the real God. Even in so-called 'free worship', when the worship leader insists on a giving a running commentary on the songs or the song-leader insists on working relentlessly through the list of songs previously selected, then, in both cases, sensitivity to the moods of the Spirit is lost, liminal space is denied and no extra-dependency occurs.

Daniel Albrecht has shown from his fieldwork that contemporary Pentecostal/Charismatic churches do intuitively provide recognisable ritual activity to enable extra-dependence. 'Pentecostals participate in forms of ritual liminality.'[68] Ritual space is provided even if not in specifically religious buildings, which are sanctified by the use made of them. In fact the otherwise secular use made of such buildings may actually heighten the liminal dimension when commandeered for worship. Ritual roles are undertaken by all and ritual actions are encouraged. Above all, ritual time is crucial. For the worshipper in the Spirit, time stands still so that God can be experienced as eschatological presence. This is why extended periods of time are given over to praise and worship. So Barry Liesch explains that 'longer sections of praise allow time to offer the whole person – mind, heart, emotions – to the Lord. Humanly speaking, we need a longer frame of time to prepare ourselves psychologically to offer genuine adoration'. He quotes Jim Packer as saying that repetitious charismatic singing is understandable on the basis that 'you don't move on from any thought about our relationship with God until time has been given for everyone to feel it'.[69]

Graham Hughes suggests the need for leaders of worship to have 'absorbed deeply into themselves an awareness that the work in which they are engaged is a "boundary" or "liminal" (threshold) event; that it takes place at a kind of virtual "edge" of what we can manage conceptually and emotionally; that the event is nullified if it is permitted (as it threatens continually to do) to fall back into domesticity or "routinisation"'.[70] By risking extended liminal time and space, Albrecht concludes, room is made for the effects of liminality to take place. 'Communitas' occurs with a deeper bonding between people who may or may not have either status or community outside the church. Reflexivity is made possible so that worshippers together can safely risk exploring uncharted realms of mood and behaviour. Reorientation occurs so that effective change takes place whether conversion or emotional release, healing or empowerment.[71] As Victor Turner rightly said, 'Liminality is the mother of invention.'[72]

4

Holy Love: Transcendent Otherness *and* Transforming Immediacy

> The coal is lifted from the fire and held to (Isaiah's) lips. Thus the fire of godliness is passed on and on. A community, a circle about the fire, is not merely warmed by the fire, but touched by the fire, marked indelibly.[1]

God is never 'cool' but always a consuming fire. In pursuit of the polarities inherent in worship, then, nothing could be more important than to probe the polarities inherent in the way God relates to us – or how we conceive he relates to us – which shape our worship of him. How we envisage and encounter God obviously determines the way we worship God.

Worship practices mirror a doctrine of God, however ill-defined. This opens up a vast area of study in which one could easily go missing without trace, so this chapter will seek to narrow the field. It aims to explore how a deficient understanding of God – in particular of *God's transcendence and immanence* – fosters a false dichotomy between 'hard' and 'soft' attitudes to God and experiences of God as these are expressed in worship.

Transcendence or Immanence: A False Antithesis?

The concepts of transcendence and immanence are still central to any theological quest, even when other terminology is preferred. The usefulness of the concepts has been demonstrated by Stanley Grenz and Roger Olsen, who employ them as interpretative tools to review the whole of twentieth-century theology. 'At its best,' they assert, 'Christian theology has always sought a balance between the twin biblical truths of the divine transcendence and the divine immanence.'[2] God's transcendence they define as God being 'self-sufficient apart from the world', God as 'above the universe', who 'comes to the world from beyond'. On the other, in his immanence, God is 'present to creation . . . active within the universe, involved with the processes of the world and human history'.[3] The way theologians – and we shall argue, worshippers – handle these twin truths becomes a touchstone of theological sensitivity. Grenz and Olsen introduce their project by arguing that 'because the Bible presents God as both beyond the world and present to the world, theologians in every era are confronted with the challenge of articulating the Christian understanding of the nature of God in a manner that balances, affirms and holds in creative tension the twin truths of the divine transcendence and the divine immanence'. The operative words here are 'balance' and 'creative tension'.

Confusion occurs, it could be argued, when, in practice, we dissolve the 'creative tension' by choosing between transcendence and immanence as if they were opposites. Whether consciously or not, when we envisage God as transcendent we emphasise his majesty or remoteness; whereas God's immanence suggests warmth and intimacy. The result is polarised worship. In the one case, the God who is worshipped is distant and aloof, best served by long-distance respect. In the other, God is rendered indistinguishable from us and courted with over-sentimental love-songs.

One way of preserving the 'creative tension' is offered by Walter Brueggemann's own doctrine of God. At first sight, though, Brueggemann appears not to be on the side of the angels at all – especially as 'signals of transcendence'.[4] He contends that Christian theology has long practiced what he calls a 'flight to the transcendent' and argues, in characteristic fashion, that it needs the dialectical dimension of the Old Testament view of God to keep its feet on the ground. Brueggemann makes a distinction between a God 'above' and 'in the fray', noting that 'the God of Israel is characteristically "in the fray". Conversely, the God of Israel is rarely permitted, in the rhetoric of Israel, to be safe and unvexed "above the fray"'.[5] On this view, God can never really be disentangled from his historic relationship with Israel. What is at issue is not an all-embracing omnipresence but a God with whom Israel has to do business, whether he withdraws and hides his face (*panim*, or presence), or dwells with his people and smiles with favour on them. The point of texts like Amos 9:2–4 and Psalm 139 – traditionally used to bolster the image of a God who fills all space – is not, Brueggemann argues, 'the pervasive immanence of Yahweh but Yahweh's dangerous inescapability'.[6]

In a stimulating symposium devoted to evaluating Brueggemann's concept of God, Terence Fretheim, comments on Brueggemann's dialectical approach, and, in particular the phrases 'God "above the fray"' and 'God "in the fray"'. 'This distinction', says Fretheim, 'seems to correspond to the traditional distinction between transcendence and immanence'.[7] Leo Purdue agrees with this assessment. 'These basic images of God as "above the fray" (i.e. transcendent and absolute) and "in the fray" (i.e. immanent and humane) correspond to the two fundamental polarities present in the Christian imagination.'[8] Purdue's words, however, in off-setting 'absolute' and 'humane', lead to the suspicion that transcendent is regarded as a pejorative term – as it certainly is in some feminist theology. Fretheim's view is more subtly nuanced and better able to sustain a creative tension. He questions Brueggemann's 'above' and 'in the fray' as problematic. 'The biblical God,' Fretheim points out, 'is transcendent within relationship (never "above" it); the God active "in the fray" and "embracing pain" is so engaged as the immanent and transcendent one.'[9]

It is instructive to note, at this point, two texts which are usually associated with the polarities under discussion: Isaiah 57:15 and Jeremiah 23:23–24. In the first the 'high and lofty One' who 'lives for ever, whose name is holy' says, 'I live in a high and holy place but also with him who is contrite and lowly in spirit, to revive the spirit of the lowly and to revive the heart of the contrite' (Is. 57:15). Typically Brueggemann eschews metaphysical comment and points up the sociological rather than theological impact of the statement. 'The juxtaposition of high-holy and lowly-crushed is at the core of Yahweh's self-disclosure, the mystery of God who is the subject of biblical faith.' This juxtaposition, he adds, 'is not to be reduced to speculative categories like "transcendence" and "immanence" but is a royal metaphor for the great sovereign who from the exalted throne room extends the royal presence and the royal concern to the most lowly and undeserving of subjects'.[10]

The Jeremiah passage moves in the other direction to the Isaiah oracle in stressing the transcendence of God. It involves a critique of false prophets and an assertion of the essential otherness of God. '"Am I not a God nearby", declares the Lord, "and not a God far away? Can anyone hide in secret places so that I cannot see him?" declares the Lord. "Do not I fill heaven and earth?" declares the Lord' (Jer. 23:23–24). Brueggemann remarks on this that 'God is not near and available (v. 23). God is unavoidable (v. 24). That God should be "near" is a promise from the Temple cult. The assertion that God is distant thus stands over against the Temple ideology' which seeks to 'draw God too near to favourite arrangements and to minimize God's sovereign freedom'.[11] Such worship is fed by false prophets whose cosy reassurances bring God too 'near', hollow out his name, dumb down his word, make his presence insubstantial, and his blessings 'lite' (23:25–32).

Here is a recognition that misuse can go either way. Worship can either push God to the margins of effectiveness by making him remote from everyday life, or it can serve to control or tame God by containing him within familiar patterns of response. The real God cannot only be lost in a flight into transcendence away from reality but can be dissolved into comfortable cultic regularity that does not disturb the status quo. True worship precisely cannot play one kind of God off against another. This God retains his sovereign freedom and is not accessible on our easy terms. In Fretheim's words, 'God does enter deeply "into the fray" but not in such a way that God ceases to be God'.[12]

Brueggemann comes closer to saying this later in his *Theology of the Old Testament* when he draws a picture of the tension between what he calls the 'Priestly and Deuteronomic strategies'.[13] The Priestly strata in the Torah highlights the glory of God as the visible manifestation of God, often in cloudlike form, which evokes worship. 'And the glory of the Lord appeared to all the people. Fire came out from the presence of the Lord and consumed the burnt offering and the fat portions on the altar. And when the people saw it, they shouted for joy and fell face down' (Lev. 9:23–24). In Brueggemann's words, '"Glory" is a way of speaking about Yahweh's powerful, sovereign, transcendent presence, without making a claim that is flat, one-dimensional or crassly material.'[14] So the glory-cloud fills the Tabernacle and later the Temple (Ex. 40:34–35; 1 Kgs. 8:10–11) and, according to Ezekiel's priestly theology, is sinned away by Israel at the time of the Exile (Ezek. 10:15–22).

Elsewhere Brueggemann speaks of 'God's shattered transcendence' maintaining that the Exile has radically affected God and made him vulnerable in a new way.[15] But the reappearance in exile of the glory seems to suggest that God is not diminished by his people's failure. On the contrary he enters into the 'fray' of exile with them to demonstrate his glory in a new way in all his 'transcendent immanence'.[16]

Brueggemann adduces another trajectory in the Torah which is the Deuteronomic emphasis on the 'name' of God residing in the sanctuary. In this so-called 'name theology', the Deuteronomist is taken to be hedging his bets – as it were – by asserting that Yahweh's name is there in the Temple but his full self is elsewhere, in heaven, immune from ideological compromise. Even as God's earthly dwelling place is being inaugurated by Solomon with appropriate ceremony, the warning is given that God is not contained by buildings, not even by heaven and earth. That Yahweh's name is in the Temple encourages boldness in prayer but his answers come from heaven as does his forgiveness (1 Kgs. 8:27–30). The holding together in creative tension of God's transcendence and immanence is expressed, metaphorically, in the paradoxical image of the brightness of God's glory dwelling in a dark cloud.

Brueggemann's discussion evidently draws on the work of one of his teachers, Samuel Terrien. According to Terrien, the phrase, 'the thick darkness where God dwells', 'admirably fitted the ambiguity of the Hebraic theology of presence, for the meaning which it carried, gloom, also conveyed the symbol of the hiddenness of God at the exact moment of his proximity'.[17] Terrien also poses the issue of name or glory. Commenting on 1 Kings 8, Terrien says, once again, we witness a profound tension between two opposite views of presence: the story of the introit of the ark objectifies the psychological awareness of presence and localizes it in a man-made structure . . . sacred space. Solomon's long prayer, on the contrary, attempts to safeguard a theology of spatial transcendence; it even demythicizes 'heaven' as the spatial container of divinity. At the same time it accommodates to the needs of man the belief in the elusiveness of presence and recognises within the sacred edifice a reality which justifies its construction.[18]

Brueggemann himself adds, intriguingly, that 'the Priestly trajectory is what one might call "high church", and leads in a visual, artistic direction that is open to receive many cultural expressions. The Deuteronomic trajectory, by contrast, is "low church", depending primarily on utterances, and issues in a "theology of the word" as is evident in "sermons" in Deuteronomic history, and it tends to a separatist direction.'[19] This statement is as teasing as it is sweeping and Brueggemann does not develop his insight for the purpose of this book. But it is reasonable to infer that his comment serves to illustrate the dangerous false polarity over God's being which is shown in the polarised worship that I am arguing against here. Brueggemann comments on the twin strategies of the Priestly writers and the Deuteronomist, as he has drawn them out, that 'it is important that the canonizing process retained both, assigned both to Moses, and refused to choose between them'.[20] He acknowledges how problematic the idea of 'presence' is and how vulnerable it is to polarisation and observes that

> it is clear that ecumenical or pre-ecumenical Christianity has not done well at maintaining the fruitful and essential tension that is a key insistence of Israel's canon . . . Presence too closely claimed for the temple belittles Yahweh's true character, but presence too leanly affirmed leaves Israel excessively exposed. Therefore no single, simple articulation of presence will suffice. The canonical testimony of Israel provides ample evidence for both a 'catholic' sacramentalism and a 'protestant' protest against a controlled, controlling sacramentalism.[21]

If then a fruitful and essential tension is to be maintained, the concepts of transcendence and immanence in theological usage must not be over-pressed as spatial metaphors. On this basis God is deemed to be transcendent in the sense of being distant, remote and aloof and – in consequence – his 'hard' attributes are invoked – power, sovereignty, judgement, holiness. Immanence then suffers a reductionist downgrading into God's 'soft' virtues – amiability, unconditional acceptance, and non-judgemental cosiness. If this mistake is made, albeit unthinkingly, God appears as one kind of God when we construe him as transcendent and another kind of God entirely when we view him as near. The result is polarised worship. Rather, God remains the transcendent one even when he is immanent. It might be better to speak of his otherness and his immediacy. God remains the transcendent God of majesty and greatness when – precisely when – he manifests his immediate presence, his holy love, as it were, close up. 'The Presence is no less transcendent for its immanence in the faithful community and in all other things under heaven.'[22]

The Domestication of Transcendence

Further confirmation of the need for this synthesis is provided by William Placher's seminal study *The Domestication of Transcendence*. The heart of Placher's case is a detailed technical argument to the effect that seventeenth-century theology underwent a decisive shift in its understanding of transcendence from that posited classically by Aquinas and the Reformers. Where once, before the seventeenth century, 'Christian theologians were struck by the mystery, the wholly otherness of God, and the inadequacy of our human categories as applied to God', later philosophers and theologians 'increasingly thought they could talk clearly about God.'[23] Cultural pressures no doubt contributed to this shift in thinking so that a predictable and well-contained God would not upset the precarious social order. So Thomas Hooker, in rebuking Anne Hutcheson for teaching too radical a grace, conceded that wild joy did exist in the world like wild flowers, but that God's well-cultivated 'garden love and garden joy' were much to be preferred![24] Transcendence then began to be talked of as 'one of the definable properties' of God. The result was an unattractive picture of God as cold, unfeeling and remote. This is a misuse of transcendence as if it implied what is 'beyond' in a spatial sense.

However, as Placher, argues, 'it is not that God is transcendent and therefore distant, unrelated, and not at all immanent, but that our human categories of closeness, distance, relatedness, stand-offishnesss and the like, radically break down when we try to apply them to God'.[25] God is not an object in the world to be clarified and evaluated and analysed like other objects. What preserves this mystery from being sheer mystification is, of course, God's own self-revelation especially in Jesus Christ through whom the mystery is made known to us. If God is never an object in the world, he can be, and is, the subject of his own self-disclosure. And it is as fully transcendent that he condescends to make himself known to us.

The wrong turn taken by theology, which Placher is examining, occurs then as a development away from classical theism and as an effective domestication of God's transcendence. Placher writes:

> Increasingly, writers in the seventeenth century, since they did not want to think of God as utterly beyond their comprehension, thought of God's otherness in terms of distance and remoteness from the world. Though they did not use the terms, they were in effect contrasting transcendence with immanence. Such a 'contrastive' account of transcendence – I am using Kathryn Tanner's terminology – makes divine transcendence and involvement in the world into a zero-sum game the more involved or immanent, the less transcendent, and vice-versa.[26]

But if transcendence is not a metaphysical statement about God, still less a quasi-attribute of God, but a way of referring to God's ineffable mystery and otherness, the issue of God's involvement with the world is not foreclosed but opened up. In Kathryn Tanner's own words:

> God's transcendence and involvement with the world vary inversely . . . only when God's transcendence is defined contrastively . . . a non-contrastive transcendence of God suggested an

extreme of divine involvement with the world . . . extending to everything that is in an direct manner . . . Such an extreme of divine involvement requires, one could say, an extreme of divine transcendence. A contrastive definition is not radical enough to allow a direct creative involvement with the world in its entirety.[27]

There is a sense is which transcendence stands for the very god-ness of God who is all and in all. Placher again cites Tanner, who comments,

> (Such) a radical transcendence does not exclude God's positive fel-lowship with the world or presence within it. Only created beings, which remain themselves over and against others, risk the distinc-tiveness of their own natures by entering into intimate relations with one another. God's transcendence alone is one that may be properly exercised in radical immanence by which God is said to be nearer to us than we are to ourselves.[28]

Only God's self-revelation in Christ worked out in Trinitarian full-ness can both guarantee divine freedom and safeguard human freedom.[29] Placher concludes that 'Christian faith finds here con-firmation of God's triune character: We come to know this gracious God not merely in revelation but in self-revelation in Jesus Christ, and we come to trust that we do know God in Christ through the work of the Holy Spirit.'[30] As Henri Blocher has pointed out in a recent biblical assessment of the terms, transcen-dence is undoubtedly expressed in 'spatial' terms like height and depth. But this is to be linked always to the *transcendence of grace*, whose riches are described in hyperbolic language as surpassing and unsearchable. God's grace is superabundant as a mark not just of quantity but quality. Its effusiveness and lavishness are not measurable precisely because they are an overflow of the life and love of the One whom Jesus habitually styled the 'how much more' God. Similarly, as Blocher points out, if immanence is con-strued as containing God within the world, then we are no longer talking about the biblical God at all. It is better to view immanence as referring to God's indwelling of his creation, not as construed by pantheism or panentheism, but as a pervasive presence in it which does not impugn or threaten his transcendence.

Even within explicitly Trinitarian formulations, Blocher suggests, transcendence is 'undoubtedly appropriated to the Father' while 'immanence shows a similar affinity with the Spirit' but the 'Son, the second person in Trinitarian order, prevents us from understanding transcendence and immanence in dialectical fashion . . .'[31] Part of the challenge Christ makes to us in incarnation and suffering is to re-imagine what God might be to us and might say to us as God – and not as some super-charged, divinity-added-on, supplemented version of what already makes us feel comfortable or secure. For example, Rowan Williams has illuminated this by focusing on the 'still turning point of the world' as the humiliated Christ stands before his accusers. In the 'I am' of this enigmatic figure a transcendence is disclosed which is utterly different from any category which we might previously have slotted him into – whether good teacher, miracle worker or, even, long-awaited messiah. Only now as he exhausts our explanations and speculation, and goes beyond the limits of our speech and understanding, can Jesus disclose his real identity. 'We cannot properly speak of transcendence merely by projecting what we know and what seems to help and reassure us to the highest point imaginable. Transcendence meets us, and surprises us, when we are shown simply that the way of the world is not the final truth.'[32] Our worshipful response might well be silence, or awe, or astonishment.

This is of a piece with, and the paradoxical culmination of, the encounters with the divine recorded in the Old Testament. From the 'awesome place' where Jacob felt fearful and astonished surprise that 'the Lord is in this place and I was not aware of it', to the burning bush where Moses 'hid his face because he was afraid to look at God', and to the Temple where the prophet Isaiah was caught within the magnetic field of God's incandescent holiness and confessed 'woe is me, I am ruined' – such encounters produced self-abasement and made the human participants subject to God's will.[33] In every case God remained transcendent even when immanent.

Following Placher's lead, both defenders and critics of divine impassability agree on the need to avoid a contrastive polarisation of transcendence and immanence. Thomas Weinandy has recently argued persuasively that 'from the biblical perspective . . .

for God to be transcendent does not mean that there are certain aspects of God's being or nature which are distinct from those aspects of God's nature which allow him to be immanent'. He goes on, 'to say that God transcends the created order of time and history does not mean that there are properties within God which make him unlike the created order and which then differ from those properties which allow him to act within the created order'.[34] Again we see the fatal error – which Weinandy sees emerging in much modern theology – of opting for one pole or the other, which, in fact, in current fashion, usually leads to the pressure to diminish this kind of transcendence in favour of an increased immanence. The Old Testament, Weinandy urges, never conceives of God's transcendence in opposition to his immanence. Rather, he states, 'that which makes God divine, and thus wholly other and so transcendent, is that which equally allows him to be active within the created order and so to be immanent'.[35]

Weinandy refers to Old Testament theologian Terence Fretheim's discussion of God's vulnerability and suffering – an overall position Weinandy is questioning – to support this particular point. Fretheim recommends that 'immanence' should be thought of as 'relatedness' of which 'presence' is a special feature, while 'transcendence' should be deprived of its narrow spatial connotations and used to speak of 'the way in which the godness of God manifests itself in this "relatedness" – for God, a permanent state of affairs'.[36] Fretheim draws attention to Hosea 11:9, 'I will not carry out my fierce anger . . . For I am God and not man – the Holy One among you.' The phrase 'the Holy One among you', Fretheim notes, is especially instructive for it is as the Holy One that God is present with his people. It indicates that holiness – which is one important Old Testament indicator of transcendence – and presence do not stand in polar opposition to each other. Nor is it that they stand in tension with each other. No: 'the transcendence of God is thus manifested by the way in which God is present among his people'.[37] God in all his intense holiness is present in and with his people precisely at the point where he is disclosed as vulnerable to their plight and in inner turmoil over what to do with them (Hos. 11:8). This is truly holy love in action. The conjoining of holiness and love in the phrase 'Holy love' is a way of expressing 'the unity of his transcendence and his condescension'.[38] This was a keynote of P.T. Forsyth, who characteristically wrote:

> The chief bane of current religion, the loss of miracle, awe, and wonder, from its sense of love and tone of worship, is due to its neglect of the holiness of God; as if it were but a theological theme compared with His love, and one which might be relegated to the attention of those circles that discuss the divine attributes. Whereas it is no attribute unless love is. It is the first thing in God, His very being. His love is divine only because it is holy, and not because it is immense or wide; it is victorious and eternal only as holy, only as the Father is King in righteous majesty, mystic and infinite. God's holiness is the absolute monarchy of His righteous love.[39]

It is worth noting, furthermore, that the stark anthropomorphic language of Hosea's prophetic oracle reveals God as engaged in a profoundly emotional inner debate about the need to judge a people from whom his covenant love refuses to disentangle him. As Adrio König has passionately argued, it is precisely these anthropomorphisms which seem to define God in human terms that are said in the text to differentiate him from human categories – 'I am the Holy One, and not man'! 'The anthropomorphisms of the Bible teach that God differs from man'.[40]

Again the implications for worship are clear. No overwhelming sense of God's immanence and presence should lead us to dilute his godness. To worship God as 'abba', with songs that place us in daddy's lap for a cuddle or 'God-is-my-girlfriend' responses to the divine lover, is seriously to misread his anthropomorphic condescension, and dissolve his transcendence into a misconceived cosy immanence. God is no less transcendent when he is, as it were, close up to us. In authentic worship, immanence shuts us in to God's true transcendence. 'The God who is present is both immanent and transcendent: both are appropriate words for a constant state of affairs. God is "transcendent in relationship".'[41] As Heschel said, 'God remains transcendent in His immanence and related in His transcendence.'[42]

The Domestication of Transcendence Today

In the post-modern context in which the church now worships, escape into transcendence is a less noticeable tendency than the absorption in immanence, but it has not gone without comment. It scarcely needs pointing out that classical liturgy can become formal and remote, a high-vaulted if not necessarily 'high church' worship, often guarded by elitism as if it were a protected species. Respectful but passionless, dutiful but joyless, such worship is easily categorised as 'empty or vain repetition'. In the words of liturgical theologian Jeremy Begbie, 'Christian history is replete with thousands of one-levelled Eucharistic performances where each celebration is effectively flattened on to one theological level of significance', characterised by 'an exaggerated sense of stability, little sense of participating in a movement of divine longing beyond this particular act, of being caught up in the work of the Spirit . . . little sense of being drawn into a larger, wider hope for the world.'[43] As Brueggemann recognises, 'the liturgy could be routinised so that we did not notice what we were doing. We only exhibited the clichés one more time, each time in the liturgy. We went through the motions, sang the songs, said among the nations, ascribed glory, trembled, but it contained no bite of threat or gift'.[44]

Even at its most creative, such worship may not evade this danger. Jeremy Begbie's astute appraisal of the sacred music of the leading contemporary composer John Tavener is a case in point. Begbie concedes the beauty and appeal of Tavener's church music, which draws on Eastern Orthodox theology and praxis and tunes in with the minimalist fashion of the day. But in its very ethereal, transcendent quality, Tavener's work may teeter on the brink of the semi-gnostic. It comes perilously close to becoming detached from reality by escaping into a timeless spiritual 'decompression chamber'. It runs the risk of degenerating into the kind of 'mood music' much in vogue that covers the spectrum from Gregorian chants and singing nuns to Celtic harps and sounds of the surf, and serves to ease the angst of an overstressed consumerist society. Tavener's intentions and the theology which sources his music no doubt steer his music clear of this particular 'black hole'. But Begbie asks four questions to articulate his concern.

Firstly, Begbie wonders whether Tavener's work sufficiently recognises that God's eternity has been made known in the 'world's temporality' and history climaxing in the incarnational reality of Jesus Christ. 'There seems more than a hint in Tavener of the idea that the more deeply we relate to God, the more we will need to abstract ourselves from time, develop an immunity to time's opportunities and threats.'[45] Secondly, Begbie asks if due attention has been given to the 'conviction that God's eternity has been enacted through a human life which has embraced our fallen humanity, including the experiences of deprivation, fear, anxiety, hunger, loss, frustration and disappointment'.[46] This is not a plea for music which is less exultant or for liturgies which are more morbid. But rather it reaches out for the kind of distinction made light-heartedly but with serious intent by Barth when he compared Bach to his favourite composer Mozart. 'It may be,' wrote Barth, in playful mood, 'that when the angels go about their task of praising God, they play only Bach. I am sure however, that when they are together *en famille*, they play Mozart and that then our dear Lord listens with special pleasure.' Mozart's uniqueness, for Barth, lay in his ability to incorporate into his joyous music the shadow side of humanity – meaning by this not specifically what is evil and sin, but everything in us that is marked by limitation and frustration and which lurks on the edge of 'non-being'. Mozart's genius stemmed from his ability to hear

> the harmony of creation to which the shadow belongs but in which the shadow is not darkness, deficiency is not defeat, sadness cannot become despair, trouble cannot degenerate into tragedy and infinite melancholy is not ultimately forced to claim undisputed sway. Thus the cheerfulness in this harmony is not without its limits. But the light shines all the more brightly because it breaks forth from the shadow.[47]

'In Tavener,' Begbie suggests, 'the cool cathedral is in danger of bearing little relation to the sordid life on the streets.'[48]

Thirdly, Begbie questions whether Tavener's music comes to terms adequately with death, in particular the cross of Christ. From his Orthodox point of view, Tavener reads everything in the light of the Resurrection, but Begbie still wonders if he gives due weight to the suffering as the road to glory. Fourthly, Begbie asks about the eschatology inherent in Tavener's vision. Tavener's music certainly evokes eternity but whether it points to the renewal of heaven and earth – in a restored cosmos or to a timeless spiritual continuum – remains for Begbie an open question.[49]

When we turn to the opposite danger – to what might be called 'low church' liturgies, especially of an Evangelical/Pentecostal flavour – a more readily available target presents itself. Graham Hughes sounds the warning here: 'In drawing cultural norms such as informality and immediacy as deeply into worship practices as they have, evangelicals risk a great deal at this point.'[50] Critics have not been slow to expose the risk.

The sociologist of religion, Martyn Percy, is a particularly astringent critic of much contemporary charismatic worship. In an extended study of the songs and worship practices associated with the late John Wimber and the Vineyard movement he founded, Percy has honed his critical skills. His critique is broadly along three lines.

Firstly and primarily, he perceives that chiefly through its songs and music, the Vineyard movement's worship functions as *unhealthy ideology*. It does so, Percy contends on the basis of an analysis of its hymnody, through a curious conjunction of power and love – both of which are ascribed to God. In Vineyard worship, he argues, the Trinity is undifferentiated and 'assumes the same dissolved character throughout; intimate, loving, precious, refreshing, fulfilling, mighty and omnipotent, all without qualification'. All this, he maintains, suggests that 'it is not so much God who is being addressed but rather favourable concepts of God – an ideology – that has rooted itself in the individual and corporate identity of the worshippers'.[51] In this context worship functions as an agent of divine power but it is a power detached from incarnational qualification and divorced from the cross. 'The self-giving love of Christ on the Cross – surely the acme of God's power – does not feature significantly in Wimber's canon of worship songs. The power portrayed is usually that of supernatural brute force, rather than the ambiguous power of Calvary.'[52] The response expected of the worshipper is then construed as largely 'unresisting and submissive' although it is a

'passivity that does not include sufferance, abstinence or pain
. . .'[53] In this scheme of things, Percy suggests, 'You' as directed to
God functions as a code word for intimacy and love, while 'Lord'
acts as metaphor for power.[54] Here is further evidence of the
tragic mistake of subconsciously adopting a 'contrastive' view of
transcendence and immanence with the result that transcendence
is equated solely with power and immanence with love.

Percy levels a second charge against the kind of worship which
he observed in the Vineyard movement, particularly at the
Airport Christian Fellowship in Toronto. He indicts it for what he
terms *subliminal eroticism*. Worshippers, he observes, are regularly urged to become 'hot, wet, powerless and passionate as a
prerequisite to knowing power'.[55] Revivalism is a form of surrogate romanticism. Not surprisingly, it has 'produced the most
mood-enhancing, emotive kinds of worship of recent years, some
of which could almost be described as "smoochy"'.[56] The vocabulary used, Percy alleges, is predominantly the language of
sexual consummation with worship being described as 'making
love to Jesus' and the Spirit as a 'brooding lover' – language
which Percy admits has parallels in the medieval mystics. The
sighings, groanings, ecstatic yelps of delight, piercing screams of
ecstasy, abundance of rhythmic movements – including two
women doing pelvic thrusts sitting astride their chairs – passing
out, shaking and quaking – is all very akin to sexual behaviour.[57]
Of course such charges have been levelled at revivalist spirituality before. The Marxist historian, E.P. Thompson, made even
more high-handed, scornful and, in fact, scurrilous comments on
the eighteenth-century Methodist Revival.[58] Such evaluations
sound even more hysterical than the hysteria they purport to
decry. One suspects with Thompson totally – and even a little
with Percy – that a very big chip on the shoulder has become a
large log in the eye!

But stripped of the histrionics, Percy again has a point and his
strictures confirm the diagnosis of a theological confusion in
which immanence has degenerated into intimacy and has lost
touch with transcendent holiness. Percy furthermore points up
what he perceives as the *immaturity* associated with the kind of
worship which he encountered in Toronto and which was encouraged by the leaders. The most frequent scenario, Percy alleges,

used to describe the relationship with God is that of a teenager in love. 'Thus, "wearing a stupid grin", "starry-eyed" expressions, "unable to speak properly", "uncontrollable feelings" of elation or ecstasy, "a rosy glow", "not able to concentrate" or "helpless laughter" are seen as . . . desired behaviour.'[59] This is defended as the return to a 'first love'. But it downplays spiritual maturity and adulthood in favour of 'soppiness' and sells people short in their spiritual quest by offering them 'romantic regression under the guise of restoration'.[60] Since worship is a powerful vehicle of personal formation and social change then Percy's criticisms, if true at all, expose a serious deficiency in style of worship that is not conducive to human character development. Immanence that is reduced to wallowing in one's own subjectivity is stuck adolescence. Certainly – at least in the extreme cases described – one questions whether worship is going on at all, or even whether this is a real encounter with God or only an elevated emotional state. What is a real concern, as Percy has expressed it, is that 'although the immediacy of God is celebrated in Vineyard worship, it is a nearness that does not permit worshippers to be fully human . . . since the operating power is force'.[61]

At this point, it is worth noting that the loss of transcendence in theology and worship has been reflected in the recent theory and practice of church architecture.

Reflecting on his own experiences of Protestant worship spaces constructed in the last forty years, liturgical theologian Graham Hughes concludes that 'they wish to minimise in so far as they can a sense of alterity, and, conversely, strongly encourage a sense of sociability, of "at-homeness", of familiarity, of intimacy'.[62] Since 'sanctuaries' are signs, 'the meeting must never feel like a living room'.[63]

The designing of the 'sanctuary' as a multi-functional space further serves to reveal the 'immanent convictions of those who constructed it'.[64] Such a move tends to endorse the implicit notion that 'nothing special' is expected of the people who enter it and that 'nothing special' happens within it. Though this viewpoint gives less than credit to the Holy Spirit's ability to make a 'silk purse from a sow's ear', the point is nevertheless taken.

This contemporary 'stripping of the altars' is only to be expected perhaps as in the genes of a Protestant dissenting heritage. So supposedly religious artefacts are jettisoned as non-user-friendly. But all this has the damaging effect of further detaching current evangelical/Charismatics from historic orthodoxy. 'The long-term question, then, is: how long does a form of worship remain "Christian" which untethered itself from Christian tradition so forthrightly as evangelicalism has?'[65]

Such tendencies, moreover, further fuel the gnostic bent of charismatic and Pentecostal Protestantism – which for all its reputation for being 'happy-clappy' – remains uneasy with embodied worship, suspicious of symbolism, and shows little interest in the visual arts in worship.

Popular impressions on this score are confirmed by careful study. Mark Torgerson has traced the way in which the design of church buildings has mirrored theology in tending to emphasise God's immanence over God's transcendence. Torgerson ends his fascinating survey by concluding, 'Immanence will remain important for future church design. Many of the churches we occupy today demonstrate the positive qualities of spaces that accent the theological affirmation of a God who is present in us and active through us.' But, he argues, 'immanence alone is inadequate in conceiving of the fullness of God. Attention to God's transcendence needs to bring a healthy tension to the church buildings we occupy. Our challenge to creatively express both the immanence and transcendence of God through material means is not new, but it remains critical to the spiritual formation of the faithful and public proclamation of the God we serve.'[66]

Transcendence, Immanence and Human Freedom

Torgerson's point about sacred space contributing – or otherwise – to the spiritual formation of the worshippers connects with the claim made by Percy that worship of the type he observed in the Vineyard movement cramps human freedom and inhibits truly human growth. This is a provocative argument which – if true at all – has important implications. If God is construed as a threat to our humanness who will invade our space, then we will resist in either of two ways. We will forego intimacy and immanence and push God away into a distant transcendence, thus remaining inert, passive, formal, dull, and stiff in our worship of God. Or, we will opt for an immanent God, dissolving transcendence in our own subjectivity, and in doing so, will reject any liturgical order or structure in worship which is 'over' us or 'above' us, perceiving it as a threat to our spontaneity, self-expression and liberty. This view of how worship goes wrong in its understanding of God's sovereignty and presence, is strengthened by the findings of William Placher in the work considered earlier. In analysing how modern thinking about God went wrong, Placher concludes that 'the relation between human and divine contributions has become a zero-sum game, and thus the power of grace is finally the enemy of human freedom'.[67]

This issue has been helpfully explored by Alistair McFadyen in a discussion of sin as an assault on God's freedom.[68] Sin is essentially an assertion of our freedom and autonomy because we conceive – in fact, misconceive – God's freedom as inimical to our own. 'At its root,' McFadyen argues, 'lies a way of thinking about transcendence (otherness) and freedom in terms analogous to objects and relations in physical space. If transcendence is thought of in terms of physical spatiality then, by definition, it must be opposed to immanence.'[69] If God can only be God to us by closing down human space and curtailing our freedom, then we can only express our liturgical freedom by turning away from fixed forms and inherited traditions. Just as feminist theology rejects transcendence because it associates it with patriarchy, so charismatic practice tends to be suspicious of liturgical order as a form of bondage. McFadyen notes that 'on this account, since transcendence and immanence are bound to be opposed, human and divine freedom must in essence be competitive'.[70]

But to turn away from order into the supposed freedom of subjectivity is to move in an idolatrous direction. Again, McFadyen insists, 'idolatry involves a mistake about transcendence. God's transcendence is either so stressed that relation to the world is threatened, or else the divine is located in some aspect of the world'.[71] But Christians worship a God who is characterised by a particularly radical self-giving which creates free and responsive others. This derives from his own life in Trinity. Orthodox Christology is the ground of our submission and our freedom in worship. God's full transcendence is preserved – indeed is demonstrated – through his incarnational immanence in the real humanity of his Son. God's transcendent presence is compatible with a full and free human response evoked and enabled by the Spirit. As Daniel Hardy and David Ford state, 'the idol could be a transcendent God who is not really free to take a personal part in history; or a divine human being who himself receives all worship; or a God who is within human beings or in some other way immanent in the world. Those three basic ways of absolutising one dimension of the Christian God,' Hardy and Ford continue, 'roughly correspond to the Father, Son and Holy Spirit. Taken together as a unity, the Trinity continually dispels illusions and fantasies about God. It applies a corrective to any one type of language, whether talk about the transcendence in analogies, or sacramental and historical accounts of God's character and presence, or subjective, experiential witness to the immediacy of God.'[72]

Transcendence and Immanence: Twin Invasions of Grace

Because God has graciously drawn near to us in Christ, we have been 'brought near' by the blood of the Cross and therefore can be exhorted to 'draw near' in worship. We are recipients of God's grace and revelation and Spirit and return this movement towards us by moving towards God in praise and worship (see chapter 8).

Worship invites a redeemed humanity to be 'at full stretch', reaching out and up to the God whose transcendent grace invites us, whose mystery teases us, whose beauty attracts us, whose holiness fascinates us, whose fullness evokes our hunger and thirst, whose love draws us up and out of ourselves in astonished awe or exuberant joy or repentant praise. We worship 'by expanding into the space created by a God for us and with us in this manner . . . respectful of the divine sovereignty in the gift of grace, wherein we are given our freedom'.[73] Hardy and Ford call this the 'ecology of blessing' in which our praise 'returns all reality to God, and so lets all be taken up into the spiral of mutual appreciation and delight which is the fulfilment of creation'.[74]

By his immanence the transcendent God has moved savingly into our history so that we 'taste and see' his grace in the immediacy of his Word and Spirit. His manifest transcendence in turn invites us to reach up beyond ourselves to explore his otherness, his mystery and majesty. In this scenario both order and freedom, structure and spontaneity are accommodated. God's transcendent Word, once incarnated among us, now comes from 'beyond us' in liturgy and preaching to impact us afresh; God's empowering Spirit flows out from 'within us' so that 'our whole life is continually thrown into the air in praise in the trust that it will be caught, blessed, and returned renewed'.[75] It is precisely by attending to God as God – to his sovereign freedom in transcendence – that we open ourselves and our space to his transcendent immanence. 'The effect of praise is to open "space" for the recipient to be himself . . . without confinement or coercion . . . So when, in what is perhaps the most characteristic feature of Christian praise, God is in praise found to be ever more totally present, this is a profound intuition of the way he actually is.'[76] New Testament scholar Luke Johnson helpfully summarises that 'transcendent' must be understood in 'its full richness, not as a "going beyond" that involves distance alone but also as a "going beyond" that enables the most intense intimacy and communication . . . a "going across"' which suggests 'closeness'.[77]

In the words of P.T. Forsyth, God's 'transcendence in the Old Testament does not cease in his condescension in the New. It even rises to the place the Holy Spirit takes there as a constituent of Godhead. His love is homeward bound as well as outward bound. If it goes forth, it also returns incessantly on Himself.'[78] The phrase 'homeward bound' love connects with Brueggemann's metaphor for salvation as homecoming from exile. Homecoming, in Brueggemann's terms, is the leaving of all alternative 'Babylonian' world-views and cultural attachments in order to embrace the prophetic (and gospel) vision of Yahweh's kingdom.[79] But the God we 'come home to' is not easily assimilated but is a God both of 'threat and gift'.

To explore this dialectic between otherness and immediacy, Brueggemann draws on the object-relations theory of the paediatric psychiatrist, D.W. Winnicott.[80] The theory holds that in order to grow with a strong centre of personal identity, the baby must assert its omnipotence so that the mother is unqualifiedly attentive to its needs. Conversely, if the mother holds herself aloof, always in control, always the only one who makes sovereign decisions, then, as Brueggemann puts it, 'the baby learns quickly that the way to get along in the world is to please mother, to comply, conform, obey, flatter, be docile', so developing 'a "false self" that must live a life of pretence and fake, engaged in denial of true self'. Brueggemann draws the conclusion for worship practice that 'if God is experienced in doxology as always unqualifiedly good, fixed, sovereign, in charge, never acting, never impinged upon, it leads to worshippers who are docile, passive, and who finally act in bad faith to please God, whatever they may feel'.[81]

The psalmist employs the parent-child analogy in expressing the conviction that 'though my father and mother forsake me, the Lord will receive me' (Ps. 27:10). Afraid of being a spiritual orphan, the psalmist responds to the consoling voice and seeks the comforting face of the Lord. The voice – perhaps of the father – and the face – perhaps the mother's – which the child needs for its identity to be formed and reassured, correspond to the two key facets of immanence: God's name and God's face (*panim*). Brueggemann notes that while never confusing 'the parental relationship with one's relation to God . . . the psalmist also knows about this delicate and definitive relation between parental intimacy and God's transcendent fidelity'.[82] 'We must return', adds Brueggemann, 'both theologically and emotionally-liturgically, to the most elemental intimacies wherein we may glimpse the shape of transcendent fidelity.'[83] God practices covenanting with transcendence and covenanting with intimacy and Israel best 'learned to relate to this God . . . by the sustained, delicate practice of praise and lament'.[84] It is this polarity which the next section addresses.

5

Going to Extremes: Praise *and* Lament

'Liturgy leads regularly to the edge of chaos' and, says Aidan Kavanagh, 'from this regular flirt with doom comes a theology different from any other.'[1] This comment flags up the next polarity to be considered as it affects worship: that of *praise and lament*. These two features of Israel's worship constitute a going to the extremes, an embrace of limit experiences. Such limit experiences are the stuff of life, whether the death of a spouse or the birth of a grandchild, defeat in battle or a successful harvest. Liturgy formalises, channels and expresses the emotions, positive and negative, evoked by these limit experiences.[2]

This point connects to two earlier discussions: on liminality as experienced in worship and on the transcendence-immanence of the God we encounter in it.

As regards liminality, we may note the remarks of Jill Crainshaw, who writes that

> To embrace the liminal in liturgical practices is to invite people to enact an alternative mode of being through face-to-face encounters with one another. In this way the church can reclaim communitas . . . without abandoning the traditional structures of worship . . . In its liturgical remembering, the church must work to restore the metaphorical nature of those traditional structures . . . by restoring the tensive quality of celebration and lament, singing and silence, confession and forgiveness, and law and gospel.[3]

As regards the God encountered in worship, and as noted previously, Brueggemann translates the traditional categories of 'transcendence' and 'immanence' in typically dialectic fashion into a view of God as 'above the fray' and 'in the fray'. On the one hand, where God appears, or is presented, as having attitudes and actions similar to other gods in the ancient world, he is viewed as 'above the fray'. But he is also shown to be inexorably involved in the actual historical contingencies of Israel and so is God 'in the fray'. This has important consequences for Israel's worship – both in its use and misuse – and in the forms of praise and lament characteristic of it.

Structure Legitimation and the Embrace of Pain

Drawing once more on the work of Norman Gottwald, Brueggemann contends that 'statements about God are now also understood as statements about the misuses of human power and the proper use of human power'.[4] It follows that 'high claims for God' – a God who is everywhere present, all powerful and just, punishing the wicked and rewarding the obedient – can be construed as 'high claims of political authority in Israel'. This is grounded in the Sinai covenant and stands in opposition to the authoritarian claims of Egyptian Imperial power. But the development in the Deuteronomic tradition of a contractual or covenantal theology of blessings and curses, sanctions and rewards, establishes a new form of authoritarian orthodoxy, whose validity is confirmed by the verdict of the Deuteronomic history that follows. Both the Torah and the prophets make the linkage between this 'way Israel is governed' and the 'way in which the world works' according to creation. In this scenario, Brueggemann argues, 'the Torah is not human rules but it is the way creation has been ordered'.[5]

Seen in these broad and basic terms, Old Testament theology is structure legitimating, offering a view of God 'above the fray' not impinged upon by social realities. Positively, it is an assertion of creation theology, celebrating the sovereignty and goodness of God in providing a stable and coherent world. But, negatively, it is liable to be seized on by the ruling powers, who can utilise creation theology to buttress their own 'imperial propaganda and ideology'.[6] This point will be picked up later, but suffice it to say here that structure-legitimating theology is the majority voice in the Old Testament – popularised and no doubt distorted as in Job's friends. In the modern Christian world, it flourishes in its popular and clichéd version in prosperity teaching, which seeks to tap into the laws of the universe and to make reality bend to the laws of faith. In the Old Testament world, Brueggemann suggests, it allowed no room for dissent, failed to deal with the problem of dysfunction and stumbled over the issue of pain. Carried over into worship, such an approach fosters an unthinking and mechanical praise, which muffles the cries of the hurting and settles down into an unruffled flattery of the God 'above the fray'.

The polar opposite which lives in unresolved tension with structure legitimation is what Brueggemann calls 'the embrace of pain'. Here can be heard the minority voice which acknowledges breakdown in personal and social coherence and even a fracturing of one's relationship with God. Brueggemann is careful to insist that the tension must not be relaxed. On the one hand, merely to opt for 'the embrace of pain', would be to escape into a self-absorbed, if grim, romanticism. On the other hand, the stifling of the voices expressing pain is equally damaging. The danger emerges of 'oppression without compassion', 'competence without mercy'.[7] Genuine discontent with the way things are, however, is not readily quenched. As is demonstrated by the daring intercession of Moses, the dogged protest of Job and the bold self-expression of Jeremiah, there is pressure to move beyond the accepted ceiling set by the common theology and conventional wisdom based on creation-order. This finds its voice within Israel's liturgical development in the lament.

The lament is the crucial safety-valve that allows Israel's worship to breathe honesty and integrity. The lament is a 'dramatic, rhetorical, liturgical act of speech, which courageously refuses to settle for the way things are. Laments are not 'self-pitying meditations on trouble' but 'acts of protest' directed to God.[8] Lament risks breaking with the consensus and status quo in order to reach the God beyond the prevailing ideology and so to break through to dimensions of God's character unknown before. Lament penetrates to new depths of God's sensitivity and grace. Without lament, we deprive ourselves of such life-changing repristinations of God. Brueggemann notes how laments have dropped out of the modern liturgical repertoire, a process accentuated by the demise of psalm singing. 'The laments are not widely used among us, not printed in most hymnals, not legitimated in our theology' perhaps because we think them 'superseded by some Christological claim'. There is more merit to this last supposition than Brueggemann concedes at this point, but he is surely right when he asserts that 'unwittingly, by silencing the break of embraced pain, we have embraced the uncritical faith of structure legitimation'.[9]

This is as applicable – if not more so – to triumphalist charismatic worship than to classical worship. The place of personal testimony in contemporary charismatic worship, for example, always tends to favour the successful, those who have triumphed; it rarely if ever gives witness to those who are still struggling albeit bravely and faithfully in the midst of trials or disability. The unrelentingly cheery praise, as Martyn Percy's research discloses,[10] rarely articulates the deep theology of the cross. It also firmly maintains the leadership's view that this is a smart and confident outfit to belong to where all answers are held in reserve and all problems are inherently solvable. The absence of lament in contemporary worship practices is therefore a great loss. It closes off one avenue of healing for those in pain and grief. It misses an opportunity for solidarity which would build fellowship and promote brother-sister love. Moreover it prevents worshippers breaking through to a new appreciation of and experience of God.

In another essay, Brueggemann approaches the bipolar scheme from a slightly different angle to show the juxtaposition of two emphases that live in vital and apparently irresolvable tension.[11] Brueggemann extends his 'God in the fray'/ 'God above the fray' distinction by talking of the 'aniconic' and 'iconic' tendencies within Israel and the social consequences to be drawn from them. The 'aniconic' element is central to Israel's understanding of God: namely that God cannot and must not be represented by any visible form. Such an imageless view of God 'accompanies a social vision and social practice of equality and justice'. Conversely an 'iconic' understanding of God inevitably accompanies 'inequities of social power in society'. Brueggemann does not suggest that Israel was in the habit of literal idol-making, though the Golden Calf incident shows the propensity. Rather, this propensity took the form of a psychological need to locate God somewhere, to pin him down in the interests of an assurance that God was always available. This tendency presumably lay behind the 'inviolability of the Temple' mentality against which Jeremiah inveighed so strongly. In any case, whether we posit the distinction of the polar pairs in terms of a characterisation of God ('above' and 'in the fray'), or in terms of their sociological effects ('structure legitimation' and 'embrace of pain'), or indeed in terms of its liturgical components (praise and lament), the tension must be maintained if worship is to remain truthful. And that truthfulness rests on the liturgy's inherent faithfulness to the tradition of Israel's redemptive roots in the Exodus.

The Exodus: A Pattern for Praise and Lament

The book of Exodus – as the foundational story of Israel's national existence – establishes that Israel's praise was based firmly on redemption. Significantly, in the overall structure of its narrative, the book moves from slavery to worship. In Terence Fretheim's words, 'it moves from Israel's bondage to Pharaoh to its bonding to Yahweh . . . from the enforced construction of buildings for Pharaoh to the glad and obedient offering of the people for a building for the worship of God'.[12] Similarly, the book moves from describing in the opening pages an oppressive situation from which God seems absent to depicting, in its concluding chapters, the erection of the Tabernacle which God invades with his glorious presence. Israel is a people redeemed to worship – as is made clear by the instructions given to Moses at the burning bush: 'When you have brought the people out of Egypt, you will worship God on this mountain' (Ex. 3:12). It will be the refusal of Pharaoh to allow the Israelites out into the desert to worship their God in sacrificial offerings that is the ostensible pretext for God's judgement on Egypt and the bringing to a head of his controversy with its gods (Ex. 3:18; 12:12).

Significantly for our purposes, the trigger for God's redemption action is the cry of the oppressed people for God's saving attention and help. 'The Israelites groaned in their slavery and cried out, and their cry for help because of their slavery went up to God. God heard their groaning and he remembered his covenant with Abraham, with Isaac, and with Jacob. So God looked on the Israelites and was concerned about them' (Ex. 2:23b–25). Israel's God in his response is revealed as a covenant-keeping God, loyal to his previous promises, and a compassionate God who listens to the current cries of his people. Brueggemann comments, 'This odd drama of hurt noticed and voiced on earth, heard and obeyed in heaven, becomes incorporated into Israel's liturgy.'[13]

The truth of this is confirmed, as Fretheim points out, by the realisation that 'all of Exodus 1–15 is patterned according to a distress, lament, divine word and deed, song of praise structure . . .'[14] The pattern looks like this: 'the oppression and cries of distress (Ex. 1–2); God's response in word (3:1–7:7) and deed (7:18–14:31); and the praise (Ex. 15)'.[15] Fretheim further observes that the pattern is also visible in chapters 14–15. 'The fearful people speak the lament (14:10–12); Moses proclaims the oracle of salvation (14:13–14); the deed of salvation follows; and the people respond with praise.'[16]

If Exodus 2:23–25 is formative for the wider lament-praise structure, then the Song of Moses in Exodus 15 is paradigmatic of much subsequent celebration. Firstly, God is acclaimed as warrior-king (Ex. 15:1–10). The song utilises the Ancient Near Eastern imagery of creation as a conquest of chaos – an image later exploited by Israel's psalm-singers (Ps. 19:15; 74:13–14; 77:15–20). In Fretheim's words, 'Egypt is considered a historical embodiment of the forces of chaos threatening to undo God's creation.'[17] This throws light on a curious practice in contemporary pentecostal/charismatic worship of using praise in so-called spiritual warfare. Lengthy phases of singing – indeed on some occasion, whole meetings devoted to praise – are given over to this activity with songs of worship being directed at the devil or evil powers. This seems a strangely perverse misdirection of true worship which is meant to be addressed to God. To the contrary, Israel's marching songs were battle hymns of the theocracy, not employed as weapons in war but in proclamation of Yahweh's victory over the forces of chaos and evil. Even an incident much misused in some charismatic quarters, shows this. When Jehoshaphat sends out the choir in advance of his army against

Moab and Ammon, it is notable that they do not sing martial songs nor taunt the enemy nor even call down curses on them; rather, in confident response to a prophetic oracle assuring them of Yahweh's victory, they sing the time-honoured tribute to God's covenant-love – 'give thanks to the Lord, for his love endures for ever' – which already assures them of victory (see 2 Chr. 20:1–30; cf. Ex. 15:13). In John Kleinig's words, 'while the Chronicler clearly asserts the Lord's intervention occurred as the song began, he does not claim that the army attacked the enemy with song, or that the song caused the divine intervention'.[18] Yahweh's presence at the head of his troops was secured and symbolised by the singing of the sacred song; a function elsewhere performed by the carrying of the ark into battle. For God's people, then, 'praise was their chief defence against the enemies who threatened their survival. The power of praise lay in its connection with the prophetic word of God and in its proclamation of his holy name . . . Praise proclaimed that the Lord needed no assistance from his people to vanquish their enemies.'[19]

The second feature of the Song of Moses which merits attention is the conjunction of creation and redemption themes as a way of heralding Yahweh's universal lordship over the nations. 'The nations will hear and tremble' (15:14). As the shock waves of the exodus reverberate through the nations affected by this act of God, they tremble in prospect (here told in retrospect) of the conquest of Canaan for it was not the power of Yahweh's army but of his arm that did it (Ex. 15:15). Already, it seems clear, the exodus pattern is being used typologically within the song itself to compare the conquest of Canaan with the conquest of Egypt. As Israel has 'passed through the sea, so they will 'pass' through the nations, which, like Pharaoh's troops will drop 'like a stone' (Ex. 15:16; cf. 15:5).

Thirdly, it is worth noticing that the song encompasses what the whole book of Exodus encompasses and the whole subsequent Temple history elaborates – namely the building of a palace-cum-sanctuary for the conquering king. 'You will bring them in and plant them on the mountain of your inheritance – the place, O Lord, you made for your dwelling, the sanctuary, O Lord, your hands established' (Ex. 15:17).

Fourthly, and lastly, the exuberance of Miriam's music-making and dancing legitimises a format for praise of full emotional and bodily involvement in worship that is amply exemplified in the Psalms. The self-transcendence achieved by the women in their joyous dancing typifies the freedom of the saving experience.[20] Without being unduly heavy-handed about this, van Olst's observation is true that 'the Bible is free from prejudice against the bodily experience, an experience and acceptance that is basic to the liturgical celebration in which sensory and motor skills are totally included. Experience is a central component here because celebration is totally absorbing, involving all parts of the person.'[21] Israel's 'going to the extremes' in worship is bound, at this point, to be a standing rebuke to over-cerebral, modern, Western fears about bodily expression in worship.

Two additional implications follow this analysis. The pattern of distress-deliverance, lament-praise derived from the exodus is so well embedded at the heart of Israel's liturgy that subsequent generations of worshippers are enabled to enter into freedom as they joyfully renew acquaintance with this God. So paradigmatic is the exodus event as a ground of future acts of salvation that Isaiah can even, remarkably, invert the motif to give hope to Egypt as well as Israel so that Egypt when oppressed, cries to the Lord and is delivered (Is. 19:19–25).[22] This dialectical worship – incorporating praise and lament – has the potential to rise afresh in every generation and to reach beyond national or cultural boundaries with the good news of something to make a song and dance about. Brueggemann concludes, '"We cried out – God heard our cry". This formula stands at the centre of the old credo recitals. That formula governs Israel's songs of thanksgiving, which reiterate earlier songs of complaint that have now been answered and resolved.'[23]

Praise and Lament in the Psalms

The pattern of the exodus event, it has been argued, proved formative for the subsequent shape of Israel's liturgical practices. Tracing this lasting imprint of the exodus on the dynamic polarities inherent in truthful worship can best be done by considering the place of praise and lament in the Psalms. All modern discussion on this theme acknowledges its debt to the seminal work done during and after the Second World War by Claus Westermann who spoke of praise and lament as the 'two poles' which 'determine the nature of all speaking to God'.[24] This stance has been recently reaffirmed by, among others, Craig Broyles, who speaks in similar terms of God-laments and praise and asserts that 'this new understanding of the polar opposites of the Psalter helps to clarify the extremes of psalmic expression'.[25] This roughly corresponds to Paul Ricoeur's language when he speaks of 'limit experiences' (crisis and culmination) that are matched by 'limit expressions' (laments and celebration).[26]

'Lament' is a fairly loose category whose usefulness has been questioned by Hans-Joachim Kraus in his magisterial commentary on the Psalms. Firstly, he doubts if there are any isolated, individual lamentations at all. Rather the solo voices are representative individuals in and for the community. Secondly, Kraus considers 'lament' itself to be a problematic view, claiming that there is little outright lamentation in evidence.[27] Craig Broyles has more subtly nuanced the category of lament by dividing it into two types: psalms of plea in which the needy person cries out to God for help, and the protest psalm in which is heard a complaint to or against God. Failure to make this subtler distinction would leave the implication that the distinction is based only on the underlying situation. But, Broyles argues, the issue is not just situational but relational; not just a matter of a distressful context for prayer but one in which the psalmist's conception of God is altered. 'In the psalms of praise and plea,' Broyles maintains,

> God is approached as benevolent, in the psalms of complaint as indifferent or hostile. In the former he is believed to be an ally, but in the latter he is regarded to be either an aloof bystander or an active antagonist. These protest psalms depict how the distress and the tradition collide, thus showing that the psalmist's dilemma is not simply his own but one that threatens the integrity of Yahweh's character.[28]

Given these qualifications, lament will serve in this book as a broad category for those traumatic experiences where negative emotions are confronted and expressed, and in which the believer's (or believing community's) relationship with God is called into question.

Brueggemann's own oft-quoted division of the Psalm collection is into three broad groups which he terms *orientation, disorientation,* and *re- or new reorientation.*

But typically, he sees the polarity as involving two movements. The first move from orientation into disorientation is an act of relinquishment, characteristically expressed in lament. The second move is a step of glad surprise from disorientation into new orientation, marked by hymns and songs of thanksgiving.[29] In both of these moves to the extremities of life, worshippers are moved to express extreme emotions. This point will be touched on later, but first it is necessary to explicate how Brueggemann views these three classifications of psalms.

1. By *psalms of orientation,* Brueggemann means those songs which reflect the 'satisfied seasons of well-being' that express gratitude for the 'constancy of blessing' and the 'goodness, coherence and reliability of God, God's creation and God's governing law'.[30] These are songs in which there is 'no tension to resolve', sung by people in a 'serene location' who assume the 'orderliness . . . of life'.[31] They are chiefly represented by creation psalms (e.g. Ps. 104) or those which celebrate creation and law (Ps. 19). They culminate in the extravagant expressions of the final psalms in the Psalter (Ps. 146–150).

Psalm 104, for example, celebrates the sheer *magnificence and splendour of creation.* It pictures Yahweh, clothed majestically in a cloak of light, sweeping through the world, with angelic assistants in train, giving life to all he touches (vv. 1–4). The psalmist rejoices in the earth's *stability,* which reflects God's own faithfulness as limits are fixed and chaos is held at bay (vv. 5–9). He relishes Yahweh's gift of earth's *fecundity;* earth's prolific and luxuriant growth relativises any need to revert to Baalism or any other fertility religion (vv. 10–18). He praises God for the *orderliness of creation,* which in the modern world has made empirical science possible (vv. 19–23). He exults in the dazzling *variety* in created things which banishes greyness and drab conformism and mirrors the multi-faceted wisdom of God (vv. 24–26; cf. Eph. 3:10). The psalmist rejoices too, in the earth's continual *replenishment;* its resources not being in danger of exhaustion, because God's recreative Spirit is constantly sent forth to 'renew the face of the earth'

(v. 30). In our contemporary world where moderns are tempted to regard themselves as autonomous agents wielding technological omnipotence, this 'grand and almost overwhelming recital'[32] strikes a prophetic note. Lest we reduce the world to a scientific laboratory, a food production chain, a recreational comfort-zone, or, even, an artist's studio, psalms like this remind us that with respect to creation, we are joint-beneficiaries (vv. 14–15), active stewards (v. 23), awe-struck observers (v. 24), and above all, exuberant worshippers (vv. 1, 35). This is no sentimental picture for 'nature is red in tooth and claw' (cf. v. 21), nor is it a romantic one which denies the evil present in God's once wholly good world (v. 35). But it is an unabashed celebration of 'this world as the stunning theatre, workshop, and playground'[33] of a generous parental God.

Psalm 19 superbly joins praise for creation with worshipful appreciation of the Torah. God speaks in both the skies and the scriptures. Day and night, in morning lectures and evening classes, praise is the wordless curriculum of creation. The so-called 'laws of nature', are for the worshipper, the very 'laws of Yahweh'. The Torah is life-giving, moral fresh air, as necessary to living as the natural world, and as penetrating in its heat as the warmth of the sun. The worshipper fears to mar such beauty and to grieve such grace. The scope of praise is exemplified by Psalm 145 which encapsulates praise that is personal ('I will exalt . . .', vv. 1–7), universal ('all you have made will praise you', vv. 8–20), and eternal ('for ever and ever', v. 21). The Psalter closes with a veritable volcano of praise – five psalms of 'glad abandonment'[34] which exhaust every breath and pull out every stop in jubilant adoration of the world's One Creator God. Here the ancient singers and choirs make energetic music and give joyful voice to creation's wordless worship, acting – to paraphrase the poet, George Herbert – as the 'secretary of nature's praise'.[35] Endorsing the Psalter's final crescendo of praise, Brueggemann comments, 'what a moment when creation gets its voice for its proper, dangerous work. It is a moment of threat and of healing, of breaking down and of building up, of weeping and laughing, of mourning, dancing, of throwing away and keeping, of seeking and losing. It is a joyful noise – for all things new'.[36]

Criticism is sometimes directed at such serene and fulsome praise of God in his creation order. The suspicion is raised that since creation songs affirmed the orderliness of the world, they were particularly vulnerable to being hijacked by the 'powers-that-be' – for example the kings of Israel and Judah – for self-serving reasons. When God's interests and the kings are presented as synonymous, then the voices from below are screened out.

This danger certainly existed in Israel and was criticised by the prophets, notably Amos (see the biblical reflection at the end of this book). The abuse of worship for political ends, then and now, undoubtedly occurs. But it is extremely doubtful that the blame for this can be laid so unambiguously at the door of *creation praise*. Indeed, as, Brueggemann himself acknowledges, 'creation theology may indeed express a bold claim for the sovereignty of Yahweh against idols and false orderings of the world'.[37] Many scholars support the view that Genesis 1 is a polemic against the Babylonian gods and the system they sanctioned. Furthermore the exodus pattern itself, strongly incorporates the assertion by Yahweh, in the plague-judgements and opening of the sea, of his unique creative power and authority over against the false claims of the gods of Egypt represented by Pharaoh. The prophets, too, were not shy of appealing to this very uniqueness of Yahweh as the One Creator God in order to penetrate and open up the consciousness of a people lulled into sin by a complacent and self-serving social environment and practices. So Amos is noted for interspersing his prophetic oracles with 'creation hymns' (1:2; 4:13; 5:8–9; 9:5–6) precisely in those contexts where he is indicting Israel's royally endorsed social injustice and phoney worship.[38] David Hubbard observes that the

> use of the hymnic material suggests that the celebration of Yahweh's power as sovereign Creator was part of Israel's worship at the beginning of the prophetic era . . . There is probably a touch of irony intended, as Amos takes Israel's familiar hymnody in which the people would have found great joy and comfort (5:23) and turns it back on them as evidence of God's right and power to judge them.[39]

There is, then, nothing intrinsically socially conservative about creation praise. It is not necessary to buy into Brueggemann's whole critique of Israel's creation praise in order to note his warning about the potential misuse of psalms of orientation. Worship which is perpetually all sunshine, may indeed lull the worshipper into a passive contentment that 'God is in his heaven and all's right with the world', though lethargy, boredom and cultural assimilation will also play their part. There appears to be no evidence in the text of the *songs of orientation* for the misuse Brueggemann and other critics are wary of. If 'praise is an audacious act' of 'basic trust' and 'of self-abandonment done without grudge',[40] then there seems no good reason not to apply this generous verdict to the songs of orientation as much as to the songs of reorientation. Worshippers need not be timorous in heralding the God of creation order, faithfulness and fruitfulness. Brueggemann issues an unequivocal call to worship to his readers. 'Everything depends upon your courage to engage finally in this subversive, useless act that lets the world be the world God intends. It is time for the "secretary" to read the minutes.'[41]

2. Brueggemann's second grouping for the psalms is what he calls the *psalms of disorientation* and includes lament, complaint and contrition. All these, whether individual or corporate, are 'ways of entering linguistically into a new distressful situation in which the old orientation has collapsed'.[42] Brueggemann chooses to emphasise the 'complaint' element in these songs and petitions since they are not merely expressions of self-pity, still less sighs of stoic resignation and acceptance characteristic of some Christian piety.[43] In these liturgical statements there is nothing censored or suppressed, but a realistic recognition that the old order of things has collapsed. Nostalgia is temporarily replaced by a desperate looking forward, often expressed in a vow to God or an assurance that God has heard, which gives hope for the future. The typical lament structure involves an introductory address and cry for help, the lament or complaint, a confession of trust, a petition, an assurance of being heard, a vow of praise, and (if the situation has been resolved) responsive praise of God.[44] Brueggemann describes the movement implied in such laments as a turning from 'resentful remembering to a fresh anticipation of an equilibrium that is a gift from God, genuinely new and not a restatement of the old'.[45]

Psalm 22 is a case in point, albeit an extreme one, which concentrates the lament genre into one searing example, a psalm in which the structural elements of a typical lament are almost obliterated by the ferocity of feeling. The singer is like a drowning man who comes up for air three times; three times crying out in desperation, three times hanging on to some vestige of faith. He utters a piercing cry of spiritual abandonment (the address), and complains that God does 'not answer' (vv. 1–2). But with some kind of spiritual sixth sense (a confession of trust), he pleads a remembered sense of God's transcendent enthroned holiness (v. 3), which has given Israel a saving history (vv. 4–5). Then, repeating this pattern of lament, he describes himself as emotionally overwhelmed, so mocked and scorned that all self-esteem has left him, and worm-like, he feels he is 'not a man' (vv. 6–8). In extreme agony of mind, he clings to a very narrow ledge of memory, envisaging himself at his most vulnerable and dependent moment in his mother's womb where, he dares to believe, God was working for him (vv. 9–10). Lastly, he confesses to being physically broken (is this Psalm part of a liturgy for the sick perhaps?), dramatically portrays his enemies and vividly describes the effects (vv. 11–18), and pleads God's saving strength (vv. 19–21). Between verse 21 and 22 the psalmist has evidently received an answer of sorts – perhaps through a prophetic oracle – so that his tone changes. He addresses God with a vow of praise (v. 22), and addresses the congregation (v. 23) with the confidence that further recruits for worship will be found among the sufferers (v. 24), the seekers after God (v. 26), in all the ends of the earth (v. 27), whether poor (v. 26) or prosperous (v. 29), whether dying (v. 29b), living (v. 30), or as yet unborn (v. 31).

This psalmist then achieves resolution but only by embracing with honesty and candour the 'radical dissonance'[46] that evokes his lament. Brueggemann notes how extreme voices express extreme emotions in wild words and angry questions. These are the voices of caged people, trapped in oppressive situations of pain, grief, despair or guilt. Often, as in Psalm 22, they describe themselves as surrounded by wild beasts – 'bulls and dogs' in the case of Psalm 22. In this way, Brueggemann asserts, worshippers are faced up with their own beastliness. 'The juices flow and the animal is loosed.'[47]

The case of the imprecatory psalms in worship is even more vexed than that of lament. Their harsh tones and hate-filled lyrics would seem to have no place in Christian worship. They may certainly be cathartic in allowing for the release (and healing) of negative feelings in the presence of God. The God of Israel's praise is neither deceived about the darkness that lurks in the hearts of his worshippers nor embarrassed by the realism with which they approach him.[48] Emotionally and spiritually, such songs can thus be 'accepted as a sign of health'.[49] At least such anger is directed to God to be absorbed rather than vented destructively on others.[50] Viewed positively, expressions of such raw pain might represent a passionate longing for God's justice to be done and an empathetic siding with the victims of oppression.[51] The imprecatory psalms remind us that evil must be hated because God hates evil, and that the enemies envisaged are the enemies of God.[52]

Can these psalms be sung or prayed in Christian worship as they are? 'No,' says Reformed Old Testament scholar Tremper Longman, for the New Testament has shown us that our controversy is not with persons.[53] 'Yes,' says reconstructionist David Chilton, for whom liturgical calling down of blessings and curses is part of the spiritual warfare of the church.[54] Others tentatively see the spiritual warfare dimension as a possible use of these psalms, albeit with the strong proviso that vengeance belongs to God not to us.[55] Many see a necessary Christological channel for the songs of vengeance as if they are cleansed by being on the lips of the Messiah or spoken in his name.[56] Michael Jinkins warns against glibly seeking to strain out the offensiveness of these raw cries straining them through 'a Christian colander'.[57] Rather we should recognise the brutal realism of such prayers, which both reveal the harsh truth about ourselves, and at the same time, echo in a dim way the zeal of God for justice. It can be argued that we must indeed transcribe these psalms into a Christian key, not because God has 'become a romantic'[58] but because these psalms lead us to the cross where all hate and lust for vengeance are absorbed by the suffering of the vilified messiah and where God's supreme justice is done. 'And so,' in Brueggemann's words, 'we are driven to the crucifixion, in which God has decisively dealt with the reality of evil which must be judged . . . There is no less of vengeance in the New Testament.

But God has wrought it in "his" own person and so the world has been cleansed and purged and grace has overcome.'[59]

There is, in other words, a way through these imprecatory songs but not a way round them. Again the issue at one level is that of denial or reality. This is reminiscent of the type of argument used by Martyn Percy in his criticism of Vineyard-style worship which fixes God in a transcendent power-and-love mode and so reduces the human capacity for free response.[60] Likewise, worship which censors lament dehumanises the worshippers. If we arrive at worship too easily convinced of a well-ordered world rooted in the stability of heaven, we will eventually find that stability to be 'such heaviness that it crushes, it denies honour to us and in the end does not take us seriously'.[61] Furthermore, ideological dangers lurk, as Percy also noted with Vineyard worship. In Brueggemann's words, 'Uncritical celebrative liturgy turns out to be an ideological legitimation for the status quo that announces that the system is working well and needs only to be honoured and trusted.'[62] This is true for 'high church' praise that conforms to the establishment ethos, and true for 'charismatic praise' that confirms people in their submission to the current leadership structure. Authentic praise is a true song of thanksgiving which does not override lament but views the lament, joyously and wonderingly, from the side of resolution and transformation.

3. This leads to a consideration of Brueggemann's third category of psalm – *the psalms of re- or new orientation*. These songs describe the movement from disorientation and dislocation to a new sphere of grace, the movement from lament to praise. Such songs are not glib recitals, as if nothing had happened, but substantial outpourings of relief and humbled excitement. The old order of things did break up, the bottom did drop out of the world, but a new creation has been given, and with a joyful surprise at the saving turn of events. In the songs of thanksgiving there is usually a crux – a 'but as for me . . .' (e.g. Ps. 31:14) – where the sufferer's trust is invested in God. Then in retrospect, the experienced transformation in fortunes is celebrated. God's disfavour is real but it 'lasts only a moment' while 'his favour lasts a lifetime'; 'weeping may remain for a night but rejoicing comes in the morning' (Ps. 30:5). 'I waited patiently for the Lord,

he turned to me and heard my cry and lifted me out of the slimy pit . . .' (Ps. 40:1).

The positive outcome is then as expansively felt and unrestrainedly expressed, as was the negative plight. As Brueggemann puts it, 'the extremity of re-orientation is as shattering as disorientation'.[63] The songs of thanksgiving go to the extremes in exuberance and celebration. 'You have turned my wailing into dancing; you removed my sackcloth and clothed me with joy, that my heart may sing to you and not be silent . . .' (Ps. 30:11). The psalmist wishes for 'a thousand tongues to sing our great redeemer's praise', for the Lord's wonders are too numerous for one singer to tell (Ps. 40:5). The reluctance of God to waste good praise is appealed to as an argument for help and perhaps even immortality. 'What gain is there in my destruction, in my going down into the pit? Will the dust praise you? Will it proclaim your faithfulness?' (Ps. 30:9). In being rescued and reorientated, the redeemed feel swept up in a tidal wave of gratitude and an overflow of praise. As David Ford has reminded us, the overwhelming crises we face which put us out of our depths, are matched by the overwhelming grace that saves, and this redounds, in turn, in overflowing joy and extravagant praise that cannot be contained. It is not merely that in these psalms the joy and release are an 'answer' to the trials and the bitter laments they evoked. Rather, tragedy and resolution are, in a strange way, taken together 'in a much more richly complex picture of multiple overwhelming that has only one sure orientation – God'.[64]

The previous hermeneutic of suspicion that produced the doubt and angry questions is now replaced with a 'hermeneutic of surprise'. But it is not as if the old pre-critical days had been resumed, without being reflected on or evaluated. It is that the sufferer has come through to a new naivety,[65] not one which is thin and shrill but one textured by trauma. In Brueggemann's words, 'the ones who give thanks and sing genuinely new songs must be naïve or they would not bother to sing songs and give thanks. But it is a praise in which the anguish of disorientation is not forgotten, removed or absent.'[66] Yet praise speaks and sings audaciously as if it could enrich God's resources or enhance his status, using the language of 'blessing, magnifying and glorifying God'. As lament 'rescues' pain by naming it and sin by shaming it, so praise names and honours what is perfect, and in the act of praising, 'paradoxically perfects perfection'.[67] The loss of praise, typified at an interpersonal level, by the substitution of the language of congratulation, is as costly as the loss of lament.[68]

Genuinely uninhibited, celebratory rejoicing is rare even in charismatic churches where either 'easy-listening' praise songs smother the real emotions of the worshippers or heavy-rock style music psychologically suppresses them altogether. Heschel's words seem even truer now than when he first said them: 'the man of our time is losing the power of celebration. Instead of celebrating, he seeks to be amused or entertained.'[69] Heschel points out that celebrating is an action, while being entertained is passive. Entertainment is a mere diversion, a distraction of the heart and mind; celebration is a concentration, a focusing of heart and mind, 'a giving attention to the transcendent meaning of one's actions . . . To celebrate is to share in a greater joy, to participate in an eternal drama'.[70] We shrink the horizons of the gospel and of people's lives when we tailor worship too tightly to the worshipper's tastes or the seeker's musical comfort-zones. The reduction of worship to entertainment already seems well set. The basic problem here is the culturally acquired habit to make worship 'do' something. This pragmatic approach to worship ultimately destroys it. By its very nature, worship is a 'useless' activity which does not calculate returns but voices the sheer disbelief that God has done more than we can ask or imagine or hope for. Glossolalia, Paul argues, is a test-case at this point: it enables us to see that worship can be meaningful even when it is not intelligible (1 Corinthians 14). But then all doxology 'is an irrational act that pushes beyond control, summons us beyond our cherished rationality, rescues us from anxiety, transcends despair, overrides arrogance, strips us of self-sufficiency, and leaves us unreservedly and entirely entrusted to this one other who cares for us more than we care for ourselves'.[71]

Praise is the extravagant antidote to a despairing unbelief, which, in Paul's penetrating analysis in the first chapter of his letter to the Romans, curves in on itself so losing the truly human scale and dimension in the process. Conversely, and paradoxically, only 'in the useless play of celebration is life taken seriously as gift of God'.[72] Emboldened praise is also the cure for what

Brueggemann calls 'an overpolite idolatry' – a religious attitude of mind which 'imagines that God is fragile . . . and easily offended'.[73] Worship then becomes either flat, grim and dutiful, or prim, decorous and inexpressive. But there is, as Brueggemann points out, 'something intrinsically boisterous, and from a certain perspective disordered and disruptive, about Israel's praise . . .'[74]

Praise and Lament: A Eucharistic Synthesis?

'As there is no embarrassment in Israel's praise,' Brueggemann comments, 'so there is no trepidation in Israel's complaint'.[75] Both are pursued with equal vigour and both now need to be accommodated in the church's worship without encouraging exhibitionism. Authentic worship needs to sustain the creative tension between the polar opposites of lament and praise. It needs to do this without an artificial bolting together of items in the liturgy which sit incongruously alongside each other. Integrated worship, it is worth repeating, is not an eclectic rearrangement of otherwise incompatible elements in a contrived attempt at liturgical novelty. A rigorously thought-through, theologically articulate, well-prepared fusion of classical liturgical elements which maximises participation, and allows space for spontaneity, spiritual gifts and the free flow of the Spirit in praise – this still seems to be the best framework for a biblically responsible 'going to the extremes' in worship.

In current charismatic theology and practice, it is particularly the lament dimension that appears conspicuous by its absence. Yet, as Brueggemann maintains, 'Covenant minus lament is finally a practice of denial, cover-up, and pretence which sanctifies the status-quo.'[76] It follows, Brueggemann contends in similar vein, that covenant worship, without any acknowledgment of the shadowside, is 'mistaken, dishonest, and destructive . . . because it requires persons to engage in enormous denial and pretense about how life really is'.[77] At worst this can induce guilt since if God is so unconditionally forthcoming and the rest of the church so visibly favoured, then, if there is distress or trouble, the needy feel they only have themselves to blame. But if praise is to be an extravagant self-abandonment to God, lament must be allowed to be a whole-hearted assertion of self before God.[78]

For its part, praise is authentic when it is not a naive buying into an illusion but is sourced by the brokenness of the cross, and expressed as the lavish and exuberant overflow of grace. It is worth recalling that our typical lament – Psalm 22 – was evidently in the heart and mind of Jesus during crucifixion. According to the evangelists, the Israelite psalmist's grief became the representative Israelite's saving dereliction. Only broken fragments of the song passed his parched lips but bystanders heard him croak the first words of the psalm – 'My God, why have you forsaken me?' – 'and its final words – 'It is finished.' They were perhaps the first to begin to perceive the mystery of the cross that beneath what was being endured, something was being done, that the agonised abandonment masked a momentous achievement. If Christ in atonement has absorbed our sin and forsakenness and with it, in a profound sense, our pain and questions, then it is only so that the weight of deeper experience will raise the quality of praise and worship. Out of dark underground depths, uttered in lament, the purest stream of praise flows. In the dynamics of Trinitarian theology, our worship is gathered up by the Holy Spirit in Christ's worship of the Father. According to the writer to the Hebrews, it is not only in dying that our Messiah echoes Psalm 22, but in his ascended glory as our great high priest. Applying the words of the psalmist to himself, he declared, '. . . in the presence of the congregation I will sing your song' (Heb. 2:12; cf. Ps. 22:22). So the glorified Christ is pictured at the centre of the church's worship, acting by the Spirit, as both worship leader and leading worshipper.[79] Through the voices and song of his people whom he has been pleased to save and call his own, and whom he is not embarrassed to call his family, Jesus offers worship to the Father. By the Spirit and in Christ, that is, the singing church becomes the outlet for his song, the mouthpiece of his praise.[80]

The extremes of lament and praise are best maintained when worship is centred around the Eucharist. It is significant that 'eucharist' is derived from 'ευχαριστεω' (*eucharisteo*), which is the characteristic New Testament word for 'thanksgiving'. The church might have avoided so much eucharistic controversy if it had focused its attention not on the elements – asking 'what does the bread become or symbolise?' – but on the actions, asking 'what should we do here to remember Christ in the "Do this" which he ordained?'. And the 'doing' would involve, taking, breaking, giving and eating as an act of giving thanks. More awareness of this and the communion services might be less like a funeral wake and more like a feast. That this term *'eucharisteo'* has attached itself historically to the Lord's Supper is perfectly right. Here is the fountain of all praise which comes out of the deepest depths of suffering, lamentation and atonement and which overspills into a lifestyle of thanksgiving. Worshippers are caught up in the Son's sacrificial doxology, so that even 'in the midst of great endurance and patience' we can 'joyfully give thanks to the Father . . .' (Col. 1:10). Thanksgiving is reinstated as our native language so that we 'overflow with thanksgiving' in ways that transform our relationships and our prayers (Col. 2:7; 3:15; 4:2). Thanksgiving dissolves self-pity and enables us to 'rejoice always' not because we are playing mental tricks on ourselves but because, informed by the cross, we are learning to turn everything in the direction of God in 'repentant praise'.

Brueggemann, whose insights have stimulated so much of this discussion, himself concludes,

> Finally we may suggest that the structure of cry-response that gets expressed as petition and praise dramatizes the movement that came to be experienced by the early church as crucifixion-resurrection. The psalms of lament in their two principal parts of before/after reflect precisely the experience of death and the gift of new life. The church's resurrection faith is consistent with Israel's petition and praise, the sure conviction that God hears and sees and acts decisively.[81]

6

Creative Repetition: Tradition *and* Innovation

In the oft-quoted dictum of church historian, Jaroslav Pelikan, 'tradition is the living faith of the dead; traditionalism is the dead faith of the living'.[1] The latter we may safely jettison; the former we cannot do without. This statement serves to introduce another polarity to be discussed in connection with worship which is – in its broadest terms – that between old and new, between inherited patterns and contemporary innovation.

Narrative Newness

Israel's praise kept alive and fresh the foundational stories of the nation's identity. As has already been noted, the exodus event, in which Israel cried out to the Lord and was dramatically rescued from slavery, gave rise to exuberant praise and formed the paradigm for Israel's later pattern of lament and praise. This saving history, augmented by the acts of God that had brought Israel into the land, became the core of Israel's liturgical testimony. Israel's worship was not primarily a release of feelings or a reflection of its moods but a recital of the mighty deeds of God. This narrative recital was the overarching framework for Israel's worship, which was capable of being adapted to the special circumstances of the worshippers.

Psalm 136, for example, is a powerful litany which celebrates the exodus and the conquest of Canaan with the repeated refrain: 'His love endures for ever.' In whatever contexts this song is sung it is evidently intended to evoke both gratitude for the past and reassurance about God's enduring love in the present. Psalm 105, likewise, exults in the mighty deeds of God in saving Israel. Its lack of specific reference to the Sinai covenant, however, may indicate an Exilic origin for the song. In this case, devoid of land and Temple and kingship, the recollection of the earliest history of the Abrahamic covenant becomes particularly crucial for faith to be sustained (Ps. 105:8–11, 42). The psalm lauds the power of God's promise to generate energy and faith across the generations and to shape the course of history. Israel's whole story, from patriarchal wanderings (vv. 12–15) and Joseph's sojourn in Egypt (vv. 16–25), to the exodus (vv. 26–43) and conquest (v. 44), is liturgically subsumed under the one covenantal promise. Story becomes song.

The efficacy of such recitals in worship at this point stems from the mutual interaction of story and liturgy. On the one hand, it is *story that makes liturgy effective*. The way this works rests on the well-known capacity of narrative to draw the hearers into its action. Story has a magnetic and inclusive psychological power to involve its hearers in the world it is describing.[2] This explains, at least in part, the authority of the scriptural narrative. In a discussion of the interplay between Scripture and tradition, Lesslie Newbigin characteristically states that 'it is only by "indwelling" the Scripture that one remains faithful to the tradition. By this "indwelling" ("abiding") we take our place and play our part in the story that is the true story of the whole human race and of the cosmos'.[3] Liturgy is one key context in which later believers participate in the saving tradition and 'indwell' the story.

Paul Ricoeur points out that biblical narratives never stand alone. They work in interaction with other modes of discourse. So laws transcribe narratives into instruction while the narrative setting for the Torah prevents law being received as anything other than as gift. Prophecy stops the covenantal tradition from hardening into an oppressive orthodoxy. Prophecy brings to the surface the promises buried deep in the narrative that open it to the future. Narrative, for its part, furnishes prophecy with typological images and analogies for the future salvation (as in the 'new exodus' motif in Isaiah). Wisdom perpetuates and applies the lessons of the story but the underlying story prevents wisdom being reduced to bland moralisms and generalisations.

This complex interplay between narrative and non-narrative ways of discourse is focused in worship where the story is re-enacted and dramatically retold. Here the saving story, the law, the prophetic vision and the moral insight of wisdom are brought dynamically within 'indwelling' range of the believing worshipper. 'The whole range of modes (of discourse) can thus be seen as distributed between the poles of storytelling and praising.'[4]

Not only does the inherent power of narrative help to make the liturgy effective, so conversely, *liturgy makes the story effective by enacting and contemporising it.* Ricoeur notes that it is the 'privilege of worship to reactualise salvation, to reiterate the creation, to remember the exodus, to renew the proclamation of the law, and to repeat the promises'.[5] This was not achieved by an exact acting-out of the details of the original story. Passover regulations do not stipulate the painting of blood on doorposts and lintels. Rather, what occurs is a symbolic representation in worship of the theological heart and soteriological significance of the original historic event(s).

In this way, says Andrew Walker, 'liturgy as divine drama, tells again the old, old story. It is not play-acting but an acting out of God's love for the world.'[6]

The words and images, movements and food, colour and choirs by which we do this are only means to an end. 'It is unfortunate,' as Eugene Peterson remarks, 'that "liturgical" is so often identified with choreography in the chancel or an aesthetics of the sublime. There is nothing elitist about it; it is vast and dramatic "story-ing", making sure that we get into the story and don't leave anything or anyone out of the story.'[7]

Liturgy is repentant praise, a regular re-conversion in which we once again surrender our self-referential and often self-made stories in favour of involvement in the larger script and bigger story that God is writing. 'Without sufficient liturgical support,' Peterson suggests, 'we are very apt to edit the story down to fit our individual tastes and predispositions.'[8]

Old Story: New Song

In his study of Israel's worship traditions as presented by the chronicler, John Kleinig notes that the Levites were appointed by

David to perform three functions: 'To proclaim' (*zakar*; 'to make petition,' NIV), 'to give thanks' (*toda*), and 'to praise (*hillel*) the Lord, the God of Israel' (1 Chr. 16:4).[9] The first function in particular, 'to proclaim', suggests that worship was the matrix for the recording and recollecting of the saving deeds of Yahweh that form Israel's history. The word *zakar* is used twice with this sense in the composite hymn that follows. 'Remember (*zakar*) the wonders he has done, his miracles and the judgments he pronounced' (1 Chr. 16:12). And again in verse 15, where Kleinig, unlike the NIV, prefers the imperatival reading, 'Remember his covenant for ever, the word he commanded for a thousand generations' (1 Chr. 16:15). It was this recital of the historical events that constituted Israel's identity as the people of God which evoked the congregation's responsive 'amen' and betokened their embrace of their own formative story (1 Chr. 16:36b). But if the redemptive narrative settles the fixed shape of Israel's worship pattern, where is there room for the 'new song'?

Walter Brueggemann takes up this point in an evaluation of Psalm 96. In one of a series of six opening imperatives, the psalmist urges Israel to sing 'a new song' and so to 'proclaim (*basar*) his salvation day after day' (Ps. 96:2b). The Hebrew term here, *basar*, is ordinarily used of bringing news. It is speech 'which transfers the significance of an event from one place to another'.[10] It gains in theological import when employed by Isaiah to refer to the new exodus salvation God will achieve for his people beyond exile (Is. 40:9; 52:7; 61:1). Victory elsewhere only becomes effective for others in their context when it is told and heard as news by them. The 'new song' conveys the decisive effect in one situation of a salvation of God wrought in another place. In terms of content, this means that a 'new song' need not be an entirely new lyric but an earlier song renewed with fresh meaning and impact as God is praised as the one who newly saves. The remembered story of the one covenant Lord breaks afresh on the consciousness of the worshippers so that they experience God's love even in the darkest days as 'new every morning'.[11] Liturgy then tells the 'old, old story' in order to celebrate God's 'genuine newness'.[12]

Furthermore, when the psalmist urges Israel to 'say among the nations, "The Lord reigns"', he is not simply seeking a recognition of a rule of God that is always and everywhere true, an acknowledgment of what is obviously and perennially the state of affairs. He is prophetically declaring, in effect, that 'the Lord has just become king'. The paint is still wet, as it were. 'Dramatically, experientially, realistically, this liturgic formula, "the Lord reigns," is not a remembering but is an enactment, a making so.'[13]

The 'new song' becomes virtually a technical term for a victory song, which rejoices in the new situation brought about by God's kingly intervention.[14] The 'new song' causes the worshippers to feel the impact of the newness and – to coin a phrase – the nowness. Such a song transfers the significance of the saving event from the 'there and then' to the 'here and now'. In Brueggemann's words, the 'liturgic act is the moment of announcement in which old claims are made present realities, in which victories won in other places are made available as victories in this place now'.[15]

Sung in the enclosed world of exile, for example, such 'new songs' effectively dethrone the reigning gods, and usher worshippers into the new world of the kingdom of God.[16] By this account, our contemporary worship need not embark on a desperate quest for novelty or relevance but can urgently seek the revitalising of its old traditions and an immediate awareness of the saving rule of God.

Psalm 96 further shows us that the newness of which the 'new song' partakes is *eschatological*. The psalmist not only praises the Lord's great deeds in the past, not only does he celebrate the Lord's current reign, he also sings of the Lord who is coming to bring justice and salvation (Ps. 96:13). Worship here daringly and prophetically transcends the historic recital of remembered saving actions, and risks 'a proclamation of God's reign before all the evidence is in . . .'[17] When the coming of the Lord impinges on God's people in worship, it arouses intense expectation and longing so that they experience him not as distant but close in transcendent immanence. If the 'new song' in worship celebrates God's newness and evokes his nowness, then it also reverberates with a sense of his nearness. More needs to be said of this in a Christian context but suffice it to say that Israel's 'new song' is true gospel music.

Recycled Truth

Before leaving Psalm 96, it is worth noting an intriguing point made by John Kleinig in his analysis of 1 Chronicles 16. Kleinig notes that, in the song placed on the lips of the Levitical worship leaders, the chronicler conflates Psalms 96, 105, and 106 but makes subtle changes. For the benefit of his exilic audience, he changes 'they were but few in number' (Ps. 105:12) to 'you were but few in number' (1 Chr. 16:19; not reflected in the NIV). 'In this way the chronicler identified his contemporaries with the patriarchs, whose experience was of vulnerability as a landless minority.'[18] Similarly with his use of Psalm 96: since the gentile nations which he is calling on to praise Yahweh had no 'old' song to sing, he omits the call to 'sing a new song'. Paradoxically, by omitting these words, the chronicler invites the nations to sing a new song they had not sung before.

Old lyrics, it seems, are not sacrosanct but can be adapted to fresh needs. The three psalms the chronicler draws on are not simply bolted together nor crassly updated but carefully crafted into a new psalm appropriate to his purpose and setting.[19] Several psalms incorporate whole sections of previous psalms. Psalm 108 is a case in point. This psalm is a 'patchwork quilt'. It repeats part of Psalm 60 and adds to that a section of Psalm 57. Psalm 108 is 'recycled truth' – and our Bible is full of it! Reworking old songs is good not least for our humility, reminding us that we stand on the shoulders of the giants of faith who went before us. Any society which is obsessed with being trendy and is dismissive of the past is dooming itself to 'stuck adolescence'. Like the novelty-obsessed Athenians whom Paul met, it is not a sign of wisdom to be fascinated only with the latest and flashiest brands of truth on offer (cf. Acts 17). How many psalms would now be in our collection if Israel's worshippers had used only the top favourites from that year's annual festival and discarded the rest!

What God has spoken once, he speaks again in new settings and we may hear him again as if for the first time. Realising this, we may be encouraged to dig out the old wells, to rediscover ancient paths of wisdom, to ransack the 'back catalogues' of under-used praise songs, and, above all, to reaffirm the legacy of our spiritual forefathers. Awakening to a fresh dawn

(Ps. 108:1–2), we may yet say again the true things about God that have been said many times before (vv. 3-4). Facing our own unique challenges, we may tune in again to the old prophetic voices (vv. 7–9). We are under no pressure to be original as God is. We may repeat earlier prayers, and re-echo the confession of those whose earlier faith we wish to emulate (vv. 10–13).

When needs must, we too may recycle spare bits of remembered sermons, leftover prayers, scraps of old hymns, snatches of parental wisdom, bits and pieces of discarded devotion and from them fashion a living faith!

Verbal Icons

Current impatience with set forms of prayer and inherited language as vehicles for fresh devotion threatens to erase all trace of the past from contemporary Christian worship. Certainly we may feel able to dispense with 'here I raise my Ebenezer' – since we no longer feel inclined to sing Robert Robinson's great hymn 'Come Thou fount of every blessing, tune my heart to sing Thy praise'. But even here something is lost in translation: how else to commemorate the landmarks of saving history but by landmarks! The sensitivities of post-modern audiences are usually cited as the reasons for such iconoclasm; more likely ignorance and immaturity are at work.

The church historian, Robert Wilkin introduces his stimulating book *Remembering the Christian Past* by recalling how a Lutheran pastor of a long-gone generation taught Luther's Small Catechism. In the first year, he said, 'I have the students memorise the Catechism. The second year I tell them what it means.' Wilkin recalls how incredulous this sounded to his youthful ears for surely the whole point is to help young people understand the meaning of the Catechism. Now, Wilkin ruefully admits, I see the wisdom of that old pastor. 'He knew that Christian faith was a matter of words, and that what counted most in the Catechism were the words.' After all, Wilkin concludes, '. . . the meanings one learns at twelve years of age are not the fullness of the words one memorises. If a young person is fitted only with the meanings of youth, what does one return to when the words are faded and forgotten? Words, however, endure and if one has the words the meaning is never lost'.[20]

In fact, fresh meanings may spring forth from the old words. In this connection it is worth noting the occurrence within the New Testament itself of the traces of early Christian worship practices. These include the Jewish-style, *'berakah'*-type, 'Blessed be . . .' formulations (e.g. 2 Cor. 1:3ff; Eph. 1:3ff; 1 Pet. 1:3ff) – which C.F.D. Moule characterised as 'extrovert adoration';[21] doxologies (see Rom. 11:36; Phil. 4:20; 1 Tim. 6:16; 2 Tim. 4:18; Heb. 13:21); possible credal elements (Rom. 1:3ff; 1 Cor. 15:3ff); and so-called hymn fragments (e.g. Phil. 2:5–11; Col. 1:15-20 etc.). This evidence fits well with the undoubted fact that the New Testament letters were intended to be read aloud in the congregations to which they were sent (1 Thes. 5:27; Col. 4:16; Rev. 1:3; 22:18). This intended setting accounts for the inclusion of worship terms and phrases.

In David Aune's words, 'Since these formulas were derived from Christian worship, they enabled letters to fit comfortably into liturgical settings.'[22] It may be that 'very much of what now constitutes the New Testament owes its existence to the requirements of worship' and 'that worship was a very important factor in the preservation and transmission of the traditions'.[23]

Four words in particular provide us with intriguing windows on the earliest worshipping community of the church. They are *'abba'*, *'alleluia'*, *'maranatha'* and *'amen'*. These terms are especially noteworthy because they are Aramaic terms present in Greek-language texts, which are obviously known and used by congregations in the wider Christian world, far removed from the earliest Palestinian church where they originated. Such terms it seem were specially precious perhaps as signifying the key elements in Christian worship from the beginning. As Ralph Martin notes, 'Several phrases in the New Testament belong to the actual liturgical vocabulary of primitive times. They are more easily recognised by the simple fact that in the Greek of the New Testament they have been allowed to remain in their original Semitic form, sometimes with a Greek interpretative translation to accompany them.'[24]

'Abba' was no doubt preserved in use as especially precious because it linked worshippers directly with Jesus (Mk. 14:32–39; Rom. 8:15; Gal. 4:6). Through this 'abba-window' we glimpse the

first Christians confidently worshipping the Father and both expressing and seeking the assurance of relationship with him. Joachim Jeremias' influential study of 'abba' has been qualified by later research. Gordon Fee summarises Jeremias' findings with modifers.[25] 'Abba', he suggests, is an address of intimacy between child and parent in the home, though not, as is often popularly assumed, requivalent to 'daddy' or 'dada' since mature children continue to use it during their father's lifetime.

Jesus' use of 'abba' in addressing God, though not unique in all Jewish literature, was surely distinctive. Its use revealed the uniqueness of his self-understanding of his relationship as Son of the Father and was his exclusive invitation to his disciples to use this term as his extension of grace to them.

Sharing in Christ's Sonship by adoption and receiving the Spirit of Sonship, Christian believers have a share in Christ's filial awareness and so partake of his assurance and security. This is a heartfelt awareness (Rom. 8:15), a strengthening of the human spirit 'with our spirits' rather than a losing of self. That 'abba' is 'called out' or 'cried out' (Gal. 4:6) implies spontaneity and, almost certainly, the passionate urgency evoked by 'Gethsamene' contexts.

'*Alleluia*' preserves the classic Hebrew ascription of praise, 'praise be to Yah(weh)', Israel's covenant Lord. Ascriptions of praise were the pulsating centre of Israel's life. Since God's name is God's revealed character and nature, 'alleluia' reminds us that worship is a response to revelation and a celebration of it. Christians now follow their 'New David', who prays 'Father glorify your name' (Jn. 12:28; 13:31–32; 17:4–6, 26). The shout of 'alleluia' links New Testament believers with Old Testament worshippers in a song of triumph over God's enemies (Rev. 19:1–6; cf. 1 Chr. 29:11) and, at the same time, anticipates God's future salvation, God's final judgements and God's coming rule and reign. Through this 'alleluia' icon we catch a flavour of the first Christians praising the name of the Lord in joyful acclamation.

'*Maranatha*' is probably an invocation: 'O Lord come', both now and in the future (1 Cor. 16:22; cf. Rev. 22:20). God is always the coming one: never to be presumed upon but always to be relied upon to turn up. Though not all scholars agree, it may well be that the Lord's Supper was the normal setting for this invocation, in which case the cry seems to an eager invitation that the Risen Christ will come not only at the end but now to meet his people at the table and be present with them as they celebrate in his name. Christian worship exults in *both* the *presence* of the exalted Christ and the *coming* of the expected Christ; and both according to promise. Through this 'maranatha' icon we may taste the sweetness of the first Christians' anticipation.

'*Amen*' stems from the root of the Hebrew word for what is firm, sure, valid. Saying 'amen' enables us gratefully and willingly to acknowledge what is valid and binding, what is sure and steadfast. As in Ancient Israel (e.g. 1 Chr. 16:36; Neh. 8:6), 'amen' assumes 'a corporate worship setting where this word, also taken over from the Jewish synagogue, indicated whole-hearted response to and endorsement of the words of another'.[26] Again only Jesus fully uttered this cry: only he prefaced his words with it: 'amen, amen . . . truly, truly'. Hearing the Father, Jesus was entirely ready to endorse the Father's word and affirm his will in every way. And it cost him his life to say 'your will be done'. 'Amen' was his royal seal to the truth of God (cf. Jn. 3:33).

In one sense the whole of the New Testament witness is an answering amen to the testimony of Christ. Our 'amen' becomes possible only through his (2 Cor. 1:19-20). We worship 'in Christ'; we stand inside his 'yes' and echo his 'amen'.

'Amen' is important because it stands for a united response (1 Cor. 14:16). That all the people say 'amen' is a sign of mutual recognition of the gifts and offerings of others. It stirs each worshipper from individual passivity and serves to engage us when sincerely uttered in a shared responsiveness. Cultivating the 'amen' mentality is one sure way of bringing order and meaning to charismatic expressiveness, one way to create a worshipping community. Schmemann comments that

> The church is the assembly, the gathering of those to whom the ultimate destination of all life has been revealed and who have accepted it. This acceptance is expressed in the solemn answer to the doxology: 'amen'.
>
> It is indeed one of the most important words in the world, for it expresses the agreement of the church to follow Christ in his ascension to the Father, to make this ascension the destiny of

humankind. It is Christ's gift to us, for only in him can we say 'amen' to God, or rather he himself is our 'Amen' to God and the church is the 'amen' to Christ. Upon this 'Amen' the fate of the human race is decided. It reveals that the movement toward God has begun.[27]

Through the 'amen' window we emulate the first Christians gladly responding to God's word with unreserved affirmation.

This brief survey of four key watchwords of New Testament worship is intended to serve one purpose: to reaffirm that inherited terminology is no barrier to fresh and authentic worship; in fact it may best facilitate it. The current mania for personal self-expression which disdains such a possibility if worship is to be real, is short-sighted and will prove short-lived. Contemporary worshippers deserve to know that *instinctive cries lose no personal power through being expressed in learned language*. In fact they gain much. And what they gain is *historic reference and contemporary corporate resonance*. As we take up all time-honoured 'verbal icons' with new respect and fresh feelings we find ourselves praying with the whole church, past and present.

Prophetic Praise

The ability of the fixed patterns of worship to yield fresh disclosures of God and new visions of his kingdom derives from the prophetic roots of praise. These roots may be as deep as the enigmatic prophetic schools of the earliest tradition (Num. 11:24–30; 1 Sam. 10:1–13; 19:19–24). The chronicler in his time has certainly come to equate singing with 'the ministry of prophesying' (1 Chr. 25:1). The choirs, he describes, were trained, skilled in musicality, and were descended from Asaph, Haman and Jeduthan, all of whom were prophets.

Scholarly opinion suggests that these 'singers in the post-exilic second temple were the successors of the pre-exilic schools of the prophets'.[28] John Kleinig describes their fourfold prophetic function as: standing in the Lord's presence to mediate between him and the people by speaking his word to them; proclaiming the Lord's judgement on his enemies and his salvation on his people; communicating the Lord's acceptance of the people, and his approval of their sacrificial worship, and assuring the people of the Lord's help as they call on his name; and, finally, announcing the Lord's salvation to the people.[29]

Incidentally, if singing is a prophetic activity, it would be well for it to be heard! I could not agree more with Frank Senn when he comments,

> The human singing voice is a vibrating wind column: it can best be supported by other vibrating wind columns. Acoustical instruments such as winds, brass, and strings do nicely to support congregational singing: pipe organs have proved especially effective. The use of electronic instruments has the effect of stifling congregational singing. So does a cantor singing through an amplification system. In both cases, the congregation is overwhelmed and drops out.[30]

The fruits of the prophetic rooting of Israelite praise are obvious in the outpouring of new song in the Psalm collection. Descriptive praise exults in God for who he is, declarative praise applauds him for what he has done. In each case there is a prophetic forthtelling of God's name and record. But one particular feature – of special interest for the dialectic being discussed here – is the way in which the prophetic speech invades certain psalms with a new and now word from God. Westermann drew attention to this by pointing out that in certain psalms of lament, a crucial turning-point is reached, marked by a *waw* adversative, a 'but now' in the Hebrew construction.[31] The psalm hinges on this moment which, Westermann, suggested, marks the intrusion of a prophetic oracle of assurance or hope.

Psalm 12 is a case in point. The psalmist is bewailing the corruption of speech and truth in the community when suddenly, it seems, he is interrupted by the voice of the Lord who declares, 'Because of the oppression of the weak and the groanings of the needy, I will *now* arise . . . I will protect them from those who malign them' (Ps. 12:5). It is to be assumed, Westermann argues, 'that an oracle of salvation was given in the midst of the psalm and that the psalm also includes the words that follow the giving of the oracle'.[32] Psalmists with prophetic gifts were evidently available to voice the community's concern and available to God as agents of the answering prophetic word. John Eaton concurs, 'We have to expect that prophetically gifted ministers led in the appeals to God as well as bringing back his response. For it was the same gift of intimacy that was needed, whether to draw near to him with a moving request, or to bring a word from his inner council.'[33]

Psalm 32 may look like the carefully crafted and stylised joining of a hymn of thanksgiving (vv. 1–7) with a didactic wisdom-type appendage (vv. 8–11). In fact the change from testimony of sins forgiven to the admonition in the first person 'I will instruct you and teach you in the way you should go . . .' looks very much like a creative intrusion into the process of worship of a fresh reassuring divine word. Once more God has 'burst into the psalm through a prophetic oracle of priestly response'.[34]

The creativity of the prophetic Spirit reaches its apogee after Pentecost in the fullness of the messianic era. Since Jesus brings the earlier stage of God's story to its intended climax, the prophetic psalms which envisaged the future kingdom can now come into their own and are transcended by the fulfilment. Now, to paraphrase Scripture, every prophetic singer, steeped in the value of the old truth, who has been instructed about the kingdom of heaven, is like the keeper of the choir records who brings out of his repertoire new song treasures as well as old.

In a landmark article, Martin Hengel made the fascinating suggestion that the dramatic Christological statements of the New Testament were born in Spirit-inspired song as the gospel pressed for new articulation. 'The Spirit urged them on beyond the content of preaching, the exegesis of scripture and indeed the content of confessional formulae expressed in prose to express new, bolder, greater things in the "new song" of the hymn to Christ, because earthbound human language could not do justice to God.'[35] The tradition gave rise to the new song in a creative synthesis of old and new. Perhaps, as Hengel suggests, the church was singing the messianic psalms which then, under the inspiration of the Spirit and fuelled by fervent love for Jesus, burst their banks, as it were, and overflowed in a flood of new heightened revelation of the glory of Jesus Christ. Worship was the matrix of Christology issuing in the Christological 'hymns' of Philippians 2:5–11, Colossians 1:15–20 and even Hebrews 1.

The discernible roots of Israel's prophetic praise offer one further insight into the dynamic interplay between the old and new. The chronicler gives an intriguing glimpse of the connection between prophetic praise and the felt presence of God as he describes the inauguration of the Temple under Solomon. When the Levitical musicians played – including no less than 120 trumpeters – and when singers sang as with one voice, giving praise to the Lord, then 'the temple of the Lord was filled with a cloud . . . for the glory of the Lord filled the temple of God' (2 Chr. 5:13–14). In John Kleinig's words, 'the choral service evoked the divine glory'.[36] With the prophetic proclamation of the Lord's name and attributes in sacred song, God's glory was manifest in the sanctuary so that the priests were incapable of ministering. The glory was not evoked by the music alone, 'however grand it may have been, but rather by the singing of the common refrain for thanksgiving by the whole choir with musical accompaniment'.[37] This common refrain was the time-honoured hymn to God's covenant love (*hesed*): 'He is good, his love endures for ever' (5:13). In other words, the choir, in Kleinig's words, 'did not sing a special anthem composed for the occasion but the refrain for thanksgiving which was the epitome of the regular choral service (1 Chr. 16:8, 34, 41; 2 Chr. 7:3, 6)'.[38] Again it appears that novelty and innovation are not always necessary but that the old songs about the old story can still yield new manifestations of God's glorious presence.

Preaching as Worship

Preaching is often excluded from considerations of worship but it has a key role to play in the polarity we are discussing. First, it needs to be said that preaching is an essential part of worship. 'Preaching ought not to be something else than the liturgy. It is a liturgical act, a ritual, the exercise of communal faith.'[39] Preaching, as P.T. Forsyth insisted, is the 'organised hallelujah of an ordered community'.[40] The interesting conjoining of Levitical and prophetic roles in the origins of praise in Israel is relevant here. Preaching is both priestly and prophetic. As a priestly act, preaching, while addressed to people, is primarily offered to God. It is a necessary form of the church's liturgical self-expression as the church grows into faith. In the preacher, as representative figure, the church articulates its faith.[41] What the church most thankfully believes comes to grateful expression in and through preaching. It is a communal act in which people and preacher interact to offer praise for what they have received. Forsyth maintained that preaching is a sacramental act which effects the real presence of Christ.[42] Through preaching, the old gospel re-enacts itself, prolongs itself, reproduces itself and reasserts its original power afresh. The living Christ is made known in the breaking of the word.

Preaching is also a prophetic act of news telling. It is an utterance of the 'new song'. Reflecting on Isaiah's prophetic preaching to the exiles, Brueggemann observes that 'everything flows from the conviction that God is working a newness, has turned loose energy and power and promises amidst the realities of contemporary public life. This daring liturgical, rhetorical claim, voiced in passion and poetry, repositions Israel in exile, reshapes world history, rereads Israel's history, and makes a promise that comes as a demand.'[43] Christian preaching, whatever its atomised theme, is always an offer of the grace that flows from good news. It partakes of the newness and nowness of prophetic vision and word that brings home to hearers the vividness and freshness of God's victories. Precisely for this reason the preacher does not have to strive for novelty. The preacher's aim is not spontaneity of speech but spontaneity of power.[44] The preacher need not be original but true, at least not original 'in the sense of being absolutely new but in the sense of being fresh, of appropriating for his own personality, or his own age, what is the standing possession of the Church . . .'[45]

Preaching's relation to tradition and received truth is dialectical. Preaching's aim, on the one hand, is not to astonish people with the unheard of but to revive in them what they have long heard.[46] At the same time, Gordon Lathrop can talk of preaching's contribution to the breaking of tradition.[47] This is an inevitable and happy consequence of the Easter event and what makes Christian preaching different from anything analogous in the Old Testament. Since the coming of Christ, biblical revelation acknowledges deep continuity between the Testaments so that we hear the one God speaking throughout the canon. But it also witnesses to a profound discontinuity centred in the crucial Christological facts at the heart of the gospel. The old inherited traditions of revelation were fulfilled in Jesus but in being fulfilled were fractured. Previous revelation is broken open, so to speak, to disclose 'new understanding of our world and ourselves, from the old texts and rites'.[48] Christian preaching even when instructing or exhorting never degenerates into moralising. Even when it admonishes and exposes it does so as good news. In its freshness and power it remains faithful to the apostolic gospel tradition even as it sings that gospel as 'new song'.

Memory as Presence and Hope

The Passover feast established remembrance as the central dynamic in Israel's worship. It memorialised the exodus deliverance though not as a mere act of nostalgia but as a making present of the past. Remembering is not so much a harking back but, as when applied to God's 'remembering' a signal for action in the present. So liturgical memory is not a mental daydream which attempts to revisit the past but an exercise of the mind and heart whereby the past is reactivated in the present as a stimulus to action.[49] Later generations of Israelites who settled in the land were to remember the foundational history of the nation's life and to confess it in worship as if they had themselves been involved in it. Those who enter the land are told to make their 'credo', to identify with the exodus generation, and to make that story their own. So they confess that 'the Egyptians treated us harshly . . . and the Lord heard our cries . . . and brought us out of Egypt . . .' (Deut. 26:6–8).

An intriguing example of the creative interplay between old and new can be observed later in the biblical story when Isaiah urges the exiles 'to forget the former things' and not to 'dwell on the past' (Is. 43:18). When the prophet heralds the coming of the future salvation after exile, he portrays it as a 'new exodus', ransacking the imagery of the first exodus to do so. Tradition proves enormously generative of fresh revelation. 'When you pass through the waters, I will be with you says the Lord' (43:2). The

God who once made a dry way through the sea, will make streams flow in the desert (43:16–19). But so new is this new exodus that Isaiah urges his hearers not to allow nostalgia and tradition, even the exodus tradition which gave the nation its unique identity, to paralyse their hope or dull their dreams. Yet paradoxically, the new event which eclipses the old, has no other imagery but the old imagery to describe it. Newness can coexist with the tradition. This is an example not merely of borrowed terminology but of a crucial typological connection which makes the earlier language more than useful and almost inevitable. Lathrop reminds us that neither baptism nor the Lord's Supper were ex nihilo innovations.[50] Both have strong Jewish roots. Christian baptism has links with Jewish proselyte baptism even if it transcends its antecedents by its Christological revolution. Similarly the Lord's Supper reflects Jesus' own radical rescripting of the Passover meal.

What was a characteristic feature, then, of an Old Covenant worship shaped by Passover, is even truer of New Covenant worship, which is centred on the Eucharist. The church is the only organisation that cannot afford not to be backward looking. In fact in oppressive situations our memorial feasts are 'dangerous memories' which threaten the status quo.[51] The church is distinctively a 'community of memory'[52] and 'Do this in remembrance of me' stands at the heart of our liturgical commission. But we cannot have a mere memorial of a Saviour who is so alive and present with us. The distinctive 'remembrance' or anamnesis of Christian worship is well summarised by Jean Corbon.

> In the liturgical celebration the Church remembers all the saving events which God brought about in history and which had their climax and fulfilment in the cross and resurrection of Christ. But the paschal event, which occurred only once in history, is contemporary with each moment of our lives, for now that Christ is risen he has broken through the wall of mortal time. The liturgy is thus a 'memorial' of an utterly new kind. We do the remembering, but the reality remembered is no longer in the past but is here; the Church's memory becomes presence.[53]

In fact remembering is precisely not a harking back to the Upper Room to replicate the night's events or aura. In typical Catholic vein, Joyce Ann Zimmerman argues that the 'narrativity of liturgy rescues us from "going back to" or "re-enacting" what Jesus did long ago. The permanence in time ensures us of a sameness; that is, the liturgy we celebrate is an enacting of those original events'.[54]

But if the biblical story is rooted in history, it is also markedly future orientated. The story holds in deposit promises which are yet intended to shape the future. They reach out for the 'eschaton' of God's future, the coming of the true End of the biblical storyline which gives it point and meaning. Telling the story in worship helps to carry the story on into the present and into the future. Praise is a true experience of homecoming. This probably accounts for the psychological sense of peace, wholeness and self-integration that many worshippers feel at a certain climactic point in truly spiritual worship. In praise, which is our reason for living, we truly 'enter into God's rest'. In praise, says Brueggemann, we 'enact a vision of true self, true communion, true world, true creation; not escapism but an arrival, in the length of the song, at our true destiny'.[55]

In a recent discussion of the rubric 'Do this in remembrance of me', Anthony Thiselton gives qualified assent to a re-enactment theory of remembrance in worship.[56] He utilises the work of Paul Ricoeur to show that, far from boxing us in, regularised liturgical remembrance establishes our true identity in relation to past, present and future as part of a meaningful narrative plot. Memory becomes potentially transformative as '"possibility" for change interacts with foundational givens as part of a temporal plot which looks back to the past and forward to a new future'.[57] Thiselton helpfully summarises the implications of 'Do this in remembrance of me' under four heads. Remembrance of Christ's death (i) 'retains the biblical aspect of self-involving remembering in gratitude, worship, trust, acknowledgment, and obedience'; (ii) 'It also carries with it the experience of being "there" in identification with the crucified Christ who is also "here" in his raised presence'; it embraces (iii) 'a self-transforming retrieval of the founding event of the personal identity of the believer . . . and the corporate identity of the church'; and (iv) it looks 'forward to the new "possibility" for transformed identity opened up by the eschatological consummation'.[58]

So worship, especially as characterised by the Eucharist, is the point on which our storied lives pivot. Remembrance and hope, history and eschatology meet in the momentary middle so that we taste the eschatological now. God's past, so to speak, catches up with us, and God's future, as it were, comes to meet us.

Remembrance (memory)   eschatology (hope)

God's past   'now'   God's future

'Real Presence'

Ritual activity symbolically 'bridges the gap' between our narrative past and the story's expected end. The 'night in which he was betrayed' and the 'until he comes' evoke memory and hope which conjoin whenever we come together. And the fact that this regular 'whenever' of Christian meeting occurs on the eighth day only serves to heighten the eschatological note. Worship on Sunday is called 'a meeting on the eighth day because it opens toward what cannot be reached simply by more days like those of the seven-day weeks we have known. Christians believe the eighth-day meeting is already the dawning . . . of a new creation'.[59] Admittedly much contemporary worship can become a one-dimensional experience, afflicted by both amnesia and myopia.[60] But this need not be so. Ideally, in the words of liturgical theologian, Thomas Schattaeur,

> through the memory of Jesus Christ – his coming in the flesh, his life, death, and resurrection – our lives are directed in hope to the kingdom of God that Jesus proclaimed and to God's ultimate purposes for our world, just as we enjoy even now Christ's life-giving presence in the assembly of the faithful through word and sacrament by the power of the Holy Spirit.[61]

Of course, liturgical habits can dull the spiritual senses as much as awaken them and leave congregations indifferent to the crisis in their midst. So it was with the attitude taken to the Eucharist by the Corinthians, whom Paul recalls to the original sense of the Supper. Paul is not concerned with liturgical correctness, as if each word of institution must be as it was. But he rehearses the received tradition and interprets it 'in a way which he perceives to be more faithful to the context in which the words originated'.[62] The tradition, creatively reapplied, confronts the Corinthians with their misuse of the Lord's Supper. Paul reminds them of what he 'passed on' (*paredōka*) to them concerning the 'night in which Jesus was betrayed' (*paredideto*).

Intriguingly, the language of *paradosis* can have a positive or negative connotation.[63] It can mean 'handed on' or 'over' in the sense of the passing down of received truth and the transmission of tradition. Its more negative meaning comes from a legal context in which the prisoner is 'handed over' to the judiciary. Paul uses the word in both senses here for what he has received from the Lord and passed on to the Corinthians is the memory of a crucial meal held on the night in which Jesus was 'handed over' or 'betrayed' by Judas. Did the Corinthians get the point of the wordplay we wonder? It is possible faithfully to adhere to the received rubric of liturgical order while at the same time betraying their very meaning by the way the participants are approaching worship. In the Corinthians' case their flagrant disregard for the poor, their failure to 'discern the Lord's body' is a betrayal of the cross even while they may studiously follow the inherited pattern of the words of institution. To proclaim the Lord's death is more than scrupulously following the liturgical order; it is to live and behave by the spirit of the cross in concern for the poor and needy among us.

Creative Repetition and Creative Fusion

The prophetic reuse of tradition, as noted earlier, was at the heart of the Old Testament's hope of salvation, notably in the reapplication of exodus imagery by Isaiah and others to the awaited post-exilic deliverance. Paul Ricoeur describes this kind of typological hermeneutics as 'creative repetition'.[64] The musician and theologian Jeremy Begbie has developed this idea in arguing that repetition need not be the enemy of innovation.[65] Although the complexities of his musicological analysis are beyond the scope of this book, his basic point is very pertinent to it. Begbie rests his case on the way, in tonal music at least, in which metre works. Such music is made up of overlapping metrical waves. At the micro-level, the waves are generated by the downbeat of each bar, which then moves through tension to resolution to the next bar. At the macro-level, the waves so created form overarching sections, movements or indeed the whole composition. In between the extremes of the micro and macro, is a 'multi-layered texture of metrical waves'.[66] Draw a vertical line dissecting the metrical wave patterns at any point and it will show the metrical waves in varying relations to each other. This is true even if the bottom level is a chord sequence repeated over several bars. 'Each repeated component of music will have a different dynamic quality because each occurs in relation to a different configuration of tensions and resolutions.'[67] Paradoxically, then, the recurrence of certain components only serves to highlight the ever-different metrical network, so that 'repetition which might seem to be the enemy of novelty, can in fact promote it'.[68]

Begbie is well aware that liturgical sameness can dull the senses and attract the criticism of being 'vain repetition' (Mt. 6:7), but he counters by making interesting application of the musical phenomenon just described to the practice of liturgy, in particular to the regular celebration of the Eucharist. At the micro-level, the lowest level, 'each "down beat" could denote successive Eucharists; the highest wave could represent the over-arching history of God's engagement with the cosmos; and a multitude of waves, interacting and overlapping, lies in between. In so far as we are bound to Christ through the Spirit, each Eucharist introduces us to, and enables us to participate in, this abundant complexity of waves.'[69] Ironically, some contemporary worship which throws out structures and inherited order in favour of making something different on each occasion in formless spontaneity, precisely falls into a rut of sameness, working to death the same top six praise songs from the latest national Christian festival.

This is not to plead for the triumph of high culture over popular culture or of the elaborate over the plain and simple. In principle, there is no compulsion to choose between worship as an aesthetic response to the beauty of God and worship as a moral response to the holiness of God. Both the 'ah' and the 'oh' factor are at one here. As Richard Bauckham reminds us, Monet's series of Rouen Cathedral paintings was done at different seasons and times and does effectively de-historicise the subject. But impressionism, like worship we might add, is often misconstrued as an attempt to connect with eternal timelessness when it fact it gains its strength precisely from its fierce concentration on temporality, its preoccupation with an immediacy of the now. Viewed theologically, and in positive light, Bauckham argues, this amounts to an evocation of an aesthetic eschatology.[70] This is the awareness we have when impacted by any great work of art, be it painting or music, and so feel ourselves momentarily in the presence of the End. This is not a gnostic downgrading of time in favour of a flight into the transcendent. For, if, as Rowan Williams has said, 'music is the most fundamentally contemplative of the arts, it is not because it takes us into the timeless but because it obliges us to rethink time'.[71] Worship, too, accompanied as it is by music, is not release from time into some eternal realm but the breakthrough of the eternal in such a way as to redeem the time.

At the same time, as Begbie points out, the inbuilt dynamic in music of tension and resolution, creates longing and expectation. Even as it satisfies and fulfils, music, and the worship it carries, prevents premature closure and pretence. True liturgy is true to the 'already and not-yet' dynamic. Whether in the surplus of meaning in the ancient word exploited afresh by the prophets, as Paul Ricoeur suggests,[72] or the unleashing of an extravagant overflow of thanksgiving that 'adds' to the already perfect, as David Ford has it when speaking of 'non-identical repetition',[73] it is the Holy Spirit who is the great creative catalyst. 'The Holy Spirit is the improviser par excellence in every eucharistic repetition.'[74]

Pentecostal theologian Steven Land ably maintains that it is Pentecostal tradition that has most faithfully made room for this creativity of the Spirit. Pentecostalism is often maligned for being fixated with spiritual experiences for their own sake. But, says Land, 'the point of Pentecostal spirituality . . . was to experience life as part of a biblical drama of participation in God's history'.[75] For Pentecostals, living within the already but not-yet tension, the Holy Spirit is the 'bridge or bond between the ages'.[76] The Spirit acts in conjunction with the word as 'a kind of "time machine" . . . enabling the believer to travel backward and forward in salvation history, and to imaginatively participate in the events that have been and are yet to be'.[77] Land describes this as a fusion of polarities which must equally be recognised. So 'space and time are fused in the prophetic reckoning created and sustained by the Spirit of the end'.[78]

Here and now, there and then, are 'telescoped and traversed by the Spirit',[79] so evoking a recognition of the already but not-yet tension in the worshippers' response. And what is claimed for Eucharistic worship might equally be claimed for charismatic worship. In Eucharistic worship we encounter the real presence of Christ by the Spirit and so, in Christ, enter into Christ's own historic fulfilment and eschatological future. In the gathered spiritually gifted community, we receive 'intimations of immortality' in the foretastes of 'the powers of the age to come' (Heb. 6:5). Through the gift of prophecy, the congregation knows and even unbelievers realise that 'God is among us' (1 Cor. 14:25). And this is not merely a mystical experience but a profoundly moral encounter in which the secrets of hearts are disclosed. Religious overwhelming and moral conviction prostrate the hearer in what is a clear worship response.[80] Not that the spiritual gifts are by definition spontaneous.[81] At one end of the spectrum, speaking in tongues is likely to be spontaneous but teaching will surely (and hopefully) involve considerable preparation as gifted by the Spirit. Prophecy may well oscillate between the two poles of spontaneity and preparedness. Nor does prophecy introduce theological novelty which contradicts the received gospel. Rather the fresh intrusive word folds back on itself in the received truth of the Lordship of Jesus Christ (1 Cor. 12:3), which stands as the benchmark by which prophecy is judged. So charismatic gifts – whether spontaneous or otherwise – are a fresh intrusion, marking the real presence. Yet at the same time they evoke memory and longing for an even more intense presence. In this sense it is his presence not his absence that makes the heart grow fonder, inspiring cries of 'Come O Lord' ('*maranatha*'; 1 Cor. 16:22). Space between settled structures, fluidity and flow interweaving fixed forms, allows us to discover that 'liminality is a situation of immense openness to the newness of the Spirit'.[82]

7

Vortex of Love: Liturgical Work *and* Trinitarian Participation

Is worship something we do? Or is worship something done for us? Then again, is worship something we participate in? No one has addressed these questions more astutely than James Torrance. Of course, at a basic level, worship is obviously some-thing we do. Liturgy is after all the 'work of the people'.[1] Worship done by us is a healthy corrective to worship misconstrued as done for us – whether by the praise band or the robed choir – which encourages us to be passive spectators rather than involved worshippers. As Robert Webber so tirelessly reminded us, worship is a verb, and a transitive verb at that.[2] We do not 'worship' or 'have a worship experience' but we 'worship God'. Anything else is what Eugene Peterson calls 'Baal worship'. This, he says, was

> worship that sought fulfilment through self-expression, worship that accepted the needs and desires and passions of the worship-per as its raw material. Harlotry is worship which says – 'I will give you satisfaction. You want religious feelings? I will give them to you. You want your needs fulfilled? I'll do it in the form most attractive to you . . . The phrase 'let's have a worship experience' is Baalism's substitute for 'let us worship God'. The difference is between cultivating something that makes sense to an individual and acting in response to what makes sense to God . . . Worship is neither subjective only nor private only. It is not what I feel when I am by myself; it is how I act toward God in responsible relation with God's people.[3]

But even given these qualifiers, worship done *by* us can succumb in its classic form to 'liturgical Pelagianism' – a dutiful, ritualistic enactment before God rather than a direct and loving address to God. So called free-worship done energetically by us is no less vulnerable, liable to fall victim to a 'psychological Pharisaism' in which ardent worship leaders 'prime the emotional pump' to enforce an emotional correctness almost invariably of a cheery kind.

So notwithstanding our active involvement, worship is not to be viewed as what James Torrance terms – somewhat misleadingly – a *unitarian* activity. Torrance concedes he may have set up too sharp an antithesis but presses his case nevertheless.[4] Everything we do liturgically we do as response and all our responses occur only because they are authorised by Christ and energised by the Spirit. Rather worship must be viewed as what might be termed an *intra-Trinitarian activity* – our participation in the Son's honouring of the Father in the Spirit.[5]

In evaluating this viewpoint, it may be worth summarising the Trinitarian basis of Christian worship. God the Holy Father *seeks worshippers*. And as the Johannine Jesus makes clear, the Father seeks worshippers of a *particular kind*.

The Father of Jesus is actively searching for those who will worship him in spirit and in truth. This is why Jesus came to a well in Samaria to meet one Samaritan woman (Jn. 4). Since the Son of Man has come to seek and to save the lost, then, he has surely come to seek out the lost worshippers and by saving them to return them to his Father rejoicing and thankful. The conversation between the Son and the Samaritan woman takes some strange turns, starting with social embarrassment, ranging over cultural history and ending with a discussion about liturgical theology! For all these reasons it is well worth recounting.

> 'Sir, I can see that you are a prophet. Our fathers worshipped on this mountain, but you Jews claim that the place where we must worship is in Jerusalem.' Jesus declared, 'Believe me, woman, a time is coming when you will worship the Father neither on this mountain nor in Jerusalem. You Samaritans worship what you do not know; we worship what we know, for salvation is from the Jews. Yet a time is coming and has now come when the true

worshippers will worship the Father in spirit and truth, for they
are the kind of worshippers the Father seeks. God is spirit and his
worshippers must worship in spirit and in truth.' (Jn. 4:19–24)

The Samaritan woman represents a particularly ambiguous history and doubtful status. The Samaritans were descendants of
Jews left in Palestine after the eighth-century Assyrian invasion,
the offspring of mixed marriages between indigenous Jews and
Assyrian settlers. The very existence of such 'half-breeds' viol-
ated Torah, as did their having their own worship centre on
Mount Gerazim with its own sacrificial system. Such irregularity
made the Samaritans culturally suspect and despised by Jews.

If this encounter, as some scholars suggest, is reminiscent of a
betrothal scene (in particular that of Rachel and Jacob whose well
this is) then the irony is acute. 'The woman's personal history of
marriage to five husbands and cohabitation with a sixth parallels
the colonial history of Samaria.'[6] At the same time the woman
represents the elemental needs of all humanity in being thirsty.
Besides physical thirst, 'thirst' as a biblical metaphor points to the
deepest needs and longings of the human heart, the need for
eternal significance and meaning, the thirst for love and life
worth living (cf. Ps. 42; 63). Seeking to find this level of satisfaction anywhere else but in God is doomed to disappointment. The
woman has tried to find this fulfilled life in sexual experience. In
the process she has 'sucked dry' several men – and no doubt, or
more likely, been 'sucked dry' herself. Until she meets the man
who is different.

He offers her living water to quench her deepest thirst – a satisfaction that will make her a source rather than a drain – 'a
spring of water welling up to eternal life' (Jn. 4:14). Such life is
replenished supernaturally at source, so that it is renewed by giving, not exhausted by it. Such a fulfilled life overflows to others
and to God in self-giving love. In short, Jesus offers to change the
Samaritan woman from a being a *consumer* to being a *worshipper*.

As we have reminded ourselves earlier in this book, the Father
seeks worshippers not because he craves flattery or needs
stroking but because we were made to find our ultimate satisfaction, our fullest joy and final reason for living, in knowing
him and appreciating him and in enjoying a loving intimacy

with him (cf. Jn. 17:3). So what kind of worshippers does the Father seek?

The first answer to that question is: God wants worship on his own terms. 'God is spirit and his worshippers must worship him in spirit and truth' (Jn. 4:24, ESV). Since God is spirit, worship must be offered in a way appropriate to him: namely 'in spirit and truth'. In context, 'God is spirit' is not primarily a metaphysical statement about God's nature or essence (true though it is that God has no body, nor indeed any gender). Rather 'God is spirit' is a statement about God in relationship with humankind. This means, too, that the relationship between this God and those who worship him must 'be a spiritual relationship'.[7] It follows therefore that 'in spirit' must mean worshipping 'in' or 'by' the Holy Spirit. What is implied here is worship inspired by the Holy Spirit: in short, charismatic worship. Two qualifiers need to be applied here. First, worshipping 'in spirit' most definitely does *not* mean worship which is merely inward or interior – as if true worshippers should be seen and not heard! To worship 'in the spirit' does not imply an introverted spirituality concerned with states of mind and heart so redolent of a nineteenth century Romanticism which sought in this way to overcome the 'scandal of particularity' and to detach the Christian ethos from embodied worship in specific times and places. This can only be a denial of incarnational truth. 'Jesus' words . . . have been frequently used in the interests of a post-Enlightenment privatized religion, as though he were saying that religion was an inward affair of the heart, to which disputes between Judea and Samaria are irrelevant'.[8]

At the same time 'worship in spirit' carries a sharp prophetic thrust which should not be blunted. In context, 'in spirit' is set in contrast to worship bound to sacred place and temple. In George Beasley-Murray's words, 'The worship that God seeks is a worship not frozen to a sacred building or by loyalty to a particular tradition, but a worship which is living, the ever new response to God who is Spirit as prompted by and enabled by the Spirit of God.'[9]

What of the phrase 'in truth'? Almost certainly it does not carry the connotation of 'sincerely' – that is surely taken as read. Rather it implies 'according to the truth as it is in Jesus' (cf. Eph. 4:21). Gary Burge argues for taking seriously the fact that one preposition governs both 'spirit' and 'truth' (not shown up in NIV). In which case what is meant is worship grounded in, and informed by, the truth as revealed in Jesus *and* as it has been made known by the Holy Spirit. The worship sought by the Father is worship based upon the reality of all that Jesus is and did and still does as the Revealer and Saviour and Priest.

Two points strengthen this view. First, that 'truth' here has to do with revelation is supported by the contrast with the Samaritan woman's 'ignorance' – 'you . . . worship what you do nor know' (Jn. 4:22). Any god will not do: nor will any syncretistic mixture of gods. A 'god who can be equally represented by all the contradictory images of man's religious imagination is not God'.[10] Worship is not addressed 'to whom it may concern'; nor launched vaguely in the general direction of an 'unknown god' (Acts 17:22–23). Worship is offered to a God who has revealed Godself as personal and knowable and who – on his own terms – wants worship and fellowship.

Secondly, this view of 'in . . . truth' is further endorsed by the statement that 'we worship what we know, for salvation is of the Jews' (Jn. 4:22, ESV).

We can now worship because we know the climactic truth as it is in Jesus and for this the Old Testament has been the indispensable prior education. Truthful, spiritual worship presupposes the biblical revelation of a personal creator God who has chosen to make himself known in personal encounters and historic speech.

'Salvation is of the Jews' since it is through Israel's story that this God introduces himself as the God of Abraham, Isaac, Jacob, Moses and Isaiah, demonstrating in so doing his character and nature to his chosen people Israel and making plans for a decisive invasion of his world through her Messiah.

Now *the time has come* and with it a new and fulfilled way of worship. The 'time' is ripe – with the advent and achievement of Christ – for a sea-change to come in our relationship with God and therefore with worship. All previous worship patterns – whether erroneous like the Samaritans, or genuinely God-given like Israel's – are now radically relativised by the coming of Jesus and the truth uniquely made known in him.

What are sacred times? What do the traditional patterns of worship whether Jewish or Samaritan matter any longer? How the woman's fathers worshipped matters little compared to how *his Father* seeks to be worshipped now. Times have changed: the time has come for the true worshippers to worship the Father in spirit and truth. Sacred space goes the same way too. What do Mount Gerazim, or even the Temple in Jerusalem matter now? There is a new focus for worship, a new meeting place of God and worshipper – a new Temple not made with hands – which is the Risen Christ himself. John has already alerted us to this in 2:19–21. Such a claim was hurled back at Jesus at his trial in a distorted form but was, for all that, a provocative and subversive way of announcing the end for the glorious Temple in Jerusalem. This threat to the Temple was the historic, ostensible reason why Jesus was killed. But his death is the 'hour' that has come: his death, resurrection, ascension and outpouring of the Spirit will change everything. The Temple was both centre for the sacrificial system which provided atonement for sins and dwelling-place of God where the concentrated holy presence of God was said to dwell! By his dying on the cross, animal sacrifices are made obsolete and a 'new and living way' is opened up for the worship of God.

Now, we worship through Jesus, sharing by the Spirit in his complete sacrifice and self-offering to the Father. Furthermore, by the resurrection of Jesus a new temple has been raised up – the temple of his risenness – so that Jesus in his body (of blood-washed, Spirit-filled disciples) is the very dwelling place of God in the Spirit (Eph. 2:22; cf. Jn. 2:19ff). *In short, the time has come for a fully Trinitarian worship.*

Trinitarian Worship

Engaging in Christian worship is a focused experience of that larger Trinitarian reality into which we were baptised and in which we live out the whole of our new creation lives. Anthony Ugolnik summarises this glorious participation in the divine life in typically Orthodox fashion, saying, 'In the very Persons of the Godhead, "proceeding" in perfect love from their interrelationship, we experience a vortex of love that pulls us as well into its power.'[11] Its focus in gathered and ordered worship was well expressed by Yves Congar, 'The whole of the liturgy expresses and brings about a movement of God towards us and of us towards God. This movement passes from the Father through the Son in the Spirit and returns in the Spirit through the Son to the glory of the Father, who takes us, as his children, into communion with him.'[12]

James Torrance has pressed home this point in stimulating and significant ways. Echoing Congar, Torrance characterises Christian worship as a 'double-movement of grace'.[13] God's saving grace comes to us redeemingly through his Son, Jesus Christ, acting on us in the power of his Spirit and this grace *returns to him in worship* through the Son in the Spirit. Two Pauline statements may stand as representative of these movements: 'For from him and through him and to him are all things. To him be the glory for ever! Amen' (Rom. 11:36). And the answering doxological movement of the reconciled community – not least in gathered worship – is rendered 'for through him (Christ) we both have access to the Father in one Spirit' (Eph. 2:18).

In the first place Christian worship depends on a God-human-ward movement, the saving initiative and gifts of God grace. It is as if God the Father says to the assembled church,

> 'This is my Self-revealing Word – addressed to you: hear this,
>   believe this and do this in obedient and
>   loving response to me . . .'
> 'This is my Son's body – broken for you: do this in remembrance
>   of him . . .'
> 'This is my Spirit – given to you: do this in manifestation
>   of him . . .'

Given these dynamics, Christian worship can be characterised as *prophetic* and *scriptural* – as a response to, and affirmation of, the biblical revelation of God in his nature as the One Creator God of Covenant Lord. Worship on these terms is *evangelical*, rooted in a response to the gospel. 'We must ask ourselves,' says Torrance, 'whether our forms of worship convey the gospel. Are they an appropriate response to the gospel?'[14]

This appropriateness is alluded to in Paul's injunction to the Romans to 'offer your bodies as living sacrifices, holy and pleasing to God – this is your spiritual act of worship' (Rom. 12:1). The disputed adjective 'spiritual' (*'logikēn'*) – otherwise translated as 'rational' or 'reasonable' – suggests, in C.E.B. Cranfield's words, 'the worship that is consonant with the truth of the gospel'.[15] This is worship that finds expression in the bodily self-offering of the cultic community and finds outlet in a self-sacrificial lifestyle within the wider world.

This is worship which is *priestly* in function and *eucharistic* in focus, rooted in the creative achievement of Christ's cross and sacrifice and in his continuing intercession. Worship is *charismatic* and *pentecostal* – worship in which we are caught up in the 'force-field', the 'magnetic field' of the Holy Spirit.

The gracious God-humanward initiatives evoke from believers an answering movement of grace channelled in worship. So worship, viewed from this angle, is the grace of God returning to the Father through the Son in the Spirit. Worship is a thoroughly God-directed movement – 'from him and through him and to him . . .' And the key phrase here is *'through the Son'*; everything we offer in response to God's grace is offered 'through Jesus Christ' or 'in his name'. Jesus' whole saving career dramatically outlined in the 'Christ hymn' of Philippians 2:5–11 as a parabola of redemption – tends in every stage to the 'glory of God the Father'.

The battle for the exclusive God-orientation of worship was joined in the Judean wilderness when Jesus rebuffed Satan with the words of Israel's covenant charter: 'Worship the Lord your God: and serve him only' (Lk. 4:5–8). Jesus taught his disciples the 'abba' prayer, emphasising that our priority in prayer and worship is always that of hallowing God's holy name – the profaning of which had led to the Babylonian Exile (Ezek. 36:22–24). Our sense of security in worship comes from knowing this God as our Father and naming him as such as we cry to him as 'abba' with confidence and assurance of his openness to us so that by the same grace which first loved us, we love him in return.

Viewed with special clarity through a Johannine lens, the Son's entire ministry was one long doxology to the Father and his self-offering in the cross the climactic glorification of the Father (Jn. 12:27–33; 17:1–5). Especially significant in this connection is Jesus' attitude to the Temple in Jerusalem and his actions in the week of his death. Jesus threatened the Temple (Mk. 11) and envisaged its destruction and replacement by himself. As far as John is concerned, the Temple of the messianic age is the crucified and now risen Son. The Temple was the place of sacrifice for sins: now Jesus displaces the Temple by the offering of himself as the ground of our acceptance by God.

Worship Is Made Possible by the Death of Christ on the Cross

Because we have access to the holiest presence of God, we need not stay at a safe distance, as the Israelites did at Sinai, but we can come boldly and assuredly. Yet surely we come with sensitivity and an enormous sense of privilege? After all the new and living way into God's presence is a bloodstained path that cost our High Priest his life. To have access to God is not to be taken for granted but is the most sublime privilege purchased with an unspeakable price. James Denney memorably reminded the church that 'just as in the ancient tabernacle every object used in worship had to be sprinkled with atoning blood, so all the parts of Christian worship, all our approaches to God should consciously rest on the atonement'. Every song we sing, every prayer we utter, every offering we bring in approaching God, should, he said, '. . . be penetrated with the sense of Christ's Passion, and of the love with which he loved us when he suffered for our sins, the just for the unjust, to bring us to God'.[16]

Atonement is access but not merely as a one-off event, an opened door in the past. The way to God that has been opened up for us by Christ's death is not only a new but a *living* way (Heb. 10:20). Current Christian worship depends not only on what Christ once did which is now freshly remembered but on what he is still doing.

As has often been noted, the so-called 'resurrection appearances' in all four Gospels read like the outline of a gathering for worship in the early church. This is because Christ has displaced the Temple by his Resurrection Body. By the life he imparts to those who are in him, they are formed into a living Temple of God in the Spirit. In every act of worship we experience afresh the miracle of the coming of the Risen Christ to be with his followers. Coming together in Christ's name in the Spirit we form 'a dwelling in which God lives by the Spirit'. And the dynamics of such worship are *maintained by his heavenly High Priestly ministry.* 'Christian worship is . . . our participation through the Spirit in the Son's communion with the Father in his vicarious life of worship and intercession.'[17] At the heart of this is the vision of Jesus whose self-giving life and self-offering was one fulsome act of praise to the Father.

It is this perfect life and complete sacrifice which is portrayed in Hebrews as the only basis on which we can relate to God and come before him to offer acceptable worship. Furthermore, Hebrews is unique in the New Testament for painting the picture of Jesus as our Great High Priest. Jesus is alive at the Father's right hand and acts there as our High Priest. In this capacity he makes his own self-offering perpetually available as the means of our acceptance and forgiveness. He takes our petitions and the offering of our lives and makes them acceptable to God. Above all Jesus continues to make intercession for us as he pleads the merits of his blood on our behalf.

Christian worship is funded and fuelled by the ongoing mediatorial ministry of the Ascended Christ. His High Priesthood is the 'throughness' which in the Spirit alone makes our worship authentic and effective. It is his 'throughness' which gathers our praise and prayer into his own and brings it to the Father. Our worship and our intercession are made meaningful by being taken up into his continued ministry in heavenly places. This is what it means to come to God through Jesus and to pray in his name. This heavenly priestly ministry is *mediated by his presence in the midst of the congregation.*

The writer to the Hebrews utilises the Old Testament scriptures in new and exciting ways. None more so than when he takes the words of Psalm 22 and puts them into the mouth of the risen and ascended Lord Jesus: 'in the midst of the congregation I will sing your praise' (Heb. 2:12). This insight alone promises to transform attitudes to worship. Whenever the Father's children (Heb. 2:12–13) gather for true spiritual worship, *Jesus is the leading worshipper, leading us in praise.* The nineteenth-century preacher and devotional writer F.B. Meyer said it well: 'Whenever in the congregation of the saints there is an outburst of genuine song, you may

detect the voice of Jesus singing with them and identifying with it.'
How encouraging to know that when we come together to worship we are joining Jesus in his praise of the Father.

In Gerrit Scott Dawson's words: 'So in worship, we may visualize Jesus standing in the midst of our sanctuary. His arms are outstretched and his head is raised to heaven. He has gathered us all and he is offering us to his Father even as he offers his praise.'[18]

But then isn't everything we do done in the same fashion?

> Is not the bread that we break a means of sharing in the body of Christ?
>
> Is not the cup that we bless a means of sharing in the blood of Christ?
>
> Are not the songs that we sing a means of sharing in the praise Christ offers?
>
> Are not the prayers we pray a means of sharing in the high priestly intercession of Christ?
>
> Is not the body we are building with love and gifts a means of sharing in the very body of Christ?
>
> Is not the love we share a means of sharing in the mutual love of the Father and the Son?

8

Wild Goodness: Jubilation *and* Justic

Go in peace to love and serve the Lord.
In the name of Christ. Amen.

Throughout this book so far, the term 'worship' has been used in its restricted sense to refer to the cultic act when the people of God gather to offer praise and prayer. But in its wider sense the concept of worship can and should be applied to the whole of the life of faith. Worship construed in this way spills over from its concentrated cultic focus so as to permeate all our practices and determine all our dealings. Where worship, in one sense, ends, worship, in another sense, begins. 'So whether you eat or drink or whatever you do, do it all for the glory of God' (1 Cor. 10:31). Paul's injunction helps us with both the *what* and the *why* of everyday living. It helps us to discriminate between what is, and what is not, glorifying to God, and, perhaps even more importantly, encourages the intentional doxological direction of the worshippers' lives. 'Through Jesus, therefore, let us continually offer to God a sacrifice of praise – the fruit of lips that confess his name. And let us not forget to do good and to share with others, for with such sacrifices, God is pleased' (Heb. 13:15–16).

A sacrificial life is one and undivided. Though not the primary focus of this discussion (another book would be called for) something ought to be said for the holistic holiness that unites liturgy and life. A divorce here is truly fatal to the authenticity of worship. Failure here to hold the polarities together is a hypocritical contradiction that corrupts the worship and compromises the witness of God's people. No one more ruthlessly exposed the mismatch between worship and ethics, than the prophet Amos.

One of my favourite writers, Robert Macfarlane, has published a beautifully crafted book about the 'wild places' of Britain and our need to respect and rediscover the wildness of the natural world. We need 'wildness' because the wildness is an expression of independence from human direction, of that which 'acts or moves freely without restraint . . . is unconfined and unrestricted'. Our danger is to over-cultivate, regularise, domesticate, industrialise, tarmac over – or otherwise seek to tame – the wildness in the world. Much of this is right and beneficial since we are called to be culture-makers. But the danger is the hubris which imagines that everything exists to serve our interests. So it can be in our attitude to God.

We can domesticate and trivialise God; we can tame God and seek to make him manageable. It is a perennial danger of liturgical constructs to do just that. Now, as then, we need the voice of Amos warning us of the folly of trying to contain God and celebrating for us the wildness of God – in fact, the wild goodness of God. This concern is what lies behind the prophet's summons: 'Prepare to meet your God' (Amos 4:12). The real God is the wild God of creation power and majesty (4:13). The real God is often ignored in favour of the safe God we can tame and manage in our meetings.

It is worth at this point rehearsing Amos' critique of what he saw as phoney worship in the Israel of his day. God's special target is the royal sanctuary at Bethel (Amos 3:14). Bethel had an honoured place in the Israelite history books. Jacob had first named this place as the site of his famous dream. He had dreamed of a ladder on which the angels ascended and descended. So startled was he by this that he declared 'surely the Lord is in this place and I did not know it' (Gen. 28:17, ESV). In calling the place Bethel, he felt it to be the doorway giving access to God. How ironic then that Bethel is now in Amos' day to be the site of judgement for Jacob's descendants. The roots of this lie in a previous generation when the present king's namesake, King Jeroboam I had set up an idolatrous altar there (1 Kgs. 12:25–33) after the division of the kingdom.

This alternative worship centre was one of several (including Shechem and Dan) set up as a rival to Jerusalem for political reasons. A man of God immediately warned of its demise – in

1 Kings 13:1 and following – a prophecy fulfilled some 300 years later and after Amos' time when the southern king Josiah (*c.* 639 BC) ventured north to smash the shrine and its altar (2 Kgs. 23:15–16). The first Jeroboam had probably not intended his innovation to be idolatrous as such: merely a way of providing the devotion to an invisible God, Yahweh, with external and visible support. But this was sailing too close to the wind of accommodation to the local Canaanite religion of Baal. Jeroboam's action invited confusion and the temptation to mix formal devotion to Yahweh with covering all your options by paying dues to the pagan gods of fertility.

By Amos' time, Bethel has become a byword for the political manipulation of religion and for the idolatrous corruption of the true worship of Yahweh. But now, in Amos' day, at the very site of Jacob's historic encounter with the living God, that same living God is set to surprise the worshippers at Bethel by *actually turning up*! But this time it will be different. This time, those who have carelessly treated God lightly will have to take God seriously again. Bethel is indeed the gate of heaven but through it the angel-armies will stream in judgement as well as mercy. How awesome is the place when God makes his presence felt.

Amos continues his critique in sarcastic mood as he mocks Israel's false and hypocritical worship. 'Go to Bethel and sin; go to Gilgal and sin yet more . . .' (Amos 4:4). Here the prophet raises the stakes by urging Israel with massive irony to increase her sinning by worshipping more and more intensively and fervently! The worshipers are proud of their fervour at the worship centres at Bethel and Gilgal. 'Gilgal', too, like Bethel was a significant name from Israel's covenantal past. Gilgal, on the edge of Jericho, was the first sanctuary erected after the conquest of the land (Josh. 4:19; 5:9). It was where Israel's 'reproach' acquired by the wilderness wanderings had been 'rolled away' – a play on the word 'Gilgal' – by a renewed consecration and circumcision. But by now Gilgal has joined Bethel as a site of corrupt worship.

And Amos sarcastically challenges them to more of the same! Like some hyped-up worship leader or cheerleader he urges his audience to raise the roof, to give as they've never given before. Amos pours on the scorn. Let's have more songs, more thank-offerings, more sacrifices. Give yourself something to boast about. 'What a wonderful worship time we had this morning; it was so exciting. We love this kind of worship ("For this is what you love to do", Amos 4:5c). We had such a fantastic time of praise; the liturgy was so beautiful, the choirs so heavenly!' "the sort of religious show you Israelites just love" (Amos 4:5c, *The Message*). They were worshipping with great enthusiasm; there was nothing half-hearted about it, yet it only intensified their sin and guilt.

It is possible to be infatuated with worship itself, perhaps because it makes us feel good. Amos perceives that they love the sacrificial system more than they love their neighbour, more even than they love Yahweh. Worship has a habit of exposing what our true love is; do we love worshipping or do we love God? 'This is what the LORD says to the house of Israel, "Seek me and live; do not seek Bethel, do not go to Gilgal, do not journey to Beersheba. For Gilgal will surely go into exile, and Bethel will be reduced to nothing . . ."' (Amos 5:4–5).

Amos continues to emphasise that Israel's national guilt involves both unjust social practices (5:7, 10–13) and the false worship which is his primary target. But now there shines through his dark message of judgement a bright ray of hope: 'Seek God and live' (5:4, 6). He pleads with Israel not to seek God's saving presence in sanctuaries which God does not recognise and where God is not available. Israel would do well to cancel the services at the unholy trinity of unlawful worship centres at Bethel, Gilgal and Beersheba. God will bypass historic religious sanctuaries with blessed associations. Worshippers are invited to seek God but to seek him *on his terms*, not ours. There must be no more 'convenience religion' where we celebrate a God who fits into our existing lifestyles. Seek God and live is a wonderful invitation to a reprieve from a just sentence of death. A nation dying on its feet will live if it gets on its knees and repents. A church in meltdown may yet repent, seek God and find new life.

Nothing honours God more than seeking his face. As Frederick Faber said: 'Those who love God cannot love Him by measure, for their love is but hunger to love him still better.' You may not physically be able to go to some particular place. You don't have to. God draws near to you that you might draw near to him. We love only because he first loved, we seek only because he found us. As Faber wrote: 'God loves to be longed for, He loves to be sought, For he sought us Himself with such longing and love; He died for desire of us, marvellous thought! And He yearns for us now to be with Him above.'

Once more Amos unleashes the fierce metaphors for God's activity. God is a lion that roars; now he is an unquenchable *fire* (5:6a; cf. 1:4, 7, 10, 12, 14; 2:2, 5 . . .) and this God will appear again (cf. 7:4–6). Fire does not tell us all we need to know about God: it evokes many different emotions and contrasting reactions:

- fire evokes welcome and unwelcome associations;
- fire warms and sustains life; fire burns and threatens life;
- fire cooks food and generates energy; fire consumes and destroys.

But one thing you don't do with fire is play with it! And if for no other reason than this, worshippers in every age need to hear of the all-consuming fire which is God. Contemporary worshippers live in a squeamish age when even God has been rendered innocuous. The bland lead the bland and we wonder why we have lost our spiritual taste buds. The processed food the church serves us spoils our appetite for the real thing.

So we surely need these vivid, violent Old Testament pictures of God even if they are not the whole story. Jesus is the full and final revelation of God to us. But we need the images of God that prophets like Amos offer if only to prevent us making God into a cosy lap-God. We need the reminders of God's wildness and fierceness lest we tame God into being our pet. The fire of God will break out against the false worship being offered by God's people and the false worship will not be able to quench it or withstand it (Amos 5:6c).

In critiquing worship, doxologies to the God of creation – 'he who made the Pleiades and Orion' – are never far from Amos' mind and intersperse his prophecies (5:8; cf. 4:13; 9:5–6). The prophet evidently wants his hearers to avoid scaling God down to their size but to let God be God. We too may be tempted to downsize God to make him manageable and likewise need reminding that he is not. We ought never to succumb to wonder-fatigue but repeatedly to meditate with awe and joy on God's greatness and the splendour of God's creative achievement. God threw the stars into space and knows them by name better than any astronomer or, for that matter, any astrologer! Millions read their stars every-day. So do believers. But we read the stars for what they tell us of the great Creator who made them. Our future is safe in his hands. The God who makes daytime and night-time is the God who watches over our morning and evenings, our getting up and going to bed.

This is our God: the Lord of the rivers and lakes and oceans of the earth. The Lord of the amazing blue planet beneath the waves as of the glorious green planet around us! And above all, let's be thankful that the cosmos is energised and controlled not by an impersonal power but by a personal being. Behind everything that moves is not a cosmic force but a compassionate face. And we can give a name to that face. He is our Lord and God. All the more reason to eschew false worship and to prepare to meet the real God in real worship.

At the heart of Amos' concern is that phoney worship masks social injustice – the subject of perhaps his most famous oracles (5:21–27).

> I hate, I despise your religious feasts; I cannot stand your assem-blies. Even though you bring me burnt offerings and grain offer-ings, I wil not accept them. Though you bring me choice fellowship offerings, I will have no regard for them. Away with the noise of your songs! I will not listen to the music of your harps. But let jus-tice roll on like a river, righteousness like a never-failing stream. (Amos 5:21–24)

Amos asks the question we seldom ask when we are arguing over our worship preferences: *What does God think of our worship?* And the short answer is: God loathes it (5:21). God 'cannot stand' the worship meetings (5:21). As for the sacrificial offerings being made to him, God will 'not accept them' (5:22) – literally, 'will not smell them'; God will not 'regard them' or look upon them (5:22). As for the endless praise songs accompanied by over-amplified music, God will not 'listen to them' (5:23). God closes his nostrils, his eyes, and his ears to Israel's worship of him. He rejects it all.[1]

Everything here described, it needs to be said, is what God requires in the Law. There is nothing unlawful about any of the liturgical actions in themselves. What God loathes is worship activity behind which there is no authentic, loving obedience to God and beyond which is no true love for one's neighbour in society.

In other words, the prophets do not attack Israel's worship practices because they prefer some supposedly 'spiritual' worship to that offered in sacrificial ritual but 'because Israel's worship is an empty show, unmatched by sincere love for God and faithful obedience to his will'.[2] God is not impressed with solemn Eucharists or festive celebrations *in themselves* but only as offered by worshippers who love God and do justice. God does not so much mind whether the songs are noisy or the hymns sedate as long as they are sung with honest adoration by people who practice what they preach. What God desires – loving hearts and godly lives – is deeper even than what God requires.

God wants justice in the law court and stock exchange every bit as much as celebration and festivals in the worship centres. God wants righteousness in the courts and markets as much as he wants hymns and prayers in the sanctuary. 'Justice' and 'righteousness' are two of the great Old Testament words which describe Israel's covenant commitment. As the commentator James Mays points out, 'Justice' is particularly 'associated with the court in the gates and means the judicial process and its decisions by which right order is maintained in social relations, and especially the protection of weak and poor through the help of the court'. 'Righteousness' is the 'rightness that belongs to those who fulfil the responsibilities which their relationships to others involve'.[3] Loving God and loving neighbour are inextricably intertwined as covenant obligations.

There is much fashionable talk in the contemporary church of new waves of the Spirit and of fresh streams of revival. We need not ponder too greatly what these may entail because it is doubtful that God's priorities have changed. The streams of the Spirit and rivers of refreshment that God is most interested in are 'justice' and 'righteousness'. These are the infallible final marks of whether we have experienced true revival. In New Testament terms, when experiences like those at the beginning of Acts 2 –

'they were all filled with the Holy Spirit and . . .' – permeate down into our daily living to produce attitudes and communities like those at the end of Acts 2 – 'there was no needy one among them' – then perhaps we will have seen revival.

Amos warns against worship that is going nowhere, that doesn't spill over into everyday life to wash it clean. As Alex Motyer has it, worship is not a sealed compartment; it is a box we dare not enter unless the exit is clear.[4] Amos is castigating the worship being practiced at places like 'Gilgal' (Amos 5:5) and is maybe once again indulging in powerful wordplay. 'Gilgal' means 'roll away' – for this is where historically God 'rolled away' the reproach of his people before taking possession of the Land. But today's worshippers – says Amos – are not so much 'holy rollers' as '*un*holy rollers'.

What needs to 'roll down' is a rushing tide of justice to wash through society; the next big 'wave of God' that Amos says we need is a torrent of righteousness that sweeps through all business dealings and personal relationships. In other words, Israel is 'going through the motions' of worship but its heart is far from the Lord. It is doing all the right things on the Sabbath but living the rest of the week as if God did not exist. God asks poignantly if it was like this at the beginning, in the wilderness time when they only had him to rely on (Amos 5:25)? The time in the wilderness was a time of testing and failure, but the prophets see it equally as almost a honeymoon time of pure relationship between God and his people (cf. Hos. 2:14). But once comfortably settled in the land, they had been led astray to other gods (5:26). The end result, says Amos, will only be exile from the Land (5:27).

So perhaps we can hear this prophetic word today as a quality check on our own relationship with the Lord and the sincerity of our worship. Is our worship on Sunday like a never-failing stream irrigating everything we do from Monday to Saturday? Have we left our 'first love' for the Lord? Have we dabbled in idols, in anything that has displaced the Lord from being central in our affections and decisions? Do we feel estranged and cut off from the living God? Is that why the church is now in exile in a post-modern secular Europe? Bethel, Gilgal and Beersheba are synonymous with worship that is energetic and enthusiastic and tailor-made to the demands for a safe and intimate god-experience (Amos 4:4–5; 5:5). But, 'the safe God asks nothing of us, gives nothing to us. He never drives us to our knees in hungry, desperate praying and never sets us on our feet in fierce, fierce determination'.[5]

In the oft-quoted scene from *The Lion, the Witch and the Wardrobe*, Mr and Mrs Beaver take the children to met Aslan, the king who happens to be a lion.

> 'Ooh,' says Susan, . . . 'Is he quite safe? I shall feel rather nervous about meeting a lion.'
>
> 'That you will dearie, and make no mistake,' said Mrs Beaver; 'if there's anyone who can appear before Aslan without their knees knocking, they're either braver than most or just silly.'
>
> 'Then he isn't safe?' said Lucy.
>
> 'Safe?' said Mr Beaver . . . 'who said anything about safe?' 'course he isn't safe. But he's good . . . he's the king, I tell you.'[6]

God's people want a safe God because we imagine he is manageable and containable and because he seems preferable to what we imagine is the alternative: a despotic, tyrannical and cruel God. But neither the safe God nor the sadistic God is the real God.

The true God '. . . is far more loving and comforting than the safe god. And the true God is far more fierce and fearsome than the bullying and petulant god of our imagination.'[7] The safe God is not the God Amos knows. The safe God is in the pay of Amaziah and Jeroboam. The safe God tolerates sin and accommodates injustice. The safe God can be sought on our terms as and when we choose. Worship of the safe God is about customer satisfaction (Amos 4:5b). In tame worship:

- the safe God rubber-stamps our complacency;
- the safe God re-enforces our view that God can be managed and controlled;
- the safe God strives to make himself relevant to our needs and prostitutes himself to gain our attention and to stop us being bored;
- the safe God is cut down to size, domesticated to our demands;
- the safe God genially bless our plans and blandly endorses the pre-existing ideas and attitudes we parade before him;

- the safe God never confronts us, never challenges us;
- the safe God never exposes us, never holds us to account for anything;
- the safe God never scares the hell out of us, never leaves us speechless.

In tame worship we never ask what God thinks of the worship (Amos 5:21–24). Tame worship never makes room for the wildness of God. Not that the wildness of God is recognised by chaotic, disordered, anarchic, spontaneous worship. This is not about worship-styles. All worship – whether traditional or contemporary – can fall prey to this danger of trivialising and domesticating God.

In fact a measure of right order in worship and liturgy may well show our humble self-restraint and a willingness to let God be God unimpeded by our subjectivity and unrestricted by our mood swings. Walter Brueggemann catches the spirit of Amos well when he says that we live our lives before the 'wild, dangerous, unfettered, and free character of God'.[8]

Worship is not meant to insulate us from the world but to open a window on the world. Worship is not meant to domesticate God and make him bend to our needs and interests. That is consumer religion. Worship is meant to confront as well as comfort; to confront us with the real God most often in grace as welcome and acceptance; but also in scrutiny as judgement. We seek God – but too often 'the God we seek is the God we want, not the God who is. We fashion a God who blesses without obligation, who lets us feel his presence without living his life, who stands with us and never against us, who gives us what we want, when we want it. We worship a god of consumer satisfaction, hoping the talismans of guitars and candles, organs and liturgy, will put us in touch with God as we want him to be.'[9]

Worship is not designed as a means of dragooning God into waiting on our heartfelt needs: worship is a gift in space and time and structure to enable us to tune into God's heartfelt concerns – not least for the poor and needy. There is much contemporary talk about experiencing God, about immediacy and intimacy with God, about encountering the transcendent. But too often these aspirations can seem no more than the projection of our own wish list of emotions that enable us to feel better about ourselves and to overdose on the spiritual.

Traditional worship may seem the obvious culprit here. Classical liturgies can often box God in, containing him by fixed and inflexible orders of service. 'I often think of the set pieces of the liturgy,' says Annie Dillard, 'as certain words which people have successfully addressed to God without their getting killed.'[10] Following the book may be seen as the best way to guard against unruly emotional responses or disturbing divine interventions.

But contemporary, so-called 'free' worship, can have just the same effect, albeit in a different way. Such worship can effectively soften the impact of God. Its concern for intimacy can easily diminish divine transcendence, cushioning the weight of glory that might otherwise impinge itself upon us, acting like an absorbent towel so that God's otherness is soaked up in an over-familiar subjectivity. But the real God is not only warm and gentle as a summer breeze, he comes as whirlwind; not only as soft candlelight but as flaming fire. The real God is absorbing not absorbent, captivating precisely because he is not capable of being captured; gripping precisely because he is not susceptible to being held in our grip; spellbinding precisely because it is impossible to bind him with incantations whether they are choral works or praise choruses. He is not a prisoner of our boredom or a prey for our excitement.

In the words of American writer Annie Dillard,

> Does anyone have the foggiest idea of what sort of power we so blithely invoke? The churches are children playing on the floor with their chemistry sets, mixing up a batch of TNT to kill a Sunday morning. It is madness to wear ladies' straw hats to church; we should all be wearing crash helmets. Ushers should issue life preservers and signal flares; they should lash us to the pews. For the sleeping God may wake someday and take offence, or the waking God may draw us out to where we can never return.[11]

Such a God had arisen in Amos' day and Israel was ill-prepared to meet such a God. He is a lion but he is not caged and certainly not tame. He cannot be domesticated for he is the creator of all things. He is not cool but a raging fire. He cannot be lulled to sleep by lullabies of hearty songs and enthusiastic worship and homely homilies.

'God cannot be tamed. God alone lives in perfect and uninhibited freedom. God is God and will be God. There is no other . . . encountering God means you will never be the same. This is the greatest (and best) danger of worship.'[12] The polarities inherent in authentic worship which this book has so tentatively explored deserve not to be tamely balanced out, but demand to be taken to exhilarating extremes. When all is said and sung, despise not prophesying, do not quench the Holy Spirit . . . What Chesterton observed on the largest scale may be said perhaps on a smaller scale of how true worship works: '. . . the more I considered Christianity, the more I found that while it had established a rule and order, the chief aim of that order was to *give room for good things to run wild*'.[13]

Summary Reflections

The burden of this book is that a worship practice which integrates structured liturgy with charismatic freedom best reflects the polarities inherent in the Christian understanding of God in relationship to God's people. As Gordon Lathrop notes, 'the various paradoxical pairs that have been necessary to Christians in order to speak faithfully of God – human and divine, letter and spirit, now and not yet, hidden and revealed, immanent and transcendent – correspond, in conceptual language, to the ways the liturgy presents the faith'.[1] Though I have sought to explicate the 'paradoxical pairs' in ways wider than Lathrop, his statement well captures the approach to integrated worship suggested here. Some question the feasibility of such an approach on theoretical grounds. Frank Senn is a case in point. He concedes that 'formal' worship – in the sense of following a set form – need not be formal in a social-psychological sense. But he doubts that what he calls the 'effervescence' of Free Church worship can ever effectively 'be mixed with the conditions for ritualism'.[2] Certainly, it may be admitted that Western Christians are least likely by instinct and temperament to embrace extremes, reminiscent of the children in the market place of whom Jesus said: 'We played the flute for you and you did not dance; we sang a dirge and you did not cry' (Lk. 7:32). What is called for here is that 'second naivety' which has been mentioned previously so that adult childishness is replaced by mature childlikeness.

Cross-fertilisation in liturgical practice and experience may be welcomed if only to overcome the most stifling aspects of tradition on the one hand and, on the other, the more childish eccentricities of the charismatic renewal. At its most mundane, traditional worship can become perfunctory, offering what is often little more than idolatrous over-politeness, stiff-upper-lipped praise. In which case, one suspects, God would rather be praised with faint 'damns' than 'damned with faint praise'. Equally, at its most stereotyped, so-called 'contemporary' worship, can settle into mass-production praise-events, driven on by unrelentingly cheerful worship-leaders, in which praise is in danger of degenerating into mere flattery, a weekly vote of confidence in the Almighty. Embracing polarity in worship is the best antidote to such lop-sided worship experiences.

Integrated Worship Best Enables Seeking God's Pleasure to be Our Highest Good

Ordered, disciplined and theologically astute rubrics save worshippers from being reliant upon passing moods or pitching for emotional highs. Structural orthodoxy which cramps our style in godly ways serves the best interests of true self-fulfilment. Equally a ritualistic framework which is elastic enough to allow the Spirit to express himself through the worshippers helps to make our enjoyment of God not just an adrenaline rush but a means of grace and a means of growth into the uninhibited joy of Christlike character. We need worship as a way of:

- reorientating to God – against all self-determination;
- rehearsing the true story – against all self-description;
- redefining our true identity – against all self-deception;
- reordering our social world – against all self-absorption;
- reshaping our lives – against all self-complacency;
- releasing our pain and pleasure, joy and sorrow – against all self-protectiveness.

Integrated Worship Best Serves the Idea that Worship Is a World-Making Activity

While it is not difficult to see how state religion can affirm or indeed be used to endorse the way the world is currently configured, evangelical and charismatic worship is equally prone to

such corruption. In fact the very populist bent of evan-
gelical/charismatic religion – its passion for souls and obsession
with numbers – tends to drive it down the marketing route.
Marva Dawn is among the most astute critics of contemporary
evangelicalism's assimilation to a culture of consumerism.[3] Many
churches, she points out, speaking of the American scene, have
jettisoned traditional worship patterns for just such populist reasons. Where people seek instant intimacy, many churches are
offering 'instantly available feelings of coziness'.[4] In fact some
contemporary worship songs make intimacy with God sound
like infatuation with the goddess. The church adjusts also to a
sensation-seeking culture by turning worship into a thrilling and
exciting event. But, as Dawn points out, the thirst is insatiable. 'If
churches respond to this need merely by turning their worship
services into an emotional lift, however, they will have to increase
the hype constantly in order for that to remain effective.'[5]
Similarly, the church accommodates the legitimate need for communal participation and personal involvement, but without
theological boundaries or an overarching liturgical framework,
worship becomes 'private, devotional praise instead of corporate
worship'.[6]

Evangelical ethicist Jonathan Wilson observes that under pressure from the culture, much evangelical worship is so 'user-
friendly' that it reflects the therapeutic needs and entertainment
expectations of consumers. In either case the church sells the world
short. 'Worship becomes a form of mass therapy when we put the
self and the needs of the self at the center of worship and when we
define those needs in terms of our cultural situation rather than in
terms of the eschaton.'[7] Mindless praise is the cannabis, if not the
opium, of the people. This re-enforces the church's stance as
affirming the culture rather than being counter-cultural.

Wilson connects this with what has come to be styled hyperreality.[8] The term is used to describe how the Western world is
increasingly dominated by visual images which technologically
simulate reality. Through entertainment, the movies, Disney-
world, and home video games, our culture seeks heightened
experiences of everyday reality. In this way we can experience
surrogate excitement and danger which we always survive.
Wilson suggests that our worship is often corrupted by this desire

for entertainment and for an artificially heightened experience of reality. 'We want the singing, the drama, and the preaching to create an "experience" for us that heightens our sense of reality. But worship is not the enactment of "hyperreality", it is the enactment of God's eschatological redemption by the disciple community.'[9] In worship therefore, we should be able to welcome people to the 'really real' world. As Middleton and Walsh point out, the simulated world of 'image-enhanced hyperreality distances us from reality and is ultimately unsatisfying and desensitizing'.[10] In this realm of synthetic happiness, hell is not so much other people, per se – as Sartre suggested – but an eternal office party. The real drama played out in worship is our joyous participation by the Spirit in another reality, that of the kingdom of God.

Furthermore, in a simulated experience, we are experiencing sensations, not encountering reality. Worship which lacks objective, theological, structured framework and relies only on self-expression and the release of feelings will in time end up narcissistically feeding off its own emotional capital. The good feelings engendered by praising, supplant felt appreciation of the goodness of the God we are worshipping. Worship then becomes the reheating of yesterday's emotions.

Nor is the answer merely to provide alternative services for those who like traditional or contemporary or youth styles of music. This serves only to reduce worship still further to a matter of consumer taste.[11] A true integration of planned order and spontaneous freedom will best preserve worship from being a quotation of the culture and allow it to perform its symbolic task of being a world-making activity – the framing and reconstruction of the reality of the real word where Jesus is Lord, grace reigns and God's holy love prevails. From worship that is neither unrealistically world-escaping nor uncritically world-endorsing but genuinely world-making, all else follows.

Integrated Worship Best Maintains the Creative Tension Between Freedom and Order

As has been noted, authentic worship needs both structure and anti-structure. Liturgical order pays consistent respect to the varied attributes of God and the various dimensions of the gospel, while anti-structure allows for the varied responses and conditions of the worshippers. This works best when the fixed or directed elements serve as a framework which gives security and space for free expression. Liturgical forms act as stepping stones between which space is made for spontaneous response of movement, meditation, silence, gifts of the Holy Spirit in the free flow of praise. Or the fixed forms can be viewed as launching pads from which we venture repeatedly in risky trust into the uncharted realms of the Spirit, then to be brought back again and again to secure moorings. The time between the fixed elements needs to be elastic enough for the Spirit to be honoured with the liminal space to move on the worshippers 'as he wills'.

If order is so rigid as to preclude spontaneity and social intercourse in the worshipping community, then it damages human freedom and closes the liminal gaps that so powerfully reinforce the church's liminal condition as a priestly pilgrim community in the world. Such worship is too static and too safe and encourages an illusory sense of the church's established place in society. On the other hand, unrestricted freedom becomes superficial and transient, evoking surface moods rather then long-standing dispositions and convictions. When left to its own resources, emotional worship runs thin. It needs the credal, sacramental and liturgical ritual which, to use Aidan Kavanagh's terminology, 'thickens the meaning' and then 'increments meaning with style'.[12] Theologically informed, well-prepared liturgical order, then, can best reflect the various aspects of God's being and hold us to the structured outline of the gospel events. But within this structure, room is made for the free flow of God's Spirit and our varied responses to the Spirit. If special occasions call forth fresh liturgical order, why not engage the best creative thinkers, artists and theologians to create fresh liturgies every month, indeed every week. If Bach could compose a new cantata each week, then the preparation of a modest but well-crafted liturgical framework should not be beyond the scope of gifted members of the community.

Perhaps at the start of the twenty-first century, we may share the confidence Tom Smail felt at the end of the last century when he wrote:

The Spirit will be known for his faithfulness to the gospel and for his contemporary creativity and spontaneity. He who created a praiseful worship of the Father and the Son in ways that were authentic to all the cultures and centuries in which the gospel has been confessed, will do the same in new ways that are authentic to the end of the twentieth century. The prayer of the Spirit will be liturgical, in continuity with what has gone before, but it will also be free, creative and spontaneous.[13]

Integrated Worship Best Holds Together the Dynamic Dialectic of God's Transcendence and Immanence

David Wells has keenly assessed the 'weightlessness of God' in the modern world, indeed in the modern church.[14] Though God is spoken of and sung to, he has less and less bearing on the way we live and behave. In worship such a *kabod*-less or de-glorified God evokes lighter and lighter responses from worshippers. Immanence, says, Wells, has effectively diluted God's transcendence.[15] In similar vein, Marva Dawn speaks of the 'elimination of all awe and reverence from worship, in reducing God to his immanence without any sense of transcendence'.[16] But as pointed out earlier, if we polarise transcendence from immanence in order to choose between them, then God becomes a familiar backdrop to life but neither awesome or fascinating enough. He neither loves us to death nor frightens the hell out of us. He is neither rarefied enough nor raw enough. On the one hand, God is admired and given his rightful place at a safe distance – like the top-manager in the executive dining-room – but is not perceived as transcendent enough to be awesome and magnificent and mysterious and longed for as an elusive lover. On the other hand, God is made close enough to be cosily familiar but not close enough to be intimidating or a wee bit overwhelming. God's transcendence is not to be dissolved then in the subjectivity of our experience of his immanence.

We respond best to the God who is 'above' and 'beyond' us both by submission to liturgical ritual and order, bowing to what is given to us in creed, litany, word and sacrament, and by venturing 'in the Spirit' beyond ourselves in free praise, glossolalia, prophecy and awed recognition of God's holy otherness. At the same time, we respond to the God who is 'with us' – and indeed 'among us' – by releasing our joy or grief, our praise and lament, and our mutual love and forgiveness.

Integrated Worship Best Allows Due Weight to Be Given to Both Praise and Lament

Laments constitute the largest category of the Psalms but are not well represented in modern songbooks especially in charismatic circles. They are the exact opposite on the emotional spectrum to the cheerful songs of confident praise. They show that there is a place for a 'wintry spirituality' as well as a 'summery spirituality' in charismatic worship.[17] They foster integrity and real humanness because they allow negative emotions to be faced and expressed before God. This is the biblically sanctioned alternative to that grumbling and complaining in front of the world which jeopardises the reputation of God in the eyes of unbelief. But within corporate worship, the biblical lament tradition encourages us to pray our fears, tears, doubts and even anger to a God who has a great shock-absorbing heart.

Music has a crucial role to play in all this as dialectical theologian Douglas John Hall has pointed out in comments which allude to several of the polarities we have raised. 'With its strange interplay of minor and major progressions and harmonies, its never wholly predictable turns of phrase and melody, its interacting but sometimes incompatible rhythms, great music mirror's life's many-sidedness and its strange combination of order and judiciousness.'[18] Though Hall cites Johann Sebastian Bach as a case in point, this is not necessarily an elitist judgement. This is not a matter of privileging baroque over rock or – with inverted snobbery – the reverse. It is a matter of attending to the texture of the music and to its resonances; of seeking out that full-orbed music whether simple or complex which 'can and *must* call in question that within all of us that wants to embrace oversimplification and premature triumphs of the positive'.[19]

No one would dispute that time-honoured, traditional worship can have the effect of screening out the realism of life every bit as effectively as 'user-friendly' charismatic praise. Such worship can seem sanitised and hygienically correct, much like a War Museum where nothing is heard of the whining of the shells, the long howls of agony or, indeed, the unforgettable smell of battle. Aidan Kavanagh reminds us that the human story which went tragically wrong in Eden is finally resolved into the Banquet of the Lamb. 'Hebrews tells us,' he writes, 'how the resolution was accomplished, not in an orchard set in pleasant countryside but in a butcher shop located in the city's centre . . . a resolution the faint of heart, the fastidious, and the squeamish find hard to bear.'[20] Furthermore, we had, as it were, to 'look the lamb in the eye as we cut its lovely throat, and we had to keep that awful memory alive as we dined thankfully upon its flesh to live'.[21]

We must, in any event, be able to sing our 'faith in a minor key'[22] when occasion demands. Worship which is relentlessly cheerful, 'where seldom is heard a discouraging word and the skies are not cloudy or grey', is false. As Brueggemann characteristically states, 'Covenant minus lament is finally a practice of denial, cover-up, and pretense which sanctifies the status-quo.'[23]

Extravagant, exuberant praise is equally necessary. Such worship in the exhilarating liberty of the Spirit is the 'throwing of our lives into the air',[24] by 'a humanity at full stretch before God'.[25] Unbounded praise confounds conventional wisdom by being a useless activity. It rebukes a pragmatic age by not being designed to do anything and subverts a utilitarian ethos by being offered as an end in itself to the glory of God.[26] Uninhibited praise is an act of audacity, an overflow of the worshipper's whole being, a matching if inadequate response to the overflowing, extravagant grace that flows from God. Overwhelmings of both sadness and joy need to find overflowing expressions in our worship that is structured to make room for confession of sin, cries of grief, the dance of joy and shouts of acclamation.

Integrated Worship Best Blends the Old and the New, and Best Sustains Memory and Hope

It was the Christian poet R.S. Thomas who bemoaned the ruined landscape of his beloved Wales as 'worrying the carcass of an old song'.[27] So, like the debris left by a long receded tide, William Williams' great revival hymn, 'Guide me O Thou great Jehovah', emerges as the hollow anthem at Welsh rugby matches. Every tradition of churchmanship suffers from this hardening of the categories and the deadly dullness of an unchanging liturgical rut. But contemporary and spontaneous worship does not avoid the peril by evicting tradition in a desperate search for an instant rapport with the culture. 'This year's relevancies are often next year's embarrassments.'[28] In Andrew Walker's view, 'Liturgical renewal is not archaeological and antiquarian, not the restraining of the Spirit in a formal straitjacket of tradition. It is nothing less than a preparation for mission in a world where literary culture is moribund.'[29]

Robert Jenson, in a significant article, exposes the breakdown of a narratable world in modern society. 'In the post-modern world, if a congregation or churchly agency wants to be "relevant", here is the first step: it must recover the classic liturgy of the church, in all its dramatic density, sensual actuality, and brutal realism, and make this the one exclusive center of its life.'[30] On this count, even seemingly vibrant charismatic praise can become celebration without victory, a flying of a flag of convenience, since the ship of worship owns no home port of tradition to return to in order to refuel. An emphasis on the 'kingdom now' is a much needed corrective to the view that God does nothing on the Sabbath day but it tends to encourage a quick fix mentality at the expense of teaching delayed gratification. Too often contemporary worship is parasitic on the long history of the church. Its songs assume the saving narrative shape of the gospel but fail to articulate it in the way the old hymns did.

Praise stays honest when it is evangelical, not as a reflection of any current feel-good factor among the worshippers but in the sense of a genuine, never-dulled, continually amazed response to the Easter event. When worshippers are urged to be impressed by the latest phenomenon to hit the church, some may be forgiven for remaining underwhelmed: we have not yet 'gotten over' the Resurrection! And if memory lends perspective to worship, so hope keeps it sanguine. Eschatology will keep us modest in our expectations. It will remind us that all prophecy is partial, much sorrow awaits resolution, all praise is merely rehearsal for the wedding feast. Soul-numbing hype can be replaced with soul-stirring hope.

'How odd,' comments Brueggemann, 'that the new, new song is made up of the old, old story. The new doxology consists in the old songs we trusted before we succumbed, the lines we knew before we were embarrassed.'[31] Marva Dawn advocates using new music and new forms responsibly without sacrificing content and while educating the congregation to treasure gifts from the past. 'By doing so,' she asserts, 'we will help people see the value of the larger narrative, of being part of the whole Church throughout space and time, of biblical authority, of roots in tradition, of constant reformation and renewal, of anchored wisdom with fresh vitality, of all that we can learn from every epoch.'[32]

Conclusion

In the last resort, the issue is not about worship wars over style – traditional or contemporary, organ or guitar – but how and why we worship.[33] What matters is not whether our worship is up-to-date but whether it is 'truthful worship' faithful to the God we worship and to the gospel that saves.[34] What counts is that our worship is the genuine, heartfelt 'work of the people' *precisely because* it is being offered by a people caught up in the drama of the Triune God and participating by the Spirit in the Son's mediatorial hallowing of the Father's name.

Countering the cultural-assimilation of the liberalism of his day, P.T. Forsyth wrote that

> We do need more reverence in our prayer, more beauty in our praise, less dread of tried and consecrated form. But still more do we want the breathless awe, and stammering tongue, and the solemn wonder, and the passionate gratitude, which are the true note of grace, and the worship of a soul plucked from the burning and snatched by a miracle from the abyss. We want the new song of those who stand upon the rock, taken from the fearful pit and the miry clay, with the trembling still upon them and the slime still moist.[35]

Such worship will remain open to the fierce '*ruach*' of God to blow away staleness, stiffness and predictability. And all this within that theologically structured orderliness of song and prayer, confession and creed, Scripture and preaching, bread and wine, which keeps us tuned to the steady rhythm of the ongoing purpose of God.

The polarities are there to help us worship *God*.

I agree with Gordon Lathrop's conclusion that 'what is said here of God is not that God *is* these dualities, an eternal yin and yang, but that God's judgment and grace holds all these dualities together for the sake of life. The liturgy is not God. The world represented by the liturgy is not God. The juxtapositions of the liturgy are for our sake, that we might know the truth of God addressed to all of our experience.'[36]

Creative, integrated worship is worship that is both ordered by the true story and open to the great Spirit who surprises.

Is it too much to have a dream that one day the sons of liturgy and the sons of spontaneity, the sons of Passover and the sons of Pentecost, might sit down together at the table of the Lord? After all, in this context, are we not all the 'sons of former slaves', marching to the 'music of a people who will not be slaves again'?

I make the poet's wish my prayer.

> Follow poet, follow right
> To the bottom of the night
> With your unconstraining voice
> Still pursuade us to rejoice
>
> In the deserts of the heart
> Let the healing fountain start
> In the prison of his days
> Teach the free man how to praise.[3]
>
> W.H. Auden, *In Memory of W.B. Yeats*

Bibliography

Achtemeier, Elizabeth, *Minor Prophets 1*, New International Biblical Commentary (Peabody: Hendrickson Press, 1996).
—, *Preaching from the Minor Prophets* (Grand Rapids: Eerdmans, 1998).
Adam, James E., *War Psalms of the Prince of Peace: Lessons from the Imprecatory Psalms* (Phillipsburg: Presbyterian and Reformed Publishing Company, 1991).
Albrecht, Daniel E., *Rites in the Spirit: A Ritual Approach to Pentecostal/Charismatic Spirituality*, Journal of Pentecostal Theology Supplement Series (Sheffield: Sheffield Academic Press, 1999).
Allen, Leslie C., *1 and 2 Chronicles*, The Communicators Commentary (Waco: Word, 1987).
Allen, Ronald B., *Praise! A Matter of Life and Breath* (Nashville: Thomas Nelson, 1980).
Anderson, Bernhard, *Out of the Depths: The Psalms Speak for Us Today* (Philadelphia: Westminster Press, 1983).
—, *From Creation to New Creation* (Minneapolis: Fortress Press, 1994).
—, *Contours of Old Testament Theology* (Minneapolis: Fortress Press, 1999).
Anderson, E. Byron and Morrill, Bruce T. (eds), *Liturgy and the Moral Self: Humanity at Full Stretch Before God* (Collegeville: The Liturgical Press, 1988).
Arndt, William and Gingrich, Wilbur, *A Greek-English Lexicon of the New Testament and Other Early Christian Literature* (Chicago and Cambridge: University of Chicago Press and Cambridge University Press, 1964).

Aune, David, *Prophecy in Early Christianity* (Grand Rapids: Eerdmans, 1983).

—, *Revelation*, Word Biblical Commentaries (Waco Texas: Word, 1997).

Balentine, Samuel E., *The Vision of Torah's Worship, Overtures to Biblical Theology* (Minneapolis: Fortress Press, 2000).

Barr, James, *The Concept of Biblical Theology: An Old Testament Perspective* (London: SCM Press, 1999).

Bauckham, Richard, T*he Theology of the Book of Revelation* (Cambridge: Cambridge University Press, 1993).

—, 'Time and Eternity' in Richard Bauckham (ed.), *God Will Be All In All: The Eschatology of Jürgen Moltmann* (Edinburgh: T&T Clark, 1999).

Beasley-Murray, George, *John*, The Word Biblical Commentary (Waco: Word Books, 1987).

Begbie, Jeremy S., *Theology, Music and Time* (Cambridge: Cambridge University Press, 2000).

—, 'Play it (Again): Music, Theology and Divine Communication' in Jeff Astley, Timothy Hone, and Mark Savage (eds), *Creative Chords: Studies in Music, Theology, and Christian Formation* (Leominster: Gracewing, 2000).

Beisner, Calvin, *Psalms of Promise* (Colorado: Nav Press, 1988).

Bellinger, W.H., *Psalms: Reading and Studying the Book of Psalms* (Peabody: Hendrickson, 1997).

Berger, Peter L., *A Rumour of Angels* (Middlesex; Penguin Books, 1973).

—, *The Social Reality of Religion* (London: Faber and Faber, 1969).

—, *The Sacred Canopy: Elements of a Sociological Theory of Religion* (New York: Anchor/Doubleday, 1990).

—, and Luckmann, Thomas, *The Social Construction of Reality: A Treatise in the Sociology of Knowledge* (London: Penguin Books, 1991).

Berkhof, Hendrikus, *Christian Faith* (Grand Rapids: Eerdmans, 1986).

Berrigan, Daniel, *Isaiah, Spirit of Courage, Gift of Tears* (Minneapolis: Fortress Press, 1996).

Birch, Bruce C., *Hosea, Joel, and Amos* (Louisville: Westminster/John Knox Press, 1998).

Black, Clifton, 'Rhetorical Criticism' in Joel Green (ed.), *Hearing the New Testament: Strategies for Interpretation* (Grand Rapids: Eerdmans, 1995).

Blocher, Henri, 'Immanence and Transcendence in Trinitarian Theology' in Kevin J. Vanhoozer (ed.), *The Trinity in a Pluralistic Age* (Grand Rapids: Eerdmans, 1997).

Bloesch, Donald, *A Theology of Word and Spirit: Authority and Method* in *Theology*, Christian Foundations, Vol. 1, (Downers Grove: IVP, 1992).

—, *Spirituality Old & New: Recovering Authentic Spiritual Life* (Downers Grove: IVP, 2007).

Borgmann, Albert, *Crossing the Postmodern Divide* (Chicago: The University of Chicago Press, 1992).

Brown, William P., *The Ethos of the Cosmos: The Genesis of Moral Imagination in the Bible* (Grand Rapids: Eerdmans, 1999).

Broyles, Craig C., *The Conflict of Faith and Experience in the Psalms: A Form-Critical and Theological Study* (Sheffield: JSOT, Sheffield Academic Press, 1989).

—, *Psalms*, The New International Biblical Commentary (Peabody: Hendrickson, 1999).

Brueggemann, Walter, *The Prophetic Imagination* (Minneapolis: Fortress Press, 1978, revised edition, 2001).

—, *The Message of the Psalms* (Minneapolis: Augsburg Press, 1984).

—, *Praying the Psalms* (Winona: St. Mary's Press, 1986).

—, *Hopeful Imagination* (Minneapolis: Fortress Press, 1987).

—, *Israel's Praise: Doxology against Idolatry and Ideology* (Minneapolis: Fortress Press, 1988).

—, *The Creative Word* (Minneapolis: Fortress Press, 1989).

—, *Finally Comes the Poet* (Minneapolis: Fortress Press, 1989).

—, *Interpretation and Obedience: From Faithful Reading to Faithful Living* (Minneapolis: Fortress Press, 1991).

—, *Old Testament Theology: Essays on Structure, Theme, and Text*, Patrick D. Miller (ed), (Minneapolis: Fortress Press, 1992).

—, *The Bible in Postmodern Imagination: Texts Under Negotiation* (London: SCM Press, 1993).

—, *Biblical Perspectives on Evangelism* (Nashville: Abingdon Press, 1993).

—, *A Social Reading of the Old Testament*, Patrick D. Miller (ed.) (Minneapolis: Fortress Press, 1994).

—, *The Psalms and the Life of Faith*, Patrick D. Miller (ed.) (Minneapolis: Fortress Press, 1995).

—, *Theology of the Old Testament: Testimony, Disputes, Advocacy* (Minneapolis: Fortress Press, 1997).

—, *Cadences of Home: Preaching among Exiles* (Louisville: Westminster/John Knox Press, 1997).

—, *A Commentary on Jeremiah: Exile and Homecoming* (Grand Rapids: Eerdmans, 1998).

—, *The Covenanted Self*, Patrick D. Miller (ed.) (Minneapolis: Fortress Press, 1999).

Buchanan, Mark, *Your God is Too Safe* (Sisters, OR: Multnomah, 2001).

Burge, Gary M., *The Anointed Community: The Holy Spirit in the Johannine Tradition* (Grand Rapids: Eerdmans, 1987).

Chan, Simon, *Pentecostal Theology and the Christian Spiritual Tradition* (Sheffield: Sheffield Academic Press, 2000).

—, *Liturgical Theology: The Church as Worshipping Community* (Downers Grove: IVP, 2006).

Chilton, David, *Paradise Restored* (Fort Worth: Dominion Press, 1987).

Clapp, Rodney, *A Peculiar People* (Downers Grove: IVP, 1996).

Clarke, Erskine, (ed.), *Exilic Preaching: Testimony for Christian Exiles in an Increasingly Hostile Culture* (Harrisburg: Trinity International Press, 1988).

Cocksworth, Christopher, *Holy, Holy, Holy: Worshipping the Trinitarian God* (London: Darton, Longman, and Todd, 1997).

Colwell, John, *Promise and Presence: An Exploration of Sacramental Theology* (Milton Keynes: Paternoster, 2005).

Congar, Yves, *I Believe in the Holy Spirit: Vol.1, The Experience of the Spirit* (London: Geoffrey Chapman, 1983).

Copenhaver, Martin B., Robinson, Anthony B., and Willimon, William H.(eds), *Good News in Exile: Three Pastors Offer a Vision of Hope for the Church* (Grand Rapids: Eerdmans, 1999).

Corbon, Jean, *The Wellspring of Worship* (New York: Paulist Press, 1988).

Cox, Harvey, *Fire from Heaven* (London: Cassell, 1996).

Crainshaw, Jill Y., 'Embodied Remembering: Wisdom, Character, and Worship' in (ed.) William P. Brown, *Character and Scripture: Moral Formation, Community, and Biblical Interpretation* (Grand Rapids: Eerdmans, 2002), pp. 363–388.

Cullmann, Oscar, *Early Christian Worship* (London: SCM Press, 1962).

Curtis, Brent and Eldridge, John, *The Sacred Romance* (Nashville: Thomas Nelson, 1997).

Dawn, Marva J., *Reaching Out Without Dumbing Down: A Theology of Worship for the Turn-of-the-Century Culture* (Grand Rapids: Eerdmans, 1995).

—, *A Royal "Waste" of Time: The Splendor of Worshipping God and Being Church for the World* (Grand Rapids: Eerdmans, 1999).

Dawson, Gerrit Scott, *Jesus Ascended: The Meaning of Christ's Continuing Ascension* (London: T & T Clark, 2004).

de Silva, David, *Perseverance and Gratitude: A Socio-Rhetorical Commentary on the Epistle to the Hebrews* (Grand Rapids: Eerdmans, 2000).

Denney, James, *The Death of Christ* (London: Hodder and Stoughton, 1911).

Dillard, Annie, *Holy the Firm* (New York: Harper and Row, 1977).

—, *Teaching A Stone To Talk* (New York: HarperCollins, 1982).

Doran, Carol and Troeger, Thomas, *Trouble at the Table: Gathering the Tribes for Worship* (Nashville: Abingdon Press, 1992).

Drane, John, *The McDonaldization of the Church: Spirituality, Creativity, and the Future of the Church* (London: Darton, Longman, and Todd, 2000).

Driver, Tom, *The Magic of Ritual* (San Francisco: Harper Collins, 1991).

Durham, John, *Exodus*, Word Biblical Commentaries (Waco Texas: Word, 1987).

Eaton, John, *Vision in Worship: The Relation of Prophecy and Liturgy in the Old Testament* (London: SPCK, 1981).

Farrer, Austin, *A Faith of Our Own* (Cleveland: World Publishing Company, 1960).

Fee, Gordon D., *God's Empowering Presence* (Milton Keynes: Paternoster, 1994).

—, *Paul's Letter to the Philippians*, The New International Commentary on the New Testament (Grand Rapids: Eerdmans, 1995).

—, *Paul, the Spirit, and the People of God* (Peabody: Hendrickson Press, 1996).

Finney, John, *Fading Splendour* (London: Darton, Longman and Todd, 2000).

Fiorenza, Elizabeth Schüssler, *Revelation: Vision of a Just World* (Edinburgh: T&T Clark, 1991).

Ford, David F., *The Shape of Living* (Grand Rapids: Baker Books, 1997).

—, *Self and Salvation* (Cambridge: Cambridge University Press, 1999).

Forsyth, P.T., *The Taste of Death and The Life of Grace* (London: James Clarke, 1901).

—, *Positive Preaching and The Modern Mind* (London: Independent Press, 1907/1964).

—, *This Life and The Next* (New York: The Macmillan Company, 1918).

—, *The Justification of God* (London: Independent Press, 1948).

—, *The Soul of Prayer* (London: The Epworth Press, nd).

—, *Revelation Old and New* (London: Independent Press, 1962).

Fretheim, Terence E., *The Suffering of God: An Old Testament Perspective, Overtures to Biblical Theology* (Philadelphia: Fortress Press, 1984).

—, *Exodus*, Interpretation Commentary Series (Louisville: John Knox Press, 1991).

—, 'Some Reflections on Brueggemann's God' in Tod Linafelt and Timothy K. Beal (eds), *God in the Fray: A Tribute to Walter Brueggemann* (Minneapolis: Fortress Press, 1994).

Gammie, John G., *Holiness in Israel, Overtures to Biblical Theology* (Minneapolis: Fortress Press, 1989).

Geertz, Clifford, *The Interpretation of Culture* (London: Harper/Collins, 1993).

Gorman, Frank H., *The Ideology of Ritual: Space, Time, and Status in the Priestly Theology* (Sheffield: JSOT, Sheffield Academic Press, 1990).

Gottwald, Norman, *The Tribes of Yahweh: A Sociology of the Religion of Liberated Israel 1250–1050BC* (Maryknoll: Orbis, 1979; London: SCM, 1980).

Graham, M. Patrick, Marrs, Rick R., and McKenzie, Steven L., *Worship in the Hebrew Bible* (Sheffield: Sheffield Academic Press, 1999).

Green, Clifford (ed.), *Karl Barth: Theologian of Freedom – Selected Writings* (London: Collins, nd).

Green, Garrett, *Imagining God: Theology and the Religious Imagination* (Grand Rapids: Eerdmans, 1998).

Grenz, Stanley J., and Olsen, Roger E., *20th Century Theology* (Carlisle: Paternoster, 1992).

Guder, Darrell L., *The Continuing Conversion of the Church* (Grand Rapids: Eerdmans, 2000).

Guthrie, Harvey, *Theology as Thanksgiving* (New York: The Seabury Press, 1981).

Hall, Douglas John, *Bound and Free: A Theologian's Journey* (Minneapolis: Fortress Press, 2005).

—, *The Cross in our Context: Jesus and the Suffering World* (Minneapolis: Fortress Press, 2003).

Hardy, Daniel, and Ford, David, *Jubilate: Theology in Praise* (London: Darton, Longman and Todd, 1984).

Harris, Laird, Archer, Gleason and Waltke, Bruce, *Theological Wordbook of The Old Testament*, Vol. 1 (Chicago: Moody Press, 1980).

Hart, Trevor, '(Probably) the Greatest Story Ever Told?' in Tony Lane (ed.), *Interpreting the Bible: Historical and Theological Studies in Honour of David Wright* (Leicester: Apollos, 1997).

Hauerwas, Stanley and Willimon, William, *Resident Aliens* (Nashville: Abingdon Press, 1989).

—, *Where Resident Aliens Live* (Nashville: Abingdon Press, 1996).

Hauerwas, Stanley, *A Better Hope* (Grand Rapids: Brazos Press, 2000).

Hays, Richard, *First Corinthians: Interpretation Commentary Series* (Louisville: John Knox Press, 1997).

Hengel, Martin, *Between Paul and Jesus* (London: SCM Press, 1983).

Herbert, George, *The English Poems of George Herbert* (London: Dent, 1974).

Heron, Alisdair, ed., *The Forgotten Trinity. 3 A Selection of Papers presented to the BCC Study Commission on Trinitarian Doctrine Today* (London: BCC/CCBI, 1991).

Heschel, Abraham, *The Prophets* (New York: Harper and Row, 1962).

—, *Who is Man?* (Stanford: Stanford University Press, 1965).

Holmes, Urban T., *Ministry and Imagination* (New York: The Seabury Press, 1976).

Horsley, Richard A., 'Building an Alternative Society' in Richard A. Horsley (ed.), *Paul and Empire: Religion and Power in Roman Imperial Society* (Harrisburg: Trinity Press International, 1997).

Howard-Brook, Wes and Gwyther, Anthony, *Unveiling Empire: Reading Revelation Then and Now* (Maryknoll: Orbis Books, 1999).

Hurtado, Larry, *At The Origins of Christian Worship* (Carlisle: Paternoster, 1999).

—, *Lord Jesus Christ: Devotion to Jesus in Earliest Christianity* (Grand Rapids: Eerdmans, 2003).

Jacobson, Rolf, 'The Costly Loss of Praise' *Theology Today* Vol. 57, no. 3 (Princeton: Princeton Theological Seminary, October 2000).

Jenson, Peter Philip, *Graded Holiness: A Key to the Priestly Conception of Holiness* (Sheffield: JSOT, Sheffield Academic Press, 1992).

Jenson, Robert W., 'How The World Lost Its Story', *First Things*, Vol. 36, October 1993.

Jinkins, Michael, *In the House of the Lord: Introducing the Psalms of Lament* (Collegeville: The Liturgical Press, 1998).

Johnson, Luke T., *Religious Experience in Earliest Christianity* (Minneapolis: Fortress Press, 1998).

Kavanagh, Aidan, *Elements of Rite* (New York: Pueblo Publishing, 1982).

—, *Liturgical Theology* (Collegeville: The Liturgical Press, 1984).

Keesmat, Sylvia and Walsh, Brian, *Colossians Remixed* (Milton Keynes: Paternoster Press, 2005).

Kellerman, Bill Wylie, *Seasons of Faith And Conscience: Kairos, Confession, Liturgy* (Maryknoll: Orbis Books, 1991).

Kenneson, Philip D., and Street, James L., *Selling Out The Church: The Dangers of Marketing the Church* (Nashville: Abingdon Press, 1997).

Kleinig, John W., *The Lord's Song: The Basis, Function and Significance of Choral Music in Chronicles* (Sheffield: JSOT, Sheffield Academic Press, 1993).

Knight, Henry H., *A Future for Evangelical Truth* (Nashville: Abingdon Press, 1997).

Koester, Craig R., *Symbolism in the Fourth Gospel: Meaning, Mystery, Community*, 2nd edition (Minneapolis: Fortress Press, 2003).

König, Adrio, *Here Am I: A Believer's Reflection on God* (Grand Rapids: Eerdmans, 1982).

Kraus, Hans-Joachim, *Psalms 1–59* (Minneapolis: Fortress Press, 1993).

Kraybill, J. Nelson, *Imperial Cult and Commerce in John's Apocalypse* (Sheffield: JSNT, Sheffield Academic Press, 1996).

Labberton, Mark, *The Dangerous Act of Worship* (Downers Grove: IVP, 2007).

Land, Steven J., *Pentecostal Spirituality* (Sheffield: Sheffield Academic Press, 1994).

Lathrop, Gordon, *Holy Things: A Liturgical Theology* (Minneapolis: Fortress Press, 1998).

—, *Holy People: A Liturgical Ecclesiology* (Minneapolis: Fortress Press, 1999).

—, *New Creation: A Liturgical Worldview* (Minneapolis: Fortress Press, 2000).

Leaver, Robin A., 'Liturgical Music as Anamnesis' in Robin A. Leaver and Joyce Ann Zimmerman (eds.), *Liturgy and Music* (Collegeville: The Liturgical Press, 1988).

Levenson, John D., *Creation and the Persistence of Evil* (Princeton: Princeton University Press, 1988).

Lewis, C.S., *The Chronicles of Narnia* (London: Collins, 1998).

Liesch, Barry, *People in the Presence of God* (Grand Rapids: Zondervan, 1988).

Lindbeck, George, *The Nature of Doctrine* (London: SPCK, 1984).

Longman, Tremper, *How to Read the Psalms* (Downers Grove: IVP, 1988).

Longman, Tremper and Reid, Daniel, *God is a Warrior* (Carlisle: Paternoster, 1995).

Macfarlane, Robert, *The Wild Places* (London: Granta Books, 2007).

Maries, Andrew, *Worship Together Magazine* (Issue 23, Summer 1998).

Martin, Ralph, *Worship in the Early Church* (London: Marshall, Morgan and Scott, 1964).

Marty, Martin E., *The Cry of Absence* (San Francisco: Harper and Row, 1983).

Mays, James L., *Amos: Old Testament Library* (London: SCM Press, 1969).

McCann, J. Clinton, *A Theological Introduction to the Book of Psalms* (Nashville: Abingdon Press, 1993).

McFadyen, Alistair, 'Sins of Praise' in Colin E.Gunton (ed.), *God and Freedom* (Edinburgh: T&T Clark, 1995).

Meeks, Wayne, *The First Urban Christians* (New Haven/London: Yale University Press, 1983).

—, *The Moral World of the First Christians* (London: SPCK, 1986).

Middleton, J. Richard and Walsh, Brian J., *Truth Is Stranger than It Used to Be* (London: SPCK, 1995).

Miller, Patrick D., *They Cried to the Lord: The Form and Theology of Biblical Prayer* (Minneapolis: Fortress Press, 1994).

Mitchell, Nathan D., *Meeting Mystery: Liturgy, Worship, Sacraments* (Maryknoll: Orbis Books, 2006).

Moltmann, Jürgen, *The Church in the Power of the Spirit* (London: SCM Press, 1975).

Morrill, Bruce T., *Anamnesis as Dangerous Memory: Political And Liturgical Theology in Dialogue* (Collegeville: The Liturgical Press, 2000).

Motyer, J.A., *The Day of the Lion: The Voice of the Old Testament* (London: Inter-Varsity Press, 1974).

Moule, C.F.D., *The Birth of the New Testament* (London: Adam & Charles Black, 1966).

Mowinkel, Sigmund, *The Psalms in Israel's Worship* (Oxford: Basil Blackwell, 1982).

Nelson, Richard D., *Raising Up a Faithful Priest: Community and Priesthood in Biblical Theology* (Louisville: Westminster/John Knox Press, 1993).

Newbigin, Lesslie, *A Word in Season* (Grand Rapids: Eerdmans, 1994).

—, *The Light Has Come: An Exposition of the Fourth Gospel* (Grand Rapids: Eerdmans, 1982).

Nicholls, J. Randall, *The Restoring Word* (San Francisco: Harper and Row, 1987).

—, 'Worship as Anti-Structure: The Contribution of Victor Turner' in *Theology Today*, Vol. 41, No. 4, January 1985, pp. 401–409.

Norris, Kathleen, *Amazing Grace: A Vocabulary of Faith* (New York: Riverhead Books, 1998).

Parrish, Steven V., 'Walter Brueggemann' in Donald McKim (ed.), *Historical Handbook of Major Biblical Interpreters* (Downers Grove: IVP, 1998).

Pelikan, Jaroslav, *The Emergence of the Christian Tradition* (100–600), Vol. 1 of *The Christian Tradition: A History of the Development of Doctrine* (Chicago: University of Chicago, 1971).

Percy, Martyn, *Words, Wonders and Power: Understanding Contemporary Christian Fundamentalism and Revivalism* (London: SPCK, 1996).

—, *Power and The Church: Ecclesiology in an Age of Transition* (London: Cassell, 1998).

Peterson, David, *Engaging With God: A Biblical Theology of Worship* (Leicester: Apollos, 1992).

Peterson, Eugene, *Five Smooth Stones for Pastoral Work* (Atlanta: John Knox Press, 1980).

—, *Reversed Thunder: The Revelation of John and the Praying Imagination* (New York: Harper and Row, 1988).

—, 'Eat the Book,' *Theology Today* Vol. 56, No.1 (Princeton: Princeton Theological Seminary, April 1999).

Pilgrim, Walter. E., *Uneasy Neighbors: Church and State in the New Testament: Overtures to Biblical Theology* (Minneapolis: Fortress Press, 1999).

Piper, John, *Desiring God: Meditations of A Christian Hedonist* (Portland: Multnomah, 1986).

Placher, William C., *The Domestication of Transcendence* (Louisville: Westminster/John Knox Press, 1996).

Powell, Mark Allan, *Loving Jesus* (Minneapolis: Fortress Press, 2004).

Price, S.R.F., 'Rituals and Power' in Richard A. Horsley (ed.), *Paul and Empire: Religion and Power in Roman Imperial Society* (Harrisburg: Trinity Press International, 1997).

Purdue, Leo G., *The Collapse of History: Overtures to Biblical Theology* (Minneapolis: Fortress Press, 1994).

Ramsey, Arthur Michael, *The Glory of God and the Transfiguration of Christ*, (London: Longmans, Green and Co., 1949).

Ricoeur, Paul, *Figuring the Sacred* (Minneapolis: Fortress Press, 1995).

Roxburgh, Alan J., *The Missionary Congregation: Leadership and Liminality* (Harrisburg: Trinity International Press, 1997).

Saliers, Don E., *Worship as Theology: Foretaste of Glory Divine* (Nashville: Abingdon Press, 1994).

—, *Worship Come to Its Senses* (Nashville: Abingdon Press, 1996).

Sarna, Nahum, *Exploring Exodus* (New York: Schocken Books, 1987).

Schattaeur, Thomas, 'Liturgical Assembly as Locus of Mission' in Thomas Schattaeur (ed.), *Inside Out: Worship in an Age of Mission* (Minneapolis: Fortress Press, 1999).

Schmemann, Alexander, *For the Life of the World* (New York: St. Vladimir's Seminary Press, 1988).

Seerveld, Calvin, *Rainbows for the Fallen World* (Toronto: Tuppence Press, 1980).

Senn, Frank C., *Christian Worship and Its Cultural Setting* (Philadelphia: Fortress Press, 1983).

—, *The Witness of the Worshipping Community: Liturgy and the Practice of Evangelism* (New York: Paulist Press, 1993).

—, *Christian Liturgy: Catholic and Evangelical* (Minneapolis: Fortress Press, 1997).

—, *A Stewardship of the Mysteries* (New York: Paulist Press, 1999).

—, *The People's Work: A Social History of the Liturgy* (Minneapolis: Fortress Press, 2006).

Shaughnessy, James (ed.), *The Roots of Ritual* (Grand Rapids: Eerdmans, 1973).

Smail, Tom, *The Giving Gift: The Holy Spirit in Person* (London: Hodder & Stoughton, 1988).

Suurmond, Jean-Jacques, *Word and Spirit at Play* (London: SCM Press, 1994).

Swartley, Willard, *Covenant of Peace: The Missing Piece in New Testament Theology and Ethics* (Grand Rapids: Eerdmans, 2006).

Sweet, Leonard, *Soultsunami* (Grand Rapids: Zondervan/Harper Collins, 1999).

Tanner, Kathryn, *God and Creation in Christian Theology: Tyranny or Empowerment?* (Oxford: Basil Blackwell, 1988).

Tate, Marvin E., *Psalms 50–100*, Word Biblical Commentaries (Dallas: Word, 1990).

Terrien, Samuel, *The Elusive Presence* (San Francisco: Harper and Row, 1978).

Thiselton, Anthony C., *The First Epistle to the Corinthians*, The New International Greek Testament Commentary (Grand Rapids: Eerdmans, 2000).

Thomas, R.S., *Collected Poems 1945–1990* (London: Phoenix Press, 1995).

Thompson, E.P., *The Making of the English Working Class* (London: Penguin Books, 1963).

Torgerson, Mark, *An Architecture of Immanence: Architecture for Worship and Ministry Today* (Grand Rapids: Eerdmans, 2007).

Torrance, James B., *Worship, Community, and the Triune God of Grace* (Carlisle: Paternoster Press, 1996).

Torrance, T.F., *The Apocalypse Today* (Grand Rapids: Eerdmans, 1959).

Turner, Victor, *The Ritual Process* (New York: Aldine de Gruyter, 1969).

Ugolnik, Anthony, *The Illuminating Icon* (Grand Rapids: Eerdmans, 1989).

Vaileios, Archimandrite, *Hymn of Entry* (New York: St. Vladimir's Seminary Press, 1984).

Van Gemeren, William (ed.), *New International Dictionary of Old Testament Theology and Exegesis* (Carlisle: Paternoster, 1996).

Van Gennep, Arnold, *The Rites of Passage* (Chicago: University of Chicago Press, 1960).

Van Olst, E.H., *The Bible and Liturgy* (Grand Rapids: Eerdmans, 1991).

Wainwright, Geoffrey, *Eucharist and Eschatology* (London: Epworth Press, 1971).

Walker, Andrew, *Telling the Story* (London: SPCK, 1996).

Webber, Robert, *Worship is a Verb* (Waco: Word Books, 1985).

—, *Signs of Wonder: The Phenomenon of Convergence in Modern Liturgical and Charismatic Churches* (Nashville: Abbott Martyn, 1992).

—, *Blended Worship: Achieving Substance and Relevance in Worship* (Peabody: Hendrickson, 1996).

Weinandy, Thomas G., *Does God Suffer?* (Edinburgh: T&T Clark, 2000).

Wells, David, *God in the Wasteland* (Leicester: IVP, 1994).

Wenham, Gordon, *Genesis 1–15*, Word Biblical Commentaries (Waco, Texas: Word, 1987).

Westermann, Claus, *The Praise of God in the Psalms* (London: Epworth Press, 1966).

—, *Genesis 1–11* (London: SPCK, 1974).

Westermeyer, *Paul, Te Deum: The Church and Music* (Minneapolis: Fortress Press, 1998).

—, *Let Justice Sing: Hymnody and Justice* (Collegeville: The Liturgical Press, 1998).

White, Susan J., *The Spirit of Worship* (London: Darton, Longman and Todd, 1999).

Wilder, Amos, *Jesus' Parables and the War of Myths* (London: SPCK, 1982).

Wilken, Robert L., *Remembering the Christian Past* (Grand Rapids: Eerdmans, 1995).

Williams, Rowan, *Open To Judgment* (London: Darton, Longman and Todd, 1994).

—, *Christ on Trial* (London: Harper Collins, 2000).

Willimon, William, *Peculiar Speech* (Grand Rapids: Eerdmans, 1992).

Wilson, Jonathan, *Gospel Virtues* (Downers Grove: IVP, 1998).

Wink, Walter, *Engaging the Powers: Discernment and Resistance in a World of Domination* (Minneapolis: Fortress Press, 1992).

Witherington, Ben, *Conflict and Community in Corinth* (Grand Rapids: Eerdmans, 1995).

Wright, N.T., *The New Testament and the People of God* (London: SPCK, 1992).

—, *Jesus and the Victory of God* (London: SPCK, 1996).

—, *Surprised by Hope* (London: SPCK, 2007).

Wuthnow, Robert, *Christianity in the 21st Century* (New York: Oxford, 1993).

Yoder, John Howard, *The Royal Priesthood: Essays Ecclesiological and Ecumenical* (Grand Rapids: Eerdmans, 1994).

Endnotes

Introduction

[1] Robert Webber, *Signs of Wonder: The Phenomenon of Convergence in Modern Liturgical and Charismatic Churches* (Nashville: Abbott Martyn, 1992), p. x. This has been reprinted as *Blended Worship: Achieving Substance and Relevance in Worship* (Peabody: Hendrickson, 1996).

[2] Webber, *Signs of Wonder*, p. 145.

[3] Ibid.

[4] Ibid., p. 47.

[5] Ibid., p. 54.

[6] Marva J. Dawn, *A Royal Waste of Time: The Splendor of Worshipping God and Being Church for the World* (Grand Rapids: Eerdmans, 1999), p. 7. This book is a response to the discussion provoked by Dawn's widely read work *Reaching Out without Dumbing Down: A Theology of Worship for the Turn-of-the-Century Culture* (Grand Rapids: Eerdmans 1995).

[7] Andrew Maries, *Worship Together Magazine*, 23 (Summer 1998), p. 15.

[8] For some characteristically shrewd comments on the educative or diseducative effects of music in contemporary culture, and on the loss of rites of passage, see Roger Scruton, *Culture Counts: Faith and Feeling in a World Beseiged* (New York: Encounter Books, 2007), pp. 60–65.

[9] John Durham, *Exodus* (Waco Texas: Word Biblical Commentaries, 1987), pp. 424, 430; commenting on Exodus 32:17–18.

[10] Marva J. Dawn, *A Royal Waste of Time*, p. 153.

[11] Walter Brueggemann, *The Psalms and the Life of Faith*, edited by Patrick Miller (Minneapolis: Fortress Press, 1995), p. 15.

[12] Gordon Lathrop, *Holy Things: A Liturgical Theology* (Minneapolis: Fortress Press, 1993/1998), p. 80.

[13] See entry by Stephen Parrish in *Historical Handbook of Major Biblical Interpreters*, edited by Donald McKim (Downers Grove: IVP, 1998), pp. 570–575. See also Bernhard Anderson, *Contours of Old Testament Theology* (Minneapolis: Fortress Press, 1999), pp. 22–27.

[14] Anderson, *Contours*, p. 24. For a New Testament view see Clifton Black in *Hearing the New Testament*, edited by Joel Green (Grand Rapids: Eerdmans, 1995), chapter 13. For Brueggemann's own assessment see *Theology of the Old Testament* (Minneapolis: Fortress Press, 1997), pp. 64–71.

[15] Brueggemann, *The Bible and Post-Modern Imagination: Texts under Negotiation* (London: SCM Press, 1993), p. ix. See also *Theology of the Old Testament*, p. 86.

[16] George Lindbeck, *The Nature of Doctrine* (London: SPCK, 1984), p. 118.

[17] Brueggemann, *Theology*, p. 653.

[18] Ibid., p. 559.

[19] Ibid., p. 67.

[20] Brueggemann, *The Prophetic Imagination* (Minneapolis: Fortress Press, 1978), pp. 45, 13.

[21] Brueggemann, *Hopeful Imagination* (Minneapolis: Fortress Press, 1986), p. 2 (italics his); see also the very long footnote in *The Creative Word* (Minneapolis: Fortress, 1982), p. 127.

[22] Brueggemann, *Hopeful Imagination*, p. 23.

[23] Ibid., p. 25.

[24] Craig Dykstra, *Vision and Character* (New York: Paulist Press, 1981), p. 79.

[25] Trevor Hart, '(Probably) the Greatest Story Ever Told?' in Tony Lane (ed.), *Interpreting the Bible: Historical and Theological Studies in Honour of David Wright* (Leicester: Apollos, 1997), pp. 181–204.

[26] Peter Berger and Thomas Luckmann, *The Social Construction of Reality: A Treatise in the Sociology of Knowledge* (London: Penguin Books, 1991). Peter Berger, *The Sacred Canopy: Elements of a Sociological Theory of Religion* (New York: Anchor/Doubleday, 1990), previously published in UK by Faber and Faber under the title *The Social Reality of Religion*, 1967.

[27] Brueggemann, *Israel's Praise: Doxology against Idolatry and Ideology* (Minneapolis: Fortress Press, 1988), p. 13. See also Miller (ed.), *A Social Reading*, p. 213.

[28] Berger, *The Sacred Canopy*, p. 40.

[29] This anticipates the consideration of Genesis 1 and the 'new song' of Psalms and the Isaianic corpus as being prophetic protests against the 'world as constructed' by Babylonian definitions of reality. This applies also to the hymns in John's revelation as posing an alternative to the imperial 'world constructed' by the Roman Legions.

[30] Brueggemann, *Israel's Praise*, p. 11.

[31] Brueggemann, *Theology*, pp. 77–78.

[32] Brueggemann, *Old Testament Theology: Essays on Structure, Theme, and Text*, edited by Patrick Miller (Minneapolis: Fortress Press, 1992), p. 185.

[33] Brueggemann, *Cadences of Home: Preaching to Exiles* (Louisville: Westminster/John Knox Press, 1997), p. 114.

[34] Ibid., p. 126.

[35] Brueggemann, *Theology*, p. 77; see also *Old Testament Theology*, p.189.

[36] I rely for this summary on Donald Bloesch's *A Theology of Word and Spirit: Authority and Method In Theology*, Christian Foundations Vol. 1. (Downers Grove: IVP, 1992), pp. 76–81.

[37] Brueggemann, *Old Testament Theology*, p. 25.

[38] This is encapsulated in two formative essays 'A Shape of Old Testament Theology, 1. Structure Legitimation' and 'A Shape for Old Testament Theology, 2. Embrace of Pain' reprinted in *Old Testament Theology*, chapters 1 and 2.

[39] Brueggemann, *Old Testament Theology*, p. 16.

[40] Ibid., p. 17.

[41] Ibid., pp. 48, 53.

[42] Lathrop, *Holy Things*, p. 79.

[43] Leonard Sweet, *Soultsunami* (Grand Rapids: Zondervan/Harper Collins, 1999), p. 198.

[44] Webber, *Signs of Wonder*, p. 11.

1. God-sponsored Hedonism: Self-fulfilling *and* God-glorifying

[1] Cited by Barry Liesch in *People in the Presence of God: Models and Directions for Worship* (Grand Rapids: Zondervan, 1988), p. 40.

[2] See, for example, Tom Wright's typically trenchant comments on hymns and liturgies dealing with death and the afterlife in *Surpised by Hope* (London: SPCK, 2007), chapters 1 and 2.

3 Especially *Desiring God: Meditations of a Christian Hedonist* (Seven Sisters, OR: Multnomah, 1996); *The Pleasures of God: Meditations on God's Delight in Being God* (Portland: Multnomah, 1991) and in many subsequent publications.

4 Sam Storms, *Pleasures Evermore* (Colorado: NavPress, 2000), p. 43.

5 Donald Bloesch, *Spirituality Old and New: Recovering Authentic Spiritual Life* (Downers Grove: IVP, 2007), p. 172, n. 4.

6 Simon Chan, *Liturgical Theology: The Church as Worshipping Community* (Downers Grove: IVP, 2006), p. 53.

7 Ibid., p. 54.

8 Ibid., p. 55.

9 Frank Senn, *New Creation: A Liturgical World View* (Minneapolis: Fortress Press, 2000), p. 121.

10 C.S. Lewis, *Reflections on the Psalms* (Glasgow: Collins, 1962), p. 81.

2. Worship as Politics: Attending Heaven's Throne *and* Confounding Earthly Powers

1 William Willimon, *Peculiar Speech* (Grand Rapids: Eerdmans, 1992), pp. 54–55.

2 Alexander Schmemann, *For the Life of the World* (New York: St.Vladimir's Seminary Press, 1988), p. 125.

3 Ibid., p. 126.

4 Kathleen Norris, *Amazing Grace: A Vocabulary of Faith* (New York: Riverhead Books, 1998), pp. 246–250.

5 Brueggemann, *Israel's Praise*, pp. 3–4.

6 Ibid., pp. 8–10.

7 Ibid., pp. 13–28.

8 Peter L. Berger, *The Social Reality of Religion* (London: Faber and Faber 1969), pp. 3, 26.

9 David Burrell, 'Ritual and Conceptual Systems: Primitive Myth to Modern Ideology' in *The Roots of Ritual*, edited by James Shaughnessy (Grand Rapids: Eerdmans, 1975), p. 212.

10 Brueggemann, *Interpretation and Obedience*, p. 190.

11 Lathrop, *Holy Things*, p. 212.

12 Brueggemann, *Israel's Praise*, pp. 25–26.

13 Claus Westermann, *Genesis 1–11* (London: SPCK, 1974), p. 91.

14 Gordon Wenham, *Genesis 1–15* (Waco: Word, 1987), p. 10.

[15] Westermann, *Genesis 1–11*, pp. 90–91, 92; Wenham, *Genesis 1–15*, p. 38.

[16] Bernhard Anderson, *From Creation to New Creation* (Minneapolis: Fortress Press, 1994), p. 2.

[17] Ibid., pp. 210–211.

[18] Brueggemann, *Israel's Praise*, p.11.

[19] Ibid. See particularly chapter 4.

[20] Lathrop, *Holy Things*, pp. 208–209.

[21] Brueggemann, *Theology of the Old Testament*, pp. 145–164. Brueggemann repeats his earlier misgivings on pp. 149, 163.

[22] Brueggemann, *Israel's Praise*, p. 53.

[23] Ibid., p. 11.

[24] Brueggemann, *Theology of the Old Testament*, pp. 533–534.

[25] See Harvey Guthrie, *Theology as Thanksgiving* (New York: The Seabury Press, 1981), pp. 32–37, 60–63. The citation is of course from George Herbert.

[26] Brueggemann, *Israel's Praise*, p. 11.

[27] Lathrop, *Holy Things*, pp. 39–40, 211.

[28] John D. Levenson, *Creation and the Persistence of Evil* (Princeton: Princeton University Press, 1988), pp. 78–99; Terence E. Fretheim, *Exodus*, Interpretation Commentary Series (Louisville: John Knox Press, 1991) , pp. 263–278; Nahum Sarna, *Exploring Exodus* (New York: Schocken Books, 1987), pp. 213–215. William Brown, *The Ethos of the Cosmos* (Grand Rapids: Eerdmans, 1999), pp. 73–102. See also Brueggemann, *Theology of the Old Testament*, p. 533.

[29] Levenson, *Creation and the Persistence of Evil*, p. 86.

[30] Fretheim, *Exodus*, p. 269.

[31] Levenson, *Creation and the Persistence of Evil*, pp. 85–86.

[32] Nahum Sarna, *Exploring Exodus* (New York: Schocken Books, 1987), p. 215.

[33] Fretheim, *Exodus*, p. 271.

[34] Levenson, *Creation and the Persistence of Evil*, p. 86.

[35] Brown, *The Ethos of the Cosmos*, p. 88.

[36] Fretheim, *Exodus*, p. 267.

[37] Brown, *The Ethos of the Cosmos*, p. 102.

[38] Peter Berger, *The Social Reality of Religion*, pp. 26–27.

[39] Brown, *The Ethos of the Cosmos*, p. 128.

[40] Ibid., pp. 22, 28.

[41] See on this the remarkable study of Sylvia Keesmat and Brian Walsh, *Colossians Remixed* (Milton Keynes: Paternoster, 2005).

[42] Gordon Fee, *Paul's Letter to the Philippians* (Grand Rapids: Eerdmans, 1995), pp. 222–223.

[43] Acts 16:37–40.

[44] Richard Horsley in *Paul and Empire: Religion and Power in Roman Imperial Society*, edited by Richard A. Horsley (Harrisburg: Trinity Press International, 1997), pp. 206–214). *Ekklēsia* seems a deliberate choice since other terms were available to Paul by which to describe religious gatherings, as Larry Hurtado points out in *At The Origins of Christian Worship* (Carlisle: Paternoster, 1999), p. 54.

[45] John Howard Yoder, *The Royal Priesthood: Essays Ecclesiological and Ecumenical* (Grand Rapids: Eerdmans, 1994), p. 123.

[46] Horsley, *Paul and Empire*, p. 141.

[47] Bruce W. Winter, *Seek the Welfare of the City* (Grand Rapids: Eerdmans/Paternoster, 1994), pp. 131–133.

[48] Horsley, *Paul and Empire*, p. 142.

[49] Helmut Koester, 'Imperial Ideology and Paul's Eschatology in 1 Thessalonians' in Horsley (ed.), *Paul and Empire*, p. 160.

[50] S.R.F. Price, 'Rituals and Power' in Horsley (ed.), *Paul and Empire*, p. 68. Price acknowledges his use of 'constructed' as a deliberate echo of Berger's work.

[51] Ibid., p. 71.

[52] Horsley, *Paul and Empire*, p. 23.

[53] J. Nelson Kraybill, *Imperial Cult and Commerce in John's Apocalypse*, JSNT (Sheffield: Sheffield Academic Press, 1996), pp. 118–123.

[54] Ibid., p. 123.

[55] Wes Howard-Brook and Anthony Gwyther, *Unveiling Empire: Reading Revelation Then and Now* (Maryknoll: Orbis Books, 1999), p. 223 ff.

[56] Amos Wilder, *Jesus' Parables and the War of Myths* (London: SPCK, 1982), p. 37.

[57] The terminology is that of Walter Wink in *Engaging the Powers* (Minneapolis: Fortress Press, 1992).

[58] T.F. Torrance, *The Apocalypse Today* (Grand Rapids: Eerdmans, 1959), p. 11.

[59] Susan J. White, *The Spirit of Worship* (London: Darton, Longman and Todd, 1999), p. 116.

[60] Yoder, *The Royal Priesthood*, p. 129.

[61] Ibid.

[62] Richard Bauckham, *The Theology of The Book of Revelation* (Cambridge: Cambridge University Press, 1993), p. 33.

[63] Larry Hurtado, *At the Origins of Christian Worship*, p. 51. Susan J. White, *The Spirit of Worship*, p. 55.

[64] Archimandrite Vaileios, Abbot of Mount Athos, *Hymn of Entry* (New York: St. Vladimir's Press, 1984), p. 67.

[65] Schmemann, *For the Light of the World*, p. 28.

[66] Rodney Clapp, *A Peculiar People* (Downers Grove: IVP, 1996), p. 96.

[67] See Wayne Meeks, *The Moral World of the First Christians* (London: SPCK, 1986), p. 145.

[68] For this paragraph I am indebted to J. Nelson Kraybill, *Imperial Cult and Commerce in John's Apocalypse*, especially pp. 59, 117.

[69] Yoder, *The Royal Priesthood*, p. 130.

[70] David Aune, *Revelation*, Word Biblical Commentary (Waco: Word Books, 1997), pp. 310–311.

[71] Elisabeth Schussler Fiorenza, *Revelation: Vision of a Just World* (Edinburgh: T&T Clark, 1991), p. 59.

[72] Ibid., p. 59.

[73] David Aune, *Revelation*, p. 317.

[74] Eugene Peterson, *Reversed Thunder: The Revelation of John and the Praying Imagination* (New York: Harper and Row, 1988), p. 141.

[75] Kraybill, *Imperial Cult and Commerce*, p. 221.

[76] Aune, *Revelation*, p. 640.

[77] Bill Wylie Kellerman, *Seasons of Faith and Conscience: Kairos, Confession, Liturgy* (Maryknoll, New York: Orbis Books, 1991), pp. 4–5. This whole book is a powerful application of worship to political activism.

[78] Walter E. Pilgrim, *Uneasy Neighbors: Church and State in the New Testament: Overtures to Biblical Theology* (Minneapolis: Fortress Press, 1999), p. 175. Pilgrim is cited by Willard Swartley in his helpful discussion of worship in *John's Apocalypse, in Covenant of Peace: The Missing Piece in New Testament Theology and Ethics* (Grand Rapids: Eerdmans, 2006), pp. 339–355.

[79] Ibid., p. 741.

[80] This may have been an implied contrast to the 'Augustus Day' fixed to honour the Emperor. See Larry Hurtado, *At The Origins of Christian Worship*, p. 56.

[81] Stanley Hauerwas and William Willimon, *Where Resident Aliens Live* (Nashville: Abingdon Press, 1996), p. 45.

3. Crossing the Threshold: Charismatic Freedom *and* Liturgical Order

[1] Cited by Frank Senn, *Christian Liturgy* (Minneapolis: Fortress Press, 1997), p. 9. The reference is from Van Gennep's *The Rites of Passage* (Chicago: University of Chicago Press, 1960), pp. 189–190.

[2] Cited by Senn in *Christian Liturgy*, p. 9; from Gennep, *The Rites of Passage*, p. 11.

[3] Tom Driver, *The Magic of Ritual* (San Francisco: Harper Collins, 1991), p. 159. See also the very helpful summary of Turner's work and its application to worship by J. Randall Nichols, *Theology Today* Vol. 41, No. 4, January 1985.

[4] Victor Turner, *The Ritual Process* (New York: Aldine de Gruyter, 1969, 1995), p. 95.

[5] Ibid., p. 161.

[6] In this section I draw particularly on the following: John G. Gammie, *Holiness in Israel* (Minneapolis: Fortress Press, 1989); Richard D. Nelson, *Raising Up a Faithful Priest: Community and Priesthood in Biblical Theology* (Louisville: Westminster/John Knox Press, 1993); Frank H. Gorman, *The Ideology of Ritual: Space, Time, and Status in the Priestly Theology* (Sheffield: JSOT Series, Sheffield Academic Press, 1990); Peter Philip Jenson, *Graded Holiness: A Key to the Priestly Conception of Holiness* (Sheffield: JSOT Series, Sheffield Academic Press, 1992).

[7] Jenson, *Graded Holiness*, p. 43.

[8] The phrase is Nelson's; see *Raising Up a Faithful Priest*, p. 34.

[9] Gorman, *The Ideology of Ritual*, pp. 16–17.

[10] Ibid., p. 27.

[11] Jenson, *Graded Holiness*, p. 35ff.

[12] Gorman, *The Ideology of Ritual*, p. 62.

[13] Ibid., p. 90.

[14] Ibid.

[15] Ibid., p. 62.

[16] Ibid., p. 49.

[17] Nelson, *Raising Up a Faithful Priest*, p. 36.

[18] Ibid., p. 37, italics mine.

[19] Ibid., p. 85.

[20] Ibid., p. 37.

[21] Gorman sees the wilderness period as a liminal state. *The Ideology of Ritual*, pp. 147–148.

[22] See for example Brueggemann's foreword to Martin B. Copenhaver, Anthony B. Robinson and William H. Willimon, *Good News in Exile: Three Pastors Offer a Vision of Hope for the Church* (Grand Rapids: Eerdmans, 1999); and Erskine Clarke (ed.), *Exilic Preaching: Testimony for Christian Exiles in an Increasingly Hostile Culture* (Harrisburg: Trinity Press International, 1998), which includes three program-matic essays by Brueggemann. Also Alan J. Roxburgh, *The Missionary Congregation: Leadership and Liminality* (Harrisburg: Trinity Press International, 1997).

[23] See the influential and best selling work of Stanley Hauerwas and William Willimon, *Resident Aliens* (Nashville: Abingdon Press, 1989).

[24] Brueggemann, *Cadences of Home: Preaching Among Exiles* (Louisville: Westminster/John Knox Press, 1997), p. 114.

[25] Brueggemann, *Old Testament Theology* (Minneapolis: Fortress Press, 1992), p. 185.

[26] Brueggemann, *Hopeful Imagination* (Philadelphia: Fortress Press, 1987), p. 4.

[27] Jeremiah 23.

[28] Clifford Geertz, *The Interpretation of Cultures* (London: HarperCollins, 1993), p. 112.

[29] Samuel E. Balentine, *The Vision of Torah's Worship* (Minneapolis: Fortress Press, 2000), pp. 62, 250.

[30] Brueggemann, *Theology of the Old Testament*, p. 665.

[31] Marvin E. Tate, *Psalms 50–100*, Word Biblical Commentary (Dallas: Word Books, 1990), p. 418.

[32] Brueggemann, *Cadences*, p. 114.

[33] Brueggemann, *Old Testament Theology*, p. 183.

[34] N.T. Wright, *The New Testament and the People of God* (London: SPCK, 1992), pp. 268–271. *Jesus and the Victory of God* (London: SPCK, 1996).

[35] Brueggemann, *Biblical Perspectives on Evangelism* (Nashville: Abingdon Press, 1993), p. 87, italics his.

[36] Ibid., p. 88.

[37] The evidence is marshalled by James M. Scott, 'For as Many as are of the Works of the Law are under a Curse' in Craig Evans and James A. Sanders (eds), *Paul and The Scriptures of Israel* (Sheffield; Sheffield Academic Press, 1993), pp. 187–221; Craig Evans, 'Jesus and the Continuing Exile of Israel' in Carey Newman (ed.), *Jesus and the Restoration of Israel* (Downers Grove: IVP, 1999), pp. 77–100; and with reference to Qumran see C. Marvin Pate, *Communities of the Last Days* (Leicester: Apollos, 2000), especially chapter 9.

38 Brueggemann, *Evangelism*, p. 91.

39 Frank Senn, *Christian Liturgy: Catholic and Evangelical* (Minneapolis: Fortress Press, 1997), p. 13.

40 Richard Nelson, *Faithful Priest*, pp. 141–154.

41 David de Silva, *Perseverance and Gratitude: Socio-Rhetorical Commentary on the Epistle to the Hebrews* (Grand Rapids: Eerdmans, 2000), p. 70.

42 Ibid., p. 70.

43 Ibid., p. 70.

44 Brueggemann, *Interpretation and Obedience* (Minneapolis: Fortress Press, 1991), p. 208.

45 J. Randall Nichols, *The Restoring Word* (San Francisco: Harper and Row, 1987), pp. 135–136.

46 Ibid., p. 30.

47 Jurgen Moltmann, *The Church in the Power of the Spirit* (London: SCM Press, 1975), p. 262).

48 J. Randall Nichols, 'Worship as Anti-Structure: The Contribution of Victor Turner' in *Theology Today*, Vol. 41, No. 4, January 1985, p. 407.

49 Copenhaver et al., *Good News in Exile*, p. 25.

50 Jean-Jacques Suurmond, *Word and Spirit at Play* (London: SCM Press, 1994), p. 87.

51 Daniel E. Albrecht, *Rites in the Spirit: A Ritual Approach to Pentecostal/Charismatic Spirituality* (Sheffield: Sheffield Academic Press, 1999), p. 152.

52 Suurmond, *Word and Spirit*, p. 87.

53 Oscar Cullmann, *Early Christian Worship* (London: SCM Press, 1962), p. 33.

54 Ben Witherington, *Conflict and Community in Corinth* (Grand Rapids: Eerdmans, 1995), p. 151. On worship and ritual in the Pauline churches see also Wayne Meeks, *The First Urban Christians* (New Haven and London: Yale University Press, 1983), pp. 145–149. Luke T. Johnson, *Religious Experience in Earliest Christianity* (Minneapolis: Fortress Press, 1998), chapter 3.

55 Richard Hays, *First Corinthians* (Louisville: John Knox Press, 1997), p. 243.

56 Austen Farrer, *A Faith of Our Own* (Cleveland: World Publishing Company, 1960), p. 216.

57 Carol Doran and Thomas Troeger, *Trouble at the Table: Gathering the Tribes for Worship* (Nashville: Abingdon Press, 1992), chapter 3.

58 Urban T. Holmes, *Ministry and Imagination* (New York: The Seabury Press, 1976), pp. 122–123.

[59] Doran and Troeger, *Trouble at the Table*, p. 96.

[60] It's important to note that by 'anti-structure' Turner did not mean 'in opposition to structure' but that which is 'non-structure'.

[61] Daniel Hardy and David Ford, *Jubilate: Theology in Praise* (London: Darton, Longman, and Todd, 1984), p. 10.

[62] Ibid., p. 76.

[63] Ibid., p. 20.

[64] Walter Brueggemann, *The Psalms and the Life of Faith* (Minneapolis: Fortress Press, 1995), p. 58.

[65] Hardy and Ford, *Jubilate*, p. 20.

[66] Suurmond, *Word and Spirit*, p. 88.

[67] Driver, *Magic of Ritual*, pp. 159, 200.

[68] Albrecht, *Rites of the Spirit*, p. 210.

[69] Barry Liesch, *People in the Presence of God* (Grand Rapids: Zondervan, 1988), pp. 91, 94.

[70] Graham Hughes, *Worship as Meaning: A Liturgical Theology for Late Modernity* (Cambridge: Cambridge University Press, 2003), p. 301.

[71] Albrecht, *Rites of the Spirit*, pp. 209–217.

[72] Quoted by Driver, *The Magic of Ritual*, p. 166.

4. Holy Love: Transcendent Otherness *and* Transforming Immediacy

[1] Daniel Berrigan, *Isaiah, Spirit of Courage, Gift of Tears* (Minneapolis: Fortress Press, 1996), p. 33.

[2] Stanley J. Grenz and Roger E. Olsen, *20th Century Theology* (Carlisle: Paternoster, 1992), p. 11.

[3] Ibid.

[4] Peter L. Berger, *A Rumour of Angels* (Middlesex: Penguin Books, 1973), p. 70.

[5] Brueggemann, *Theology of the Old Testament*, p. 83.

[6] Ibid., p. 83, n. 59.

[7] Terence E. Fretheim, 'Some Reflections on Brueggemann's God' in Tod Linafelt and Timothy K. Beal (eds), *God in the Fray: A Tribute to Walter Brueggemann* (Minneapolis: Fortress Press, 1998), p. 27.

[8] Leo Purdue, *The Collapse of History* (Minneapolis: Fortress Press, 1994), p. 287.

[9] Fretheim, *God in the Fray*, p. 27.

[10] Walter Brueggemann, *Isaiah 40–66* (Louisville: Westminster John Knox Press, 1998), p. 181.

[11] Walter Brueggemann, *A Commentary on Jeremiah: Exile and Homecoming* (Grand Rapids: Eerdmans, 1998), pp. 213–214.

[12] Fretheim, *God in the Fray*, p. 36.

[13] Brueggemann, *Theology of the Old Testament*, pp. 670–674.

[14] Ibid., p. 671.

[15] Brueggemann, *Old Testament Theology*, pp. 183–203.

[16] The phrase is John Finney's in his *Fading Splendour* (London: Darton,Longman and Todd, 2000), p. 148.

[17] Samuel Terrien, *The Elusive Presence* (San Francisco: Harper and Row, 1978), p. 194.

[18] Ibid., p. 198.

[19] Brueggemann, *Theology of the Old Testament*, p. 673.

[20] Ibid.

[21] Ibid., pp. 674, 675.

[22] Aidan Kavanagh, *On Liturgical Theology*, p. 154.

[23] William C. Placher, *The Domestication of Transcendence* (Louisville: Westminster John Knox Press, 1996), p. 6.

[24] Ibid., p. 6.

[25] Ibid., p. 9.

[26] Ibid., p. 111.

[27] Kathryn Tanner, *God and Creation in Christian Theology: Tyranny or Empowerment?* (Oxford: Basil Blackwell, 1988), p. 89; cited by Placher in n. 1, p.111.

[28] Ibid., p.79; cited by Placher on p. 112.

[29] See chapter 7.

[30] Placher, *The Domestication of Transcendence*, p. 182.

[31] Henri Blocher, 'Immanence and Transcendence in Trinitarian Theology' in Kevin J. Vanhoozer (ed.), *The Trinity in a Pluralistic Age* (Grand Rapids: Eerdmans, 1997), pp. 121–123.

[32] Rowan Williams, *Christ on Trial* (London: HarperCollins, 2000), p. 15.

[33] See Gen. 28:16–17; Ex. 3:1–6; Is. 6:5.

[34] Thomas G. Weinandy, *Does God Suffer?* (Edinburgh: T&T Clark, 2000), p. 55.

[35] Ibid., p. 56.

[36] Terence E. Fretheim, *The Suffering of God: An Old Testament Perspective* (Philadelphia: Fortress Press, 1984), p. 70.

[37] Ibid., p. 70.

[38] Hendrikus Berkof, *Christian Faith* (Grand Rapids: Eerdmans, 1986), p. 130.

[39] P.T. Forsyth, *The Justification of God* (London: Independent Press, 1917/1948), pp. 128–129.

[40] Adrio König, *Here am I: A Believer's Reflection on God* (Grand Rapids; Eerdmans, 1982), p. 75. Konig's whole discussion is very illuminating in what is a brilliant and neglected book.

[41] Fretheim, *The Suffering of God*, p. 71.

[42] A. Heschel, *The Prophets* (New York: Harper and Row, 1962), p. 486.

[43] Jeremy S. Begbie, *Theology, Music and Time* (Cambridge: Cambridge University Press, 2000), p. 168.

[44] Brueggemann, *Israel's Praise*, p. 45.

[45] Begbie, *Theology, Music and Time*, p. 145.

[46] Ibid.

[47] Karl Barth in Clifford Green (ed.), *Karl Barth, Theologian of Freedom: Selected Writings* (London: Collins, nd), p. 323.

[48] Begbie, *Theology, Music and Time*, p. 145.

[49] Ibid., p. 146.

[50] Graham Hughes, *Worship as Meaning: A Liturgical Theology for Late Modernity* (Cambridge: Cambridge University Press, 2003), pp. 243–244.

[51] Martyn Percy, *Words, Wonders and Power: Understanding Contemporary Christian Fundamentalism and Revivalism* (London: SPCK, 1996), p. 61.

[52] Ibid., p. 79.

[53] Ibid., p. 65.

[54] Ibid., pp. 74–76.

[55] Martyn Percy, *Power and the Church, Ecclesiology in an Age of Transition* (London: Cassell, 1998), pp. 146, 104. See also Harvey Cox, *Fire from Heaven* (London: Cassell, 1996), p. 201.

[56] Ibid., p. 145.

[57] This list is taken from ibid., pp. 148, and 159, n. 34.

[58] E.P. Thompson, *The Making of the English Working Class* (London: Penguin Books, 1963), pp. 405, 407. Thompson describes it as a 'form of psychic masturbation' with a hymnody whose symbolism is, by turns, 'maternal, Oedipal, sexual and sado-masochistic'.

[59] Ibid., p. 149.

[60] Ibid.

[61] Percy, *Words, Wonders and Power*, p.77.

[62] Hughes, *Worship as Meaning*, p. 156.

[63] Lathrop, *Holy Things*, pp. 125–126.

[64] Hughes, *Worship as Meaning*, p. 156.

[65] Ibid., p. 244.

[66] Mark Torgerson, *An Architecture of Immanence: Architecture for Worship and Ministry Today* (Grand Rapids: Eerdmans, 2007), p. 226.

[67] Placher, *The Domestication of Transcendence*, p. 159.

[68] Alistair McFadyen, 'Sins of Praise' in Colin E. Gunton (ed.), *God and Freedom* (Edinburgh: T&T Clark,1995), pp. 32–56.

[69] Ibid., pp. 33–34.

[70] Ibid., p. 35.

[71] Ibid., p. 35, n. 6.

[72] Hardy and Ford, *Jubilate*, p. 55. For a Trinitarian sacramentalism (and, for example, the notion of a 'mediated immediacy') see John Colwell's brilliant study *Promise and Presence: An Exploration of Sacramental Theology* (Milton Keynes: Paternoster, 2005). My acquaintance with this book came too late for serious interaction with it.

[73] McFadyen, *God and Freedom*, p. 52.

[74] Hardy and Ford, *Jubilate*, pp. 81, 82.

[75] Ibid., p. 76.

[76] Ibid., pp. 159, 161.

[77] Luke T. Johnson, *Religious Experience in Earliest Christianity* (Minneapolis: Fortress Press, 1998), pp. 9, 59.

[78] P.T. Forsyth, *This Life and the Next* (New York: The Macmillan Company, 1918), p. 31.

[79] Walter Brueggemann, *The Hopeful Imagination* (Philadelphia: Fortress Press, 1987), pp. 92–99.

[80] Brueggemann, *Israel's Praise*, pp. 114–116. Brueggemann develops the point in a later essay '"Othering" with Grace and Courage' in Patrick Miller (ed.), *The Covenanted Self* (Minneapolis: Fortress Press, 1999), pp. 1–17.

[81] Brueggemann, *Israel's Praise*, p. 114.

[82] Brueggemann, *The Covenanted Self*, p. 5.

[83] Ibid., p. 6.

[84] Ibid.

5. Going to Extremes: Praise *and* Lament

[1] Aidan Kavanagh, *On Liturgical Theology*, p. 73.

[2] See especially Hughes, *Worship as Meaning*, chapter 8.

[3] Jill Y. Crainshaw, 'Embodied Remembering: Wisdom, Character, and Worship' in William P. Brown (ed.), *Character and Scripture: Moral Formation, Community, and Biblical Interpretation* (Grand Rapids: Eerdmans, 2002), p. 387. One need not endorse Crainshaw's feminist agenda in recognising her insightful contribution to a very helpful symposium.

[4] Brueggemann, *Old Testament Theology*, p. 7.

[5] Ibid., p. 13.

[6] Ibid., p. 16.

[7] Ibid., p. 26.

[8] Ibid., p. 29.

[9] Ibid., pp. 28–29.

[10] Martyn Percy, *Words, Wonders and Power* (London: SPCK, 1996), p. 79.

[11] Walter Brueggemann, 'Old Testament Theology as a Particular Conversation: Adjudication of Israel's Sociotheological Alternatives' in *Old Testament Theology*, pp. 118–149.

[12] Terence E. Fretheim, *Exodus* (Louisville: John Knox Press, 1991), p. 1.

[13] Brueggemann, *Old Testament Theology*, p. 48, italics his.

[14] Fretheim, *Exodus*, p. 162.

[15] Ibid.

[16] Ibid.

[17] Ibid., p. 166.

[18] John W. Kleinig, *The Lord's Song: The Basis, Function and Significance of Choral Music in Chronicles* (Sheffield: JSOT, Sheffield Academic Press, 1993), p. 178.

[19] Ibid., pp. 178, 180.

[20] Brueggemann, *Israel's Praise*, pp. 41–42.

[21] E.H. van Olst, *The Bible and Liturgy* (Grand Rapids: Eerdmans, 1991), p. 111.

[22] Michael Fishbane, *Biblical Text and Texture* (Oxford: Oneworld Publications, 1998), p. 129.

[23] Brueggemann, Old Testament Theology, p. 48.

[24] Claus Westermann, *The Praise of God in the Psalms* (London: Epworth Press, 1966), p. 152.

25 Craig Broyles, *The Conflict of Faith and Experience in the Psalms: A Form-Critical and Theological Study* (Sheffield: JSOT, Sheffield Academic Press, 1989), p. 52.

26 Paul Ricoeur, *Figuring the Sacred* (Minneapolis: Fortress Press, 1995), pp. 60–61.

27 Hans-Joachim Kraus, *Psalms 1–59* (Minneapolis: Fortress Press, 1993), p. 40.

28 Broyles, *The Conflict of Faith in the Psalms*, p. 53. See also Broyles' recent commentary on the Psalms, *The New International Biblical Commentary: Psalms* (Peabody: Hendrickson, 1999), pp. 32–34.

29 Walter Brueggemann, *The Psalms and the Life of Faith* edited by Patrick Miller (Minneapolis: Fortress Press, 1995), p. 9. *The Message of the Psalms* (Minneapolis: Augsburg, 1984), pp. 19–21. This later commentary is built around the three groupings.

30 Brueggemann, *The Message of the Psalms*, p. 19.

31 Brueggemann, *The Psalms and the Life of Faith*, p. 10.

32 Brueggemann, *The Message of the Psalms*, p. 32.

33 Calvin Seerveld, *Rainbows for the Fallen World* (Toronto: Tuppence Press, 1980), p. 23.

34 Brueggemann, *The Psalms and the Life of Faith*, p. 112.

35 George Herbert, *The English Poems of George Herbert* (London: Dent, 1974), p. 129. Brueggemann makes insightful use of Herbert's poem in *The Psalms and the Life of Praise*, pp. 129–130.

36 Ibid., p. 131.

37 Brueggemann, *Israel's Praise*, p. 101.

38 As emphasized by Bruce C. Birch, *Hosea, Joel, and Amos* (Louisville: Westminster John Knox Press, 1998), p. 209.

39 David Allan Hubbard, *Joel and Amos* (Leicester: IVP, Tyndale Commentaries, 1989), p. 163.

40 Brueggemann, *The Psalms and the Life of Faith*, pp. 114–117.

41 Ibid., p. 130.

42 Ibid., p. 11.

43 Ibid., p. 12, n. 26.

44 Claus Westermann, *The Praise of God in the Psalms* (London: Epworth Press, 1966), p. 64.

45 Brueggemann, *The Psalms and the Life of Faith*, p. 12.

46 The phrase is Brueggemann's, *The Psalms and the Life of Faith*, p. 19.

47 Ibid., p. 20.

48 Brueggemann, *Praying the Psalms* (Winona: St. Mary's Press, 1986), p. 69.

[49] J. Clinton McCann, *A Theological Introduction to the Book of Psalms* (Nashville: Abingdon Press, 1993), p. 115.

[50] Brueggemann, *Praying the Psalms*, p. 70. W.H. Bellinger, *Psalms: Reading and Studying the Book of Psalms* (Peabody: Hendrickson Press, 1997), p. 54.

[51] Michael Jinkins, *In the House of the Lord: Introducing the Psalms of Lament* (Collegeville: The Liturgical Press, 1998), pp. 96–98.

[52] Bernhard Anderson, *Out of the Depths: The Psalms Speak for Us Today* (Philadelphia: Westminster Press, 1983), p. 89.

[53] Tremper Longman III, *How to Read the Psalms* (Downers Grove: IVP, 1988), p. 139.

[54] David Chilton, *Paradise Restored* (Fort Worth; Dominion Press, 1987), p. 216.

[55] See Patrick Miller's helpful discussion, *They Cried to the Lord: The Form and Theology of Biblical Prayer* (Minneapolis: Fortress Press, 1994), pp. 301–303. Calvin Beisner makes this point well in an exposition of Psalm 109 in *Psalms of Promise* (Colorado: Nav Press, 1988), pp. 161–182.

[56] James E. Adams, *War Psalms of the Prince of Peace: Lessons from the Imprecatory Psalms* (Phillipsburg: Presbyterian and Reformed Publishing Company, 1991), p. 33ff.

[57] Jinkins, *In the House of the Lord*, p. 95.

[58] Brueggemann, *Praying the Psalms*, p. 78.

[59] Ibid., p. 79.

[60] Martyn Percy, *Words, Wonders and Powers*, p. 77.

[61] Walter Brueggemann, *Finally Comes the Poet* (Minneapolis: Fortress Press, 1989), p. 47.

[62] Ibid. p. 48.

[63] Brueggemann, *The Psalms and the Life of Faith*, p. 15.

[64] David F. Ford, *The Shape of Living* (Grand Rapids: Baker Books, 1997), pp. 66–67 and throughout.

[65] The idea of a 'new' or 'second naivety' is derived from the work of Paul Ricoeur.

[66] Brueggemann, *The Psalms and the Life of Faith*, p. 25.

[67] David Ford, *Self and Salvation* (Cambridge: Cambridge University Press, 1999), p. 115.

[68] The point is made by Rolf Jacobson in 'The Costly Loss of Praise' *Theology Today*, Vol. 57, No. 3 (Princeton; Princeton Theological Seminary, October 2000), pp. 375–385. Jacobson is mirroring

ironically Brueggemann's seminal article 'The Costly Loss of Lament' in *The Psalms and the Life of Faith*, pp. 98–111.

[69] Abraham Heschel, *Who is Man?* (Stanford: Stanford University Press, 1965), p. 117.

[70] Ibid.

[71] Brueggemann, *The Psalms and the Life of Faith*, p. 51.

[72] Suurmond, *Word and Spirit*, p. 88.

[73] Brueggemann, *The Psalms and the Life of Faith*, p. 58.

[74] Ibid., p. 114.

[75] Ibid., p. 58.

[76] Ibid., p. 102.

[77] Brueggemann, *Finally Comes the Poet*, p. 47.

[78] Brueggemann, *The Covenanted Self* (Minneapolis: Fortress Press, 1999), p. 18.

[79] See chapter 8.

[80] See chapter 7.

[81] Brueggemann, *The Psalms and the Life of Faith*, p. 83.

6. Creative Repetition: Tradition *and* Innovation

[1] Jaroslav Pelikan, *The Emergence of the Catholic Tradition (100–600)* (Chicago; University of Chicago Press, 1971), p. 9. Vol. 1 of *The Christian Tradition: A History of the Development of Doctrine.*

[2] For a helpful evangelical assessment of the role of narrative generally in theology see Henry H. Knight, *A Future for Evangelical Truth* (Nashville: Abingdon Press, 1997), chapter 6.

[3] Lesslie Newbigin, *A Word in Season* (Grand Rapids; Eerdmans, 1994), p. 89.

[4] Paul Ricoeur, *Figuring the Sacred* (Minneapolis; Fortress Press, 1995), p. 245. The paragraph summarises Ricoeur's argument on the same page.

[5] Ibid., p. 179. Ricoeur is indebted to Sigmund Mowinkel, *The Psalms in Israel's Worship* (Oxford: Basil Blackwell, 1982). It is not necessary to buy into Mowinkel's more controversial theory of an annual festival of Yahweh's re-enthronement, to feel the force of Ricoeur's point.

[6] Andrew Walker, *Telling the Story* (London: SPCK, 1996), p. 99.

[7] Eugene Peterson, 'Eat the Book' in *Theology Today*, Vol. 56, No. 1 (Princeton: Princeton Theological Seminary, April 1999), p. 16.

8 Ibid.

9 Kleinig, *The Lord's Song*, p. 135.

10 Brueggemann, *Israel's Praise*, p. 32.

11 Lamentations 3:21.

12 Brueggemann, *Israel's Praise*, p. 35.

13 Ibid., p. 34.

14 Tremper Longman and Daniel Reid, *God is a Warrior* (Carlisle: Paternoster Press, 1995), p. 45.

15 Brueggemann, *Israel's Praise*, p. 36.

16 See Brueggemann's use of Psalm 96 in connection with preaching the good news in *Cadences of Home* (Louisville: Westminster John Knox Press, 1997), pp. 86–88.

17 J. Clinton McCann, *A Theological Introduction to the Book of Psalms* (Nashville: Abingdon, 1993), p. 46.

18 Kleinig, *The Lord's Song*, p. 137.

19 Ibid., p. 139.

20 Robert Wilkin, *Remembering the Christian Past* (Grand Rapids: Eerdmans, 1995), pp. vii–viii.

21 C.F.D. Moule, *The Birth of the New Testament* (London: A & C Black, 1962), p. 19.

22 David Aune, *The New Testament in its Literary Environment* (Cambridge: James Clarke, 1987), p. 192.

23 Moule, *Birth of the New Testament*, p. 29.

24 Ralph Martin, *New Testament Interpretation*, ed. Howard Marshall (Carlisle: Paternoster, nd.), p. 224. See also Ralph Martin, *Worship in the Early Church* (Edinburgh: Marshall, Morgan, and Scott, 1964). See also more recently, Larry Hurtado, *Lord Jesus Christ: Devotion to Jesus in Earliest Christianity* (Grand Rapids: Eerdmans, 2003), pp. 110, 173.

25 Gordon Fee, *God's Empowering Presence* (Peabody: Hendrickson, 1994), p. 410.

26 Ibid., p. 231.

27 Schmemann, *For the Life of the World*, p. 29.

28 David Aune, *Prophecy in Early Christianity* (Grand Rapids: Eerdmans, 1983), p. 84.

29 Kleinig, *The Lord's Song*, p. 190.

30 Senn, *New Creation*, p. 97.

31 Claus Westermann, *The Praise of God in the Psalms* (London: Epworth Press, 1966), p. 71.

32 Ibid., p. 65.

[33] John Eaton, *Vision in Worship: The Relation of Prophecy and Liturgy in the Old Testament* (London: SPCK, 1981), p. 54. Eaton cites Psalms 14, 60, 74 and 85 as further examples.

[34] Ronald B. Allen, *Praise! A Matter of Life and Breath* (Nashville: Thomas Nelson, 1980), p. 38.

[35] Martin Hengel, 'Hymns and Christology' in *Between Jesus and Paul* (London: SCM Press, 1983), p. 95.

[36] Kleinig, *The Lord's Song*, p. 165.

[37] Ibid.

[38] Ibid., p. 166.

[39] Lathrop, *Holy Things*, p. 10.

[40] P.T. Forsyth, *Positive Preaching and the Modern Mind* (London: Independent Press, 1907/1964), p. 64.

[41] Ibid., p. 63.

[42] Ibid., p. 55.

[43] Brueggemann, *Cadences of Home*, p. 117.

[44] Forsyth, *Positive Preaching and the Modern Mind*, p. 61.

[45] Ibid., p. 60.

[46] Ibid., p. 62.

[47] Lathrop, *Holy Things*, p. 31.

[48] Ibid.

[49] E.H. van Olst, *The Bible and Liturgy* (Grand Rapids: Eerdmans, 1991), p. 16.

[50] Lathrop, *Holy Things*, pp. 22–24.

[51] Bruce Morrill, *Anamnesis as Dangerous Memory; Political and Liturgical Theology in Dialogue* (Collegeville: The Liturgical Press, 2000), p. xiii, citing the political theologian Johann Baptist Metz.

[52] Robert Wuthnow, *Christianity in the 21st Century* (New York: Oxford, 1993), p. 48.

[53] Jean Corbon, *The Wellspring of Worship* (New York: Paulist Press, 1988), pp. 5–6.

[54] Joyce Ann Zimmerman 'Liturgical assembly: Who is the subject of liturgy' in Robin Leaver and Joyce Ann Zimmerman (eds), *Liturgy and Music* (Collegeville: The Liturgical Press, 1998), p. 52.

[55] Brueggemann, *The Psalms and the Life of Faith*, p. 122.

[56] Anthony C. Thiselton, *The First Epistle to the Corinthians: The New International Greek Testament Commentary* (Milton Keynes, Paternoster, 2000), p. 879.

[57] Ibid., p. 880.

⁵⁸ Ibid.

⁵⁹ Lathrop, *Holy Things*, pp. 39–40.

⁶⁰ Robin Leaver, 'Liturgical Music as Anamnesis' in Robin A. Leaver and Joyce Ann Zimmerman (eds), *Liturgy and Music* (Collegeville: The Liturgical Press, 1998), pp. 396–397.

⁶¹ Thomas Schattaeur, 'Liturgical Assembly as Locus of Mission' in Thomas Schattauer (ed.), *Inside Out: Worship in an Age of Mission* (Minneapolis: Fortress Press, 1999), p. 12.

⁶² Thiselton, *The First Epistle to the Corinthians*, p. 868.

⁶³ William Arndt and Wilbur Gingrich, *A Greek-English Lexicon of the New Testament and Other Early Christian Literature* (Chicago/ Cambridge: University of Chicago Press/Cambridge University Press, 1964), pp. 619–621.

⁶⁴ Ricoeur, *Figuring the Sacred*, p.175.

⁶⁵ Jeremy Begbie, *Theology, Music and Time* (Cambridge: Cambridge University Press, 2000), especially chapter 6. See also in slightly more accessible form, Jeremy Begbie, 'Play it (Again): Music, Theology and Divine Communication' in Jeff Astley, Timothy Hone, and Mark Savage (eds), *Creative Chords; Studies in Music, Theology, and Christian Formation* (Leominster: Gracewing, 2000), pp. 45–75.

⁶⁶ Begbie, *Theology, Music and Time*, p. 165.

⁶⁷ Astley et al., *Creative Chords*, pp. 50–51.

⁶⁸ Begbie, *Theology, Music and Time*, p. 164.

⁶⁹ Astley et al., *Creative Chords*, p. 57.

⁷⁰ Richard Bauckham, 'Time and Eternity' in Richard Bauckham (ed.), *God Will Be All In All: The Eschatology of Jurgen Moltmann* (Edinburgh: T&T Clark, 1999), pp. 155–226.

⁷¹ Rowan Williams, *Open to Judgement* (London: Darton, Longman and Todd, 1994), p. 248.

⁷² Paul Ricoeur, *Figuring the Sacred*, p. 176.

⁷³ David Ford, *Self and Salvation* (Cambridge: Cambridge University Press, 1999), pp. 193–194.

⁷⁴ Begbie, *Theology, Music and Time*, p. 171.

⁷⁵ Steven J. Land, *Pentecostal Spirituality* (Sheffield: Sheffield Academic Press, 1994), pp. 74–75.

⁷⁶ Ibid., p. 55.

⁷⁷ Ibid., p. 98.

⁷⁸ Ibid.

⁷⁹ Ibid., p. 98.

[80] Gordon Fee, *God's Empowering Presence* (Milton Keynes, Paternoster, 1994), p. 246. Fee sees here an echo of Isaiah 45:14. See also Thiselton, *The First Epistle to the Corinthians,* p. 1130.

[81] Fee and Thiselton differ on whether the scenario of 1 Corinthians envisages free spontaneous worship in Pauline churches (Fee) or not (Thiselton). See Gordon Fee, *Paul, the Spirit and the People of God* (Peabody: Hendrickson, 1996), pp. 154–156. Thiselton sees this is an open issue (*The First Epistle to the Corinthians*, p. 1134).

[82] Brueggemann, *The Covenanted Self*, p. 66.

7. Vortex of Love: Liturgical Work *and* Trinitarian Participation

[1] On 'leitourgia' see Frank Senn, *The People's Work: A Social History of the Liturgy* (Minneapolis: Fortress Press, 2006), pp. 23–24

[2] Robert E. Webber, *Worship is a Verb* (Waco: Word Books, 1985).

[3] Eugene H. Peterson, *Five Smooth Stones for Pastoral Work* (Atlanta: John Knox Press, 1980), pp. 144–146.

[4] James B. Torrance, 'The Doctrine of the Trinity in our Contemporary Situation' in Alistair Heron (ed.), *The Forgotten Trinity: A Selection of Papers presented to the BCC Study Commission on Trinitarian Doctrine Today* (London: BCC/CCBI, 1991), p. 6.

[5] James B. Torrance, *Worship, Community and the Triune God of Grace: The Didsbury Lectures* (Carlisle: Paternoster, 1996), pp. 7–8.

[6] Craig Koester, *Symbolism in the Fourth Gospel: Meaning, Mystery, Community,* 2nd edition (Minneapolis: Fortress Press, 2003), p. 49.

[7] Gary Burge, *The Anointed Community: The Holy Spirit in the Johannine Tradition* (Grand Rapids: Eerdmans, 1987), p. 192.

[8] Lesslie Newbigin, *The Light Has Come: An Exposition of the Fourth Gospel* (Grand Rapids: Eerdmans, 1982), p. 52.

[9] I am unable to trace the source of this quotation.

[10] Newbigin, *The Light Has Come*, p. 53.

[11] Anthony Ugolnik, *The Illuminating Icon* (Grand Rapids: Eerdmans, 1989), p. 122.

[12] Yves Congar, *I Believe in the Holy Spirit Volume I: The Experience of the Spirit* (London: Geoffrey Chapman, 1983), p. 104.

[13] James B. Torrance, *Worship, Community, and the Triune God of Grace*, p. 21.

14 Ibid., p. 3.

15 C.E.B. Cranfield, *The Epistle to the Romans, Volume 2*, ICC Commentary Series (Edinburgh: T&T Clark, 1979), p. 605.

16 James Denney, *The Death of Christ* (London: Hodder and Stoughton, 1911), p. 74.

17 James Torrance, *Worship, Community and the Triune God of Grace*, p. 3.

18 Gerrit Scott Dawson, *Jesus Ascended: The Meaning of Christ's Continuing Incarnation* (London: T & T Clark/Handsel Press, 2004) p. 137. I cannot recommend too strongly this wonderful and enriching book.

8. Wild Goodness: Jubilation *and* Justice

1 See Elizabeth Achtemeier, *Minor Prophets 1: New International Biblical Commentary* (Peabody: Hendrickson, 1996), p. 211.

2 Elizabeth Achtemeier, *Preaching from the Minor Prophets* (Grand Rapids: Eerdmans, 1998), p. 43.

3 James L. Mays, *Amos: Old Testament Library* (London: SCM Press, 1969), p. 108.

4 Alex Motyer, *The Day of the Lion: The Message of Amos*, Bible Speaks Today Series (London: Inter-Varsity, 1974), p. 133.

5 Mark Buchanan, *Your God is Too Safe: Rediscovering the Wonder of a God You Can't Control* (Sisters, Oregon: Multnomah, 2001), p. 31.

6 C.S. Lewis, *The Chronicles of Narnia* (London: Collins, 1998), p. 146.

7 Buchanan, *Your God is Too Safe*, p. 33.

8 Cited by Brent Curtis and John Eldridge, *The Sacred Romance* (Nashville: Thomas Nelson, 1997), p. 47.

9 Mark Labberton, *The Dangerous Act of Worship* (Downers Grove: IVP Books, 2007), p. 66.

10 Annie Dillard, *Holy the Firm* (New York: Harper and Row, 1977), p. 59.

11 Annie Dillard, *Teaching a Stone to Talk* (New York: HarperCollins, 1982), pp. 58–59.

12 Mark Labberton, *The Dangerous Act of Worship*, p. 64.

13 G.K. Chesteron, *Orthodoxy* (London: John Lane, The Bodley Head, 1927), p. 174, italics mine.

Summary Reflections

1. Lathrop, *Holy Things*, p. 80.
2. Senn, *Christian Worship*, p. 74.
3. Marva J. Dawn, *Reaching Out without Dumbing Down* (Grand Rapids: Eerdmans, 1995) and *A Royal Waste of Time* (Grand Rapids: Eerdmans, 1999).
4. Dawn, *Royal Waste of Time*, p. 230.
5. Ibid., p. 231.
6. Ibid., p. 232.
7. Jonathan Wilson, *Gospel Virtues* (Downers Grove: IVP, 1998), p. 125.
8. Ibid., p. 126. The notion of *hyperreality* derives from the work of Umberto Eco and Jean Baudrillard. It is analysed by philosopher Albert Borgmann in *Crossing the Postmodern Divide* (Chicago: The University of Chicago Press, 1992), pp. 82–97, and assessed by Christian social commentators J. Richard Middleton and Brian J. Walsh in *Truth Is Stranger than It Used to Be* (London: SPCK, 1995), pp. 38–42.
9. Wilson, *Gospel Virtues*, p. 125.
10. Middleton and Walsh, *Truth Is Stranger than It Used to Be*, p. 39.
11. See Philip D. Kenneson and James L. Street, *Selling Out the Church: The Dangers of Marketing the Church* (Nashville: Abingdon Press, 1997), pp. 139–140.
12. Aidan Kavanagh, *On Liturgical Theology* (Collegeville: The Liturgical Press, 1984), p. 48.
13. Tom Smail, *The Giving Gift* (London: Hodder and Stoughton, 1988), p. 213.
14. David Wells, *God in the Wasteland* (Leicester; IVP, 1994), chapter 5.
15. Ibid., p. 111.
16. Dawn, *Royal Waste of Time*, p. 133.
17. The terminology is Martin E. Marty's, echoing Karl Rahner in *The Cry of Absence* (San Francisco: Harper & Row, 1983). See my reflections on this and another aspects of the spirituality of the Psalms in *Songs for All Seasons* (Farnham: CWR, 2003).
18. Douglas John Hall, *Bound and Free: A Theologian's Journey* (Minneapolis: Fortress Press, 2005), p. 78.
19. Ibid., p. 79.
20. Kavanagh, *On Liturgical Theology*, p. 34.
21. Ibid., p. 36.

[22] Bernhard Anderson, *Out of the Depths* (Philadelphia: The Westminster Press, 1983), p. 76.

[23] Brueggemann, *The Psalms and the Life of Faith*, p. 102.

[24] Hardy and Ford, *Jubilate*, p. 76.

[25] See E. Byron Anderson and Bruce T. Morrill (eds), *Liturgy and the Moral Self: Humanity at Full Stretch Before God* (Collegeville: The Liturgical Press, 1998).

[26] Paul Westemeyer in ibid., pp. 194–195.

[27] R.S. Thomas, 'Welsh Landscape' in *Collected Poems 1945–1990* (London: Phoenix Press, 1995), p. 47.

[28] Aidan Kavanagh, *Elements of Rite* (New York: Pueblo Publishing 1982), p. 102.

[29] Andrew Walker, *Telling the Story*, p. 99.

[30] Robert W. Jenson, 'How the World Lost Its Story', *First Things*, Vol. 36, October 1993, pp. 19–24.

[31] Brueggemann, *Cadences of Home*, p. 129.

[32] Dawn, *Royal Waste of Time*, p. 233.

[33] Dawn, *Reaching Out without Dumbing Down*, p. 244. See also Darrell L. Guder, *The Continuing Conversion of the Church* (Grand Rapids: Eerdmans, 2000), p. 156.

[34] Stanley Hauerwas, *A Better Hope* (Grand Rapids: Brazos Press, 2000), p. 157.

[35] P.T. Forsyth, *The Taste of Death and the Life of Grace* (London: James Clarke, 1901), p. 74.

[36] Lathrop, *Holy Things*, p. 126.

[37] Auden, W.H., *Collected Shorter Poems 1927–1957* (London: Faber and Faber Limited, 1966), p. 143.

Deep Church Series
Series Editor: Andrew Walker

The Gospel-Driven Church

Retrieving Classical Ministries for Contemporary Revitatlism

Ian Stackhouse ● 978-1-84227-290-9

Evangelicals and Tradition

The Formative Influences of the Early Church

D.H. Williams ● 978-84227-386-8

Remembering Our Future

Explorations in Deep Churchh

Edited by Andrew Walker and Luke Bretherton
978-1-84227-504-7

Worship in the Best of Both Worlds

Explorations in Ancient-Future Worship

Philip Greenslade ● 978-1-84227-614-3

Worshipping Trinity

Coming Back to the Heart of Worship

Robin Parry

If worship is God-centred and God is the Trinity then worship should be Trinity-centred. This book explores the meaning and implications of that simple claim. Written for church leaders, worship leaders and songwriters as well as those interested in theology, Robin Parry looks at why the Trinity matters and addresses pressing questions such as:

- What is the relationship between theology and worship?
- Why is the Trinity central to Christian living and understanding?
- Does the Trinity help us understand what we do when we worship?
- How can we write and select songs that foster an awareness of the Trinity?
- How can we make the Trinity central through Holy Communion, spiritual gifts, preaching, and the use of the arts?

Practical and realistic, *Worshipping Trinity* shows how we can maintain the centality of the Trinity in a fast-changing worship culture.

'An extremely valuable resource for any pastor, leader or worshipping heart.' – **Matt Redman**, songwriter and worship leader

'*Worshipping Trinity* is a sneaky book; reading it is so enjoyable one does not realize how much is being learned.' – Evangelical Review of Theology

Robin Parry is Editorial Director for Paternoster.

978-1-84227-347-0

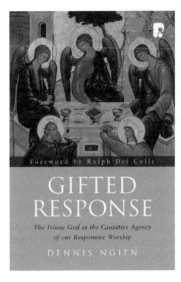

Gifted Response

The Triune God as the Causative Agency of Our Responsive Worship

Dennis Ngien

Much of the contemporary church's emphasis on worship has been on the 'how-to' aspect of worship and the discussion has been largely devoid of theological underpinning. This book seeks to fill that dangerous gap in the literature by means of an analysis of the theo-logic of worship in five major Christian thinkers:

- Basil of Caesarea
- Anselm of Canterbury
- Bernard of Claivaux
- Martin Luther
- John Calvin

The unifying theme that runs through these theologians is that worship is God's gift, in which we participate. It is primarily God's causative action in us, and secondarily our corresponding response to him.

> 'An inspiring and much-needed contribution to the growing literative on the Trinitarian character of worship.' – **Jeremy Begbie,** Thomas Langford Research Professor of Theology, Duke University

Dennis Ngien is Research professor of Theology at Tyndale University College and Seminary in Toronto.

978-1-84227-610-5

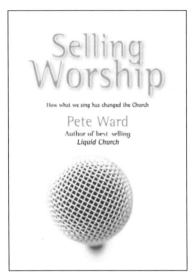

Selling Worship

How What We Sing has Changed the Church

Pete Ward

Pete Ward looks at how popular music has affected the practice and theology of worship. The evangelical church has undergone a significant change in culture and theology over the last thirty-five years. *Selling Worship* argues that this has been achieved through the adoption of a particular style of worship. In effect the songs (or rather the practice of singing and listening to the songs) carry the culture and practice of the church. This has come about through the contextualization of worship in the production, selling and consumption of associated popular music. *Selling Worship* tells the recent history of evangelicalism through the lives, actions and economic processes of fetival organisers, record companies, magazines and worship leaders. It presents a comprehensive account of how these changes have come about and offers a multilayered pattern of interpretation to show how what we sing has changed the church. The book concludes with a critical appreciation of worship and offers practical guidelines for the future.

Pete Ward is Lecturer in Youth Ministry and Theological Education at King's College, London.

978-1-84227-270-1